DISCIPLER'S GUIDE EDITION

Life in Christ

A Personalized Discipleship Notebook

Lynn Adams &
Linda Gammon

First printing 2025

Cover and text design by Diane King. dkingdesigner.com

Wheel and line diagrams adapted from *Handbook to Happiness* by Charles R. Solomon (Tyndale House Publishers), included by permission of Grace Fellowship International.

Belief system diagram adapted from *The Search for Significance by Robert S. McGee 2003 edition.*

Christ is Life diagrams adapted from Paul Travis.

Scripture quotations taken from the New American Standard Bible® (NASB) Version 2020, Copyright © 1960, 1962, 1963, 1968, 1971, 1972, 1973, 1975, 1977, 1995 by The Lockman Foundation used by permission. www.Lockman.com

Published by Grace Fellowship International

3914 Nellie St., Pigeon Forge, TN 37863

gracefellowshipinternational.com

Discipler's Guide Edition to Life in Christ: A Personalized Discipleship Notebook

ISBN 978-1-963542-03-5

TABLE OF CONTENTS

ACKNOWLEDGMENTS

I would like to gratefully acknowledge the Advanced Discipleship Training I received from Grace Ministries (1995-96), in addition to the conference, workshop, and institute training with Grace Fellowship International in November 2007.

Both seasons of discipleship were foundational to my understanding of life in Christ. I deeply appreciate the men and women who invested their time, care, and wisdom to equip me and others. This notebook is the direct result of that investment.

—*Linda*

I want to thank Linda Gammon for the countless hours she poured into my life, a living example of the biblical truths contained in this notebook.

I would also like to acknowledge the growing number of trauma-informed professionals and people helpers. Their expertise has deepened my understanding of the impact of suffering on the human spirit, soul, and body.

Most importantly, I thank the Lord, without whose life, in and through the indwelling Holy Spirit, I could not stand.

—*Lynn*

INTRODUCTION

Life in Christ is the promise and hope for Christians. What does it mean for you personally? Our **DISCIPLER'S GUIDE** notes will equip you to effectively answer this and other questions from those you come alongside for personalized, in-depth discipling.

The guide notes are on the left-sided pages of your *Life in Christ: A Personalized Discipleship Notebook,* which are directly opposite the instructional narratives and interactive materials on the right. They are designed to provide easy reference for clarification and emphasize the most valuable points of each discipleship session.

You will notice that the first two sessions of the notebook focus on an individual's family history and background. This is for the purpose of contextualizing their life and personalizing the discipleship content. Are we focusing too much on the past? Philippians 3:13 may come to mind: "forget those things which are behind." Reading the proceeding context (Philippians 3:3-8) illustrates that Paul just referred to his own past. Similarly, we are looking at the past in order to help the disciplee have a more transformative 12-session process and more freedom in the future.

A discipler's role is not the same as a professional therapist. We are primarily facilitators, trusting the Holy Spirit to illuminate and apply God's Word. We are wise to recognize our limitations as laypeople who at times benefit from consulting pastors or other professionals.

Should the discipler share any of their own personal journey? At times, this may serve to reinforce the session through illustration or to validate and encourage the disciplee. However, discernment is needed to limit one's personal references so as not to distract from the disciplee's own life experiences.

The examples provided in the **DISCIPLER'S GUIDE** are included only to support your understanding of the material.

We would enjoy responding to questions or comments about this notebook. Please email us at lindagammon8@gmail.com or ladams08.28@gmail.com

God bless and guide you as you assist others in appropriating Jesus Christ as Savior, Lord, and Life.

FOREWORD

Welcome to this personalized discipleship notebook that highlights life in Christ.

An Invitation to Accelerated Spiritual Growth

After receiving Jesus as your Lord and Savior, how have you grown in your relationship with God? Have you found a vital discipleship process?

Many believers are hindered due to minimal spiritual growth. This problem is a familiar one. The writer to the Hebrews admonishes us, "Concerning him (Jesus Christ) we have much to say, and it is difficult to explain, since you have become poor listeners. For though by this time you ought to be teachers, you have need again for someone to teach you the elementary principles of the actual words of God, and you have come to need milk and not solid food. For everyone who partakes only of milk is unacquainted with the word of righteousness, for he is an infant. But solid food is for the mature, who because of practice have their senses trained to distinguish between good and evil. Therefore leaving the elementary teaching about the Christ, let us press on to maturity ...." (Hebrews 5:11-6:1).

This notebook goes beyond the milk of the Word to solid, biblical food. Its 12-week format is ideal for accelerated spiritual growth. The weekly sessions cover many aspects of biblical teaching on living the Christian life. The authors do not present their private interpretations but stand on the shoulders of excellent source material and the ministries providing their training. Their personal studies and ministry experience have further developed the authors' teaching. As their editor, I have reviewed and endorsed the message of this notebook.

As mentioned in the introduction, this material has been developed primarily in the context of individual discipling led by a discipler and, ideally, a co-discipler. However, whether in a small group setting or one-on-one sessions, this material is intended to be experienced in conjunction with meaningful prayer, fellowship, and support.

Although the authors do not identify this as a counseling book, the in-depth evaluation, biblical insights, and personal applications can be used of the Holy Spirit to resolve many mental, emotional, and relational problems that motivate people to seek counseling.

This Edition

My wife and I have used an earlier edition of this notebook and found it very helpful and edifying. This edition reflects a revision process aimed at encouraging additional interaction, helping to personalize the disciple's learning and development.

When Grace Fellowship International invited the authors to partner with them, GFI included the "wheel and line diagrams" to facilitate sharing important diagnostic and doctrinal insights. These recently revised diagrams have helped equip discipleship counselors for over five decades and will be familiar to students of this branch of biblical counseling.

I thank my Executive Director at Grace Fellowship, Mark McKeehan, for supporting this personalized discipleship notebook project and endorsing it for use by our GFI Guides. We also thank Janet Clark Shay for her editing and publishing assistance.

Who Is Your Source?

The title of this volume celebrates the believer's relationship with "Christ, who is our life ..." (Colossians 3:4). We need to abide in Him daily. Jesus declared, "I am the vine, you are the branches; the one who remains in Me, and I in him bears much fruit, for apart from Me you can do nothing" (John 15:6).

The need for this notebook is summed up well by missionary and author F. J. Huegel:

> Christians groan, strive, and struggle mainly based on human effort, where the grace of God, though acknowledged, is scarcely operative—only to come to grief. Even at their best, they find the purpose of the Lord Jesus remains an ideal infinitely beyond their reach. The trouble lies in the fact that they are proceeding on the wrong basis.

God does not expect them to be like the Lord Jesus because of their own endeavors. He expects them to realize the utter impossibility of such a thing (as in Romans chapter 7, where Paul comes to the end of himself). He expects them to know the Lord Jesus as their very life, disowning any other. He expects them to realize their position of absolute oneness with Christ, for He '... has blessed them with every spiritual blessing in heavenly places in Christ' (Ephesians 1:3).

We pray that many disciplers, ministries and churches will discover the potential of using this notebook for grace-based personal ministry.

John B. Woodward M.Div., D. Min.
Director of Counseling and Training
Grace Fellowship International

PERSONAL TESTIMONIES

In 2005, I was Director of Women's Ministries at a large suburban church outside Minneapolis. I was delighted that Linda Gammon was referred to me as someone interested in beginning a new ministry. I had become familiar with the concepts she would teach several years earlier when reading Miles Stanford and Major Ian Thomas. Discussing the theological points of life in Christ with her was refreshing. Over time, it became apparent that many women did not clearly understand their identity in Christ and that this new ministry would be life-giving to them.

I began referring women to participate in the 12-week discipleship sessions and received glowing reports—genuinely transformational for the women being discipled. Though they were born-again Christians, they had not fully appropriated the truth of Galatians 2:20 before that time.

As the ministry continued, interest grew in other venues outside our church. In addition to one-on-one discipleship, Linda spoke for several weeks to women who were part of a Teen Challenge recovery group in their leadership track. She also taught several classes to women at our local church. I participated to some extent while still Women's Ministry Director but became more involved in my retirement. I was trained along with other women in the discipling process.

Reflecting on those days of launching this discipleship ministry, I have a deep sense of satisfaction. This ministry has truly changed lives. —*Sue Raia*

With Christ as my Savior and Lord, I was a defeated, worthless, and exhausted Christian. I wondered how this could be, as I was living an obedient life to Christ and His Word and desired to please Him. Didn't the Bible promise abundant life, peace that surpasses all understanding, and victory in Christ? Why wasn't I experiencing this when I was doing everything *right*? Whatever I did and wherever I looked, both in the church and in life, nothing sufficed.

One day at church, the women's director introduced me to Linda Gammon. During one-on-one sessions, she shared the biblical truth of union with Christ. The director could have chosen another ministry in the church, but I thank God she referred me to Linda with the message of the Cross.

Galatians 2:20 states, "I have been crucified with Christ, and I no longer live, but Christ lives in me. The life I now live in the body, I live by faith in the Son of God, who loved me and gave himself for me." Christ was my Savior and Lord, but now became my very life as I appropriated the truth that I was crucified with Him, buried with Him, risen with Him, and now seated with Him in the heavenlies in a place of victory!

This paradigm shift of tapping into Christ as my source for living and looking to Him to provide all I needed, moment by moment, was completely transformational. It was not something to attain, strive towards, or hope for. It was simply mine as a child of God. My birthright! I rested in the truth that Christ is sufficient. All glory and honor to God!   —*Cheryl Anderson*

ᴥ

I was saved soon after I was married. My husband and I served faithfully in sound fundamental churches for years. However, in recent years, I began to ask the question, if Jesus Christ brings victory, why are so many Christians—including myself—living a powerless life? Sometimes, it seemed we were all merely holding on until we went to our heavenly home.

I began to long for answers and considered enrolling in a biblical *counseling* course to minister to others. After seeking wise counsel, I committed to a biblical *discipleship* course taught by Linda Gammon. I knew from the onset the Lord had brought her into my life "for such a time as this." I soon began an intensive one-on-one 12-week discipleship course and have not regretted it for a minute.

The Lord began doing a work in my own life, awakening me to the need to fully surrender and to understand how I had often relied on my good works. No wonder I felt powerless. Galatians 2:20 took on new meaning, *"I am crucified with Christ, and it is no longer I who live, but Christ lives in me..."* I realized that I do not have to surrender authority to my flesh. While I knew this technically, I now understood it experientially. I already knew I was safe from the *penalty* of sin. Now, I more fully grasped I was also saved from the *power* of sin.

Now and then, I had done some basic biblical counseling with women who had requested it. But as I took this new course (focusing on the abundant life), I realized that much traditional biblical counseling is often only a temporary solution. While it uses Scripture, it focuses on behavior modification. I used the same method in the past when trying to help myself and others. However, altering behavior in our own power places the *doing* in the wrong place—under *our* efforts and control.

This 12-week course can and does change lives. It has changed mine. It is not a new truth. It is THE truth. The material uniquely guides students to their own conclusions through Holy Spirit illumination, rather than telling the students where their problems are rooted. I learned to identify my default behaviors and surrender them to my Lord rather than slipping into my *go-to* rut. I continue to learn. While I sometimes slip back into my default mode, I have no intention of turning back. I am still growing, but now I understand there is no reason for any Christian to live a powerless life other than a misunderstanding of Who accomplishes the work.   *—J. S.*

I went through the individualized discipleship ministry with Lynn Adams several years ago. Learning about the three-part model, spirit-soul-body, was eye-opening and changed my life.

I learned the difference between *religion* as man's attempt to reach God and the reality of the miracle of Christ in me. I was particularly impacted by the four-column exercise in the "Knowing Jesus as My Life" section.

Learning about the flesh was vital in relinquishing my self-sufficiency and turning to Christ as my source of living. I understood what true rest means. Victory is a person, not a program. Understanding the process of sanctification is a valuable tool that I constantly use in my daily walk in the Holy Spirit.
    —Bill Harnist

Have you ever experienced burdens beyond your strength—such that you even despaired of living? If you have, where did you seek help?

This was my situation six years ago. I was saved in 2006 and became involved in local churches, Bible studies, and small groups. I had a zeal for theological knowledge and enjoyed the study resources, but they were ineffective in getting me out of the darkness. I felt stuck.

I was introduced to my discipler and began a 12-week discipleship course available at my local church. Gradually, my depression lifted, and I experienced joy as a child of God. I came to personally understand His transformational grace in a way that I had never known before.

Through this personalized discipleship, I grew to understand the power of Christ and received encouragement from those who ministered to me. I was able to overcome a lifetime of depression and despair. After God delivered me from depression, I participated in training to help other women appropriate the indwelling Christ living in and through them.　　—S. A.

I sought Church counsel to show me how to live as a Christian while in a marriage that was not working. They referred me to a discipleship ministry like none other. This approach was so personal. My daily walk transformed as Lynn Adams joined me to disciple me. I learned how to appropriate Biblical truth. I started to trust in the Lord with all my heart and to lean not on my own understanding. The Bible became active in my life, piercing to divide soul and spirit, helping me to discern the thoughts and attitudes in my heart.

It has been ten years since I was first discipled, and I no longer experience that nagging pain, loneliness, and emptiness. Jesus is enough for me. His grace is sufficient!

—*Amrit Singh*

Seven years ago, my faith journey led my wife, Patricia, and me to attend a Sunday morning class at our local church. When I heard the presentation and realized the message was based on Galatians 2:20, I knew I was right where God wanted me to be. This verse was the one I picked for myself when I gave my life over to Christ. I had additional training the next year and a half, but the discipleship impact increased when I was personally discipled.

The Holy Spirit led me to start a ministry for men and guide them through Bible verses that speak to one's identity in Christ. I have since taken several men's groups through discipleship study and have seen the strengthening of their personal relationships with God. I can't say enough positive things about this discipleship message and how it is presented.   —*Steve Ranz*

I have been a believer in Jesus Christ for 64 years. I have grown so much through three years of missionary and Bible training school and six years on the mission field (three of which were in a refugee camp).

I met Linda in the great local church we both attended. She shared about the discipleship ministry she was involved with, and I became very interested. I started ministering to women who were believers but had little or no fruit and all kinds of problems. We met with them weekly for 12 sessions, and the most frequent comment we heard was, "Why am I just hearing about this now?"

I thoroughly enjoyed discipling numerous ladies and watching them grow and surrender their total lives to our wonderful Lord and Savior, Jesus Christ. I was involved in this ministry for ten years.   —*Marilyn Lovestrand*

INTRODUCTION

Life in Christ: A Personalized Discipleship Notebook

We know the grace of God is effective, and there is nothing more powerful. Yet, if this is true, why are there so many anxious and depressed Christians? Where is the abundant life that Christ came to give us? And why does the fruit of the Spirit seem so elusive?

Christians are not exempt from life's difficulties. We may experience challenging circumstances and painful relationships. Searching for answers may lead us to question our faith. Searching for relief may lead some of us to substance abuse, pornography, and other addictive behaviors.

We're taught Christ Himself is the answer and that Scripture is sufficient. How do we lay hold of these truths in our time of need? What if we could find effective, test-driven materials for individual discipleship to address these issues? What if these materials were designed to be user-friendly, even for those who do not have the gift of teaching?

We developed *Life in Christ: A Personalized Discipleship Notebook* for this very purpose. The 12-week format has proven to be transformational in both church and parachurch settings. The weekly, two-hour interactive sessions continue for three months, providing enough time to share foundational truths in a manageable commitment time frame. The authors are lay people who have ministered to hurting Christians; we are not licensed counseling professionals. We have found this notebook to be powerful and practical in short-term discipleship.

Many of the materials we share are interactive, so there is opportunity for listening and reflection during the time together. The personalized responses show the discipler what has been understood and appropriated.

If needed, further clarification can be provided before introducing the next teaching.

The notebook contains everything needed for the discipleship sessions. Twelve teaching segments, interactive materials, CONSIDER THIS homework assignments, Scripture verses, and even a place for written responses. The new discipler may especially appreciate the structure and ease of sharing in this way.

These materials will support the ongoing discipleship ministry of the local church. Pastoral or staff member referrals are the way to connect with those seeking help in this setting. When an individual has completed the discipleship sessions, we invite them to write a personal testimony about their experience. Each testimony enables church leaders to discern the value of this approach, as fruit is easy to recognize!

While the course sessions are completed in twelve weeks, growth in grace is a lifelong process. However, many have been helped to understand more fully:

- Who am I as a child of God?

- How do I live by grace and not by law?

- What does it look like to walk by the Spirit and not according to the flesh?

- What does it mean to be in union with Christ?

- How is it possible to forgive the unforgivable?

- How can I be assured the solution to my problems is life in Christ?

HOW TO USE THIS NOTEBOOK

Life in Christ: A Personalized Discipleship Notebook can be used in three different ways depending on the preferred format. For clarification, the *disciplee* is the student—the one seeking discipleship; the *discipler* is the leader—the one doing the discipling or teaching.

The Individual Method

A disciplee personalizes the notebook on their own by reading each session's narratives, filling in the interactive materials, and completing the CONSIDER THIS homework assignment.

Someone who desires to become a discipler may also choose this method in order to familiarize themselves with the process.

The Discipler/Disciplee Method

In this method, the discipler personally leads the disciplee through the notebook over a period of twelve weeks.

SESSION ONE

- The discipler administers the "Life Experience" questionnaire in order to learn more about the disciplee.

- The discipler presents an overview and explains how to personalize the interactive materials and diagrams.

- The discipler reviews the CONSIDER THIS segment, which itemizes the homework to be completed before the next session.

The interactive and homework assignments usually take one to one and a half hours outside the sessions themselves.

SESSIONS TWO THROUGH TWELVE

First hour:

- ✻ The disciplee shares his or her responses to the homework from the previous session.

Second hour:

- ✻ The discipler introduces the teaching narratives in the current week's session.

- ✻ The discipler clarifies the interactive materials and diagrams.

- ✻ The discipler reviews homework for the following week.

Small Group Method

Life in Christ: A Personalized Discipleship Notebook can be used effectively in small group settings. When selecting this option, the group should be limited to four or five disciplees and facilitated by an experienced discipler. The process is identical to that used in the individual method, with class members sharing their responses during the first hour of each week's meeting. Class members determine for themselves how many of their personalized responses they choose to share in a group setting. Often, someone who has completed a small group course may ask to repeat the sessions in a one-on-one setting.

While all three methods are effective, the discipler/disciplee approach is offered most frequently by the authors. Those who participate in one-on-one personalized discipleship seem to experience the most significant life transformation.

Discipler's Session Notes

The **DISCIPLER'S SESSION NOTES** page, located at the back of the PDN on page 279, is to be used to track your disciplee's weekly progress. Permission is granted to reproduce this page for weekly sessions with numerous disciplees.

Homework: Regular completion of the homework is important. If a disciplee has three sessions of incomplete homework, you may wish to discuss their level of commitment.

New Material: This is a helpful reminder of what was introduced in the session.

Session Notes: This information is important and meaningful to the disciplee's progress. The disciplee's own words can be helpful.

Next Session: To be covered: What is your plan for next week? Homework assigned: Notate the assignment and any additional homework given.

Key Concepts to be Grasped: The discipleship process is not linear. As you work through the notebook, information about previous or future sessions may arise.

Please make a note of this information for use when it's appropriate.

SESSION 1

Life Experience

The objective of the **LIFE EXERIENCE** survey is to get an overview of the disciplee's life. We want to understand where they are currently and what has happened to get them to this point. How do they see themselves, and do they like what they see? In conjunction with the personalization materials, we want the disciplee to discover how they attempt to meet their needs, minimize pain, and develop a *successful* life strategy.

To the greatest extent possible, determine whether the disciplee is a believer. Are they able to describe a personal relationship with Jesus (see questions 10 and 41)? This is critical for applying biblical truth being shared by the discipler.

We want to make it clear to the disciplee that they can provide only what they feel comfortable giving. While the survey aims to elicit information, we are building trust from this first meeting. We don't want the disciplee to feel interrogated; minute details are unnecessary for understanding. However, the disciplee should be doing most of the talking, and we should be listening.

Attempt to attune yourself to the disciplee, recognizing and responding to their emotional state in a way that validates and supports them. Notice a person's reactions/responses to the questions. Do they tear up, avoid certain topics, or lack memories in any areas? Make note of your observations. Also, document any *telling* comments that may shed light on emotions and belief systems in future sessions.

Listen for what is not said, as well as what is said. Is their countenance congruent with their answers?

If following up on a piece of information, ask open-ended questions, beginning with *Who? What? How?* and avoiding *Why? Why* is often difficult to answer and can create defensiveness.

IDENTIFYING INFORMATION

3 **Occupation:** Is there something about the disciplee's current position that may reveal helpful information about their current circumstances? For example, are they engaged in a highly stressful occupation, or are they in business with people who may be affecting them in an unhealthy way?

5 **Marriage:** Depending on the state of the marriage, the role of the spouse can influence one's identity and self-esteem. Factors may include the balance of individuality, partnership and healthy communication.

If a person reports feeling unsafe, this needs to be addressed. If you are not equipped to address the situation yourself, seek outside help.

6 **Single:** This may affect a person's sense of belonging. Are they suffering grief over the loss of a dream or a loved one? Are they suffering from the stigma associated with divorce (regardless of how it came about)? Do any of these influence their sense of identity?

The Life Experience survey is typically administered in a one-on-one discipleship relationship. It is a tool that can be used by the discipler to gain knowledge about the disciplee's family of origin, belief systems, current circumstances and emotional state, all of which impact our concept of God.

For those of us who use the materials on our own or with others in a small group, the questionnaire may prove beneficial in reviewing our life as we seek greater clarity and self-awareness from the Lord.

IDENTIFYING INFORMATION

[2] Name _____ *Age* _____

[3] Occupation _____

[4] Marital Status   *How long married?* _____ *First marriage?* _____

[5] Describe the marriage relationship, to include:

How would you describe the quality? _____

_____

Can you give some examples? _____

_____

If you have felt physically or emotionally unsafe,
can you describe what contributed to these feelings? _____

_____

[6] Single?   ◯ *Never Married*   ◯ *After Death of a Spouse*   ◯ *After Divorce*

[7] Are you currently in a relationship?

How long? _____

_____

How would you describe the quality? _____

_____

_____

8   Children: This may influence a person's sense of purpose, as well as their identity.

9   Are the children adults? How are the parent/child relationships? Does this impact the disciplee's beliefs about themself?

CHIEF CONCERN

10   Most people don't reach out for help unless/until a problem exists. Some people don't know the cause but only know that their life is not working for them. This may happen even when they are doing "all the right things." Do they have a specific reason for being here? What are the symptoms they describe?

If they are under a professional's care, are the *conditions serious* enough that they may need more time before they begin discipleship? The disciplee must be able to focus during the sessions and complete their homework during the week. If they are experiencing depression or anxiety, are they on medication?

11   Is the disciplee open to the Lord's solution? The Lord is always the answer to the problem. While true, the Lord is also the One in control of bringing about the solution. As disciplers, our job is to facilitate that relationship. We can point to Him, but He will work in His way, in His time. Each person has a unique experience.

PAST HISTORY

12   When taking on a people-helping role, it is wise to have at least a basic understanding of trauma and its impact. While the Lord is completely capable, we have limitations and do not want to do further harm to someone who has already been traumatized. A seemingly innocent circumstance or interaction and repeated incidents may deeply wound someone based on their personal makeup and experience.

CHILDREN

[8] How many? _____   Sexes and ages? _____

[9] Describe your current relationship (if children are adults). _____

_____

_____

CHIEF CONCERN

[10] What prompted you to want to deepen your relationship with the Lord at this time? _____

_____

_____

When did you start feeling this way? _____

Are there specific symptoms you can describe?

_____

How did they progress? ◯ *Suddenly* ◯ *Slowly, over time*

How have you dealt with the symptoms?

◯ *Medication* ◯ *Professional help*

[11] Are you open to the Lord's solution? _____

PAST HISTORY

[12] If trauma is defined as a "deeply distressing or disturbing experience" (oxfordreference.com), do you recall any traumatic events or losses in your life? Any periods of sustained stress or trauma? What if it is not just the event, but the impact it had on you? Please describe:

_____

_____

_____

13 Trauma that is presently occurring or has occurred in the recent past may impede progress and need to be addressed. Trauma, past or present, can create strong and sustained emotions. Watch for emotional reactions. Is there a pattern in who or what they are speaking about? Are there areas of their life that they seem not to remember or don't want to discuss?

If there have been times when the disciplee felt unsafe, how long ago was it? Did they do something to address the issue? Have those circumstances changed?

PARENTS

Everyone is affected by their family of origin.

14 Any of these situations can result in a positive or negative impact, largely depending on the quality of the relationship between the child and the parent/caregiver.

15 and 21 The death of a parent is a significant life event, compounded by the age of the child at death, the strength of the relationship, surrounding support, etc.

16 and 22 If so, were the parents present (both physically and emotionally) when not working? Was there quality child care, work-life balance, etc.?

17 and 23 Substance abuse can create instability in every area of a child's life. If present, is the disciplee aware of the impact? Was there support for the children?

18 and 24 A parent's faith may affect the child positively or negatively, depending on the nature of the faith and how it is practiced.

19 and 25 Attachment styles and self-worth are developed through the way a person's caregivers interact with them. Insecure attachment may lead to problems in forming relationships.

Did the disciplee grow up in an environment where they felt secure, valued, and able to express themselves?

As a person describes their relationship with each of their parents, listen for not just how they were treated but also how they felt. In addition to meeting their physical needs, were their parents able to meet their emotional needs? Emotional development is dependent on the emotional availability of the parents. Conflict resolution and communication are learned from the family of origin.

Neglect, whether physical or emotional, may lead to a sense of inadequacy.

20 and 26 Does the perception of mother and father seem to align with the person they've described?

13 If there was a time/s you felt physically or emotionally unsafe, can you describe what contributed to these feelings?

_____

_____

PARENTS

14 Raised by ◯ one parent   ◯ both parents   ◯ neither parent?

   If neither, then who? _____

15 Is mother alive? ◯ yes   ◯ no   If not, when did she die? _____

16 Was she employed? ◯ yes   ◯ no   Occupation? _____

17 Was there any substance abuse that you were aware of? ◯ yes   ◯ no

18 Did she have a faith that she practiced? _____

19 Describe your relationship with your mother (both past and present).

_____

_____

_____

20 How did you perceive your mother? _____

21 Is father alive? ◯ yes   ◯ no   If not, when did he die? _____

22 Was he employed? ◯ yes   ◯ no   Occupation? _____

23 Was there any substance abuse that you were aware of? ◯ yes   ◯ no

24 Did he have a faith that he practiced? _____

25 Describe your relationship with father (both past and present).

_____

_____

26 How did you perceive your father? _____

29 What are the sibling relationships like? If the siblings are grown, do they enjoy each other? Have they always gotten along, or have they had to work through family-of-origin issues among themselves? What impact might these relationships have had on the disciplee's self-esteem or identity?

Favoritism, sibling rivalry, and jealousy can have long-term adverse effects on all children in the home.

SCHOOL EXPERIENCE

30 Are there any memories of early childhood? Early experiences set the stage for how children perceive themselves, thus affecting both self-esteem and identity.

Grade School:

32 Positive or negative reinforcement from teachers and peers contributes to how a person sees themselves and relates to others. Were there teacher role models?

33 Does the disciplee recall receiving positive or negative feedback from teachers or friends?

Successes or struggles can shape one's self-concept, including perception of their own intelligence and capabilities.

27 Describe the relationship between your parents, if appropriate.

_____

_____

_____

SIBLINGS

28 How many siblings? _____   Sexes and ages? _____

29 Describe relationships (both past and present), to include:

Favoritism by parents _____

_____

Sibling rivalry _____

_____

Jealousy _____

_____

SCHOOL EXPERIENCE

30 Do you have memories of any significant events that happened prior to school?

_____

_____

31 Did you like **grade school**? _____

32 How was your performance in **grade school**? _____

_____

33 What were your relationships like in **grade school**?

Teachers? _____

Friends? _____

34 Did you like **middle school**? _____

Middle School:

35 Positive or negative reinforcement continues to influence one's self-image.

Acceptance or rejection plays a big role in developing identity, as there is a strong desire to fit in and belong. Belonging to a social group is balanced with exploring personal interests and values.

Successes or struggles continue to shape one's self-concept.

36 This is a critical time for identity formation, as increased independence from the family takes place. Exposure to varying morals/values helps shape beliefs about all aspects of culture. Where there are discrepancies between family and peer groups, internal conflict can result.

Life and social skills such as conflict resolution, empathy, and cooperation are honed. In addition, how a middle schooler learns to cope with stress, failure, and social challenges strongly impacts coping strategies in adulthood.

High School

38 Extracurriculars continue to help shape social identity, as interests are an integral part of our identity.

This is a time of increased self-awareness, as well as understanding and managing emotions. Successes and positive reinforcement remain important in the development of identity.

39 The relationships between student and teacher in high school can have a lasting positive or negative impact on the student's academic future, personal development, and future opportunities.

As the individual continues to learn to navigate social groups and cliques, friendships become crucial.

There is an increased grappling with moral and ethical issues, and the person's experiences are now influencing future choices in career and academics.

Many more are now exploring gender and sexual identities.

40 What did the disciplee do after high school? Do they feel good about their choices?

41 Is the disciplee able to describe an active relationship with the Lord?

35 How was your performance in **middle school**? _____

_____

Extracurriculars? _____

_____

36 What were your relationships in **middle school** like?

Teachers? _____

Friends? _____

Opposite sex? _____

37 Did you like **high school**? _____

38 How was your performance in **high school**? _____

_____

Extracurriculars? _____

_____

39 What were your relationships in **high school** like?_____

Teachers? _____

Friends? _____

Opposite sex? _____

40 What did you do after high school? _____

_____

RELIGION/FAITH/BACKGROUND

41 How would you describe your relationship with Jesus, if you have one?

_____

_____

42 Since what age? _____

The objective of the **AN ABUNDANT LIFE** exercise is to see how the disciplee is currently trying to get their needs met and to introduce them to the idea that they may be using fleshly means to do so.

This is the disciplee's initial introduction to their personal version of the flesh. In assigning this as homework (see **Session 6, CONSIDER THIS**), no additional information must be given other than that this needn't be an in-depth endeavor. Encourage the disciplee to write down the first thing that comes to mind.

The discipler should look for the following:

- Is this person seeking satisfaction in ways other than through Jesus?

- Is there an area where this person believes they are living out of a deficit?

- The thing they believe they *need* may be something that must be surrendered.

The discipler may share some or all of the following information when reviewing the homework with the disciplee. Feeling loved, secure, and significant are legitimate, God-given needs. Unfortunately, most people try to meet these needs in illegitimate ways.

People generally think that if they had something that they consider to be *lacking* in their life, they would feel differently. We frequently hear that other people, things, or certain circumstances would make them happy or provide the abundant life God intended for them.

Feelings of security (or insecurity) stem from who we think we are. Do I matter deeply to someone? Feelings of significance (or insignificance) stem from what we do. Does my life have purpose and meaning?

Through fleshly means, a self-centered person looks to others to meet these needs. A Christ-centered person gets these needs met through the Lord and is then able to help meet these needs in others. While we are best looking to the Lord to meet our needs, it is still essential to maintain Christian fellowship.

> Let us consider how to stimulate one another to love and good deeds, not forsaking our own assembling together, as is the habit of some, but encouraging one another; and all the more, as you see the day drawing near (Hebrews 10:24-25).

43 Do you have a religious affiliation; belong to/ attend a church?

_____

_____

AN ABUNDANT LIFE?

As a Christ follower, John 10:10 tells us that Jesus came so that we might have life and have it more abundantly. How might my life change if I was living an abundant life?

1 I would feel loved (that someone unconditionally has my best interest at heart) because

_____

In the past, I have tried to find love _____

2 I would feel secure (accepted, understood, and have a sense of belonging) because

_____

In the past, I have tried to get a sense of security through _____

_____

3 I would feel significant (have purpose and meaning in my life) because

_____

In the past, I have tried to gain a feeling of significance through _____

_____

4 What other things might need to happen or change for me to **truly live abundantly?**

_____

_____

_____

The objective of the **STRATEGIES AND ATTITUDES** exercise is to increase the disciplee's awareness of patterns in their behavior, indicating how they have become accustomed to getting their needs met apart from Christ.

1   While anxiety may have a physical component in certain circumstances, in this instance, we are considering anxiety stemming from our thought processes. These feelings/behaviors relate to security issues and our desire to minimize negative outcomes.

2   These *defensive* flesh responses may happen if one feels pressured or controlled by others.

3   These accommodating or submissive responses exert control by yielding to others to gain approval and acceptance and avoid confrontation. They may also result from being controlled.

4   This fleshly behavior controls others by asserting superiority (not acknowledging mistakes or weakness) and avoiding feelings of inadequacy or vulnerability.

5   Depression may also have a physical component, but for our purposes, it refers to thoughts/feelings caused by psychological and environmental factors, as well as thought processes.

6   Avoidance or denial, refusing to acknowledge or confront problems (help), is a way of managing anxiety, fear, or uncertainty.

7   Domineering or aggressive behaviors assert control over others to cause compliance or submission, achieving goals through forceful means.

8   This form of control protects a person from potential risks or harm. It may also reflect a fear of rejection and provide a temporary sense of safety.

9   These behaviors allow us to avoid dealing with underlying issues.

10 These passive-aggressive behaviors allow us to make our feelings clear without openly sharing them and becoming vulnerable.

STRATEGIES AND ATTITUDES THAT MIGHT ARISE WHEN I PERCEIVE I HAVE "UNMET NEEDS"

1 I **become anxious**, which may include a lack of peace, paralyzing fear, apprehension, or creating "what if" or "if only" scenarios.	Often	Sometimes	Never
2 I **challenge others** by resisting authority, being uncooperative, or being unreasonable.	Often	Sometimes	Never
3 I **become complaisant** by being agreeable and obliging.	Often	Sometimes	Never
4 I **have a critical attitude**, finding fault with others, myself, and circumstances around me, having difficulty admitting I was wrong, apologizing, asking for forgiveness, or expressing gratitude.	Often	Sometimes	Never
5 I **become depressed**, sad, hopeless, empty, lose interest in activities I usually enjoy, sleep too much or too little, have abnormal fatigue, have a change in appetite, and experience weight loss/gain.	Often	Sometimes	Never
6 I **deny reality**, ignore problems, and hope they will go away.	Often	Sometimes	Never
7 I **become dominant**, demanding, intimidating, or overbearing.	Often	Sometimes	Never
8 I **become emotionally inhibited**, unable to express my feelings and avoid intimacy.	Often	Sometimes	Never
9 I **escape emotional pain** through addictive behaviors, busyness, work, religious activity, screen time, sleep, etc.	Often	Sometimes	Never
10 I **fight unfairly** by using sarcasm, gossip, the silent treatment, "forgetting" things, procrastination, humor, etc., to make my point.	Often	Sometimes	Never

11 Aggressive behaviors that intimidate and exert dominance indicate difficulty managing emotions and communicating effectively.

12 These behaviors give a person a sense of control when they feel wronged or powerless, a sense of moral superiority, or a sense of purpose.

13 Inauthentic behaviors may help us to manage the impressions others have of us.

14 People may detach to protect themselves or cope with overwhelming emotions. This is often accompanied by disregard for others' emotions.

15 Trauma or prolonged stress may lead to these coping behaviors. High expectations, perfectionism, or avoiding vulnerability may also be present.

16 These may indicate self-centeredness, which leads to manipulation and authoritarian methods of control, usually accompanied by a lack of empathy.

17 These manipulation tactics attempt to control others by affecting their emotional state, often leading to emotional distress.

18 Self-aggrandizement as a way to seek admiration and use one's status to influence others.

19 Lack of emotional maturity may result in an inability to manage one's emotions. The person maintains control through emotional responses rather than constructive behavior.

20 These avoidant behaviors lead to a lack of agency and autonomy. They may serve to reduce stress and bring about comfort.

11 I **am hostile,** quick-tempered, harsh, malicious, cruel, caustic, etc., to express my anger.

Often   *Sometimes*   *Never*

12 I **hold a grudge**, becoming moody, bitter, unforgiving, resentful, and vengeful, keeping a record of wrongs.

Often   *Sometimes*   *Never*

13 I'm **inauthentic**, hiding what I really think and feel, being "phony," superficial, or "performing," to get attention or affirmation from others.

Often   *Sometimes*   *Never*

14 I **am indifferent**, uncaring, insensitive, unsympathetic, and/or unconcerned.

Often   *Sometimes*   *Never*

15 I **am too intense**, lacking joy, overly serious, unemotional, stern, overly analytical, or difficult to be around.

Often   *Sometimes*   *Never*

16 I **lack compassion**, showing no understanding, kindness, gentleness, or love.

Often   *Sometimes*   *Never*

17 I **try to maintain control** by making threats, coercion, silent treatment, passivity, shaming, or guilting.

Often   *Sometimes*   *Never*

18 I **become obsessed** with status, recognition, accomplishments, my appearance, and what others think.

Often   *Sometimes*   *Never*

19 I **operate by my emotions**, being too sensitive to criticism, taking things personally, and allowing myself to be controlled by anger, doubt, guilt, fear, etc.

Often   *Sometimes*   *Never*

20 I **become passive**, not taking risks, letting someone else make decisions, avoiding failure at all costs, procrastinating, being lazy, unreliable, or apathetic, depending on others instead of God.

Often   *Sometimes*   *Never*

21 These behaviors guard against hurt or unmet expectations. They allow one to have a *sense* of managing negative outcomes by expecting the worst.

22 People-pleasing involves approval-seeking and avoiding conflict.

23 Feeling perpetually wronged can be an attention-getting behavior that leads to sympathy and assistance from others. It can also serve as a way to avoid taking responsibility for one's behaviors and circumstances.

24 These behaviors foster maintaining control through a sense of superiority and self-importance, disregarding/dismissing the opinions of others. These behaviors allow one to avoid vulnerability.

25 Self-deprecating behavior may elicit reassurance and validation from others and can present a person as humble and modest.

26 This person attempts to maintain control by strictly adhering to rules, standards, and expectations. Their acceptance is based on their performance.

27 Self-indulgent behaviors exhibit a lack of self-control and the need to satisfy desires and urges immediately.

21 I'm **pessimistic**, preparing myself for disappointment by being skeptical, expecting the worst, never being pleased with myself or others, never being content, distrusting others, myself, God, the church, and/or the government.

Often *Sometimes* *Never*

22 I **become a people pleaser**, giving in to others, being too submissive, keeping the peace, avoiding conflict, being a doormat, telling others what I think they want to hear, having difficulty setting boundaries, saying no, or standing up for myself.

Often *Sometimes* *Never*

23 I **become self-absorbed**, feeling sorry for myself, seeing myself as the victim, becoming overly introspective, focusing on my suffering and trials, beating myself up, and doubting myself.

Often *Sometimes* *Never*

24 I'm **self-confident**, self-sufficient, proud or haughty, boastful, arrogant, a know-it-all, opinionated, conceited, and have difficulty asking for help or receiving input from others.

Often *Sometimes* *Never*

25 I'm **self-deprecating**, too hard on myself, overly apologetic, self-condemning, and critical, taking responsibility for all relationship problems, which can result in having a hard time receiving love, compliments, and forgiveness from others.

Often *Sometimes* *Never*

26 I **am self-disciplined**, perfectionistic, base acceptance of myself and others on performance, always striving, legalistic, living by *shoulds* and *oughts*, and afraid to make mistakes.

Often *Sometimes* *Never*

27 I **can be self-indulgent**, doing what "feels good," being compulsive (to satisfy an urge), being impulsive (to act without thinking), eating, drinking, using sex or pornography to satisfy cravings.

Often *Sometimes* *Never*

28 Such behaviors allow us to avoid taking responsibility for our wrongdoing, thereby momentarily reducing our guilt and shame. This enables us to maintain a positive self-image and guard against potential criticism.

29 I may experience these feelings when I realize that I can't control my environment and circumstances or am unable to manage my anxiety.

30 These behaviors are a double-edged sword. They may be a defense mechanism, protecting against perceived threats, rejection, or potential conflict. In contrast, they may be a passive-aggressive attempt to gain or maintain control in a relationship.

31 Self-pity may be a way to gain attention and sympathy, avoid responsibility through being a *victim*, or elicit validation.

32 This coercively controlling behavior gets its way by dominating others.

33 Such feelings may bolster one's self-esteem and affirm one's identity or protect against one's own fear and insecurity.

34 These behaviors show a lack of respect for others and/or prioritizing self above others, driven by a sense of self-importance.

35 Competitive attitudes want to control one's status relative to others. These attitudes are driven by insecurity or a need for validation.

28 I **become self-righteous and defensive**, justify or rationalize my behavior, avoid taking responsibility for my actions, and blame others. *Often*   *Sometimes*   *Never*

29 I **feel tense, nervous, impatient,** agitated, restless, and unable to relax. *Often*   *Sometimes*   *Never*

30 I **withdraw, pull away, or distance myself from others,** isolate myself, avoid conflict, ignore the problem, and don't openly express feelings or opinions, appearing uncaring, unsympathetic, or indifferent. *Often*   *Sometimes*   *Never*

31 I **feel sorry** for myself. *Often*   *Sometimes*   *Never*

32 I **try to get my way** (control) by manipulating, intimidating, or blaming others. *Often*   *Sometimes*   *Never*

33 I **feel morally superior** to others and can become judgmental, intolerant, harsh, or prejudiced. *Often*   *Sometimes*   *Never*

34 I **become rude** to or inconsiderate of others because I am selfish, self-centered, self-absorbed, or egocentric (pompous). *Often*   *Sometimes*   *Never*

35 I **am jealous** of what others have and become resentful, covetous, greedy, and unable to be happy for another's accomplishments. *Often*   *Sometimes*   *Never*

The objective of the **WHO DO YOU THINK YOU ARE?** diagram aims to help the disciplee determine how the *messages* they've received in life contribute to the development of their identity and resulting fleshly behaviors, aiding in the disciplee's self-awareness.

When introducing this homework to the disciplee (see **QUESTION 8, CONSIDER THIS**), explain that the disciplee should undertake this exercise after prayer and seeking the Lord's guidance. It should take roughly an hour to complete.

The disciplee will reflect on both positive and negative messages from people and events that have influenced their lives. They will seek to identify how external factors, combined with their internal world, have influenced their **BELIEFS, THOUGHTS, AND FEELINGS** about themselves. How have these perceptions fueled their **ACTIONS/CHOICES** and shaped their identity?

For as he thinks within himself, so he is (Proverbs 23:7).

These concepts will be further explored in **Session 2**.

Who Do You Think You Are?
Forming Your Identity

Examples of Messages You Received About Yourself from Pivotal People in Your Life

Dad	**Mom**	**Teachers**	**Employer**	**Friends**
I have value	I am not allowed to make mistakes	I am favored	I have great potential	They can't keep up with me
I am loved	I must be perfect	I must work hard	Join our company	I'm fun
You enjoy me	I am special	I must be the best	They want me	I'm too busy
	Achievement matters			

Significant Events in Your Life

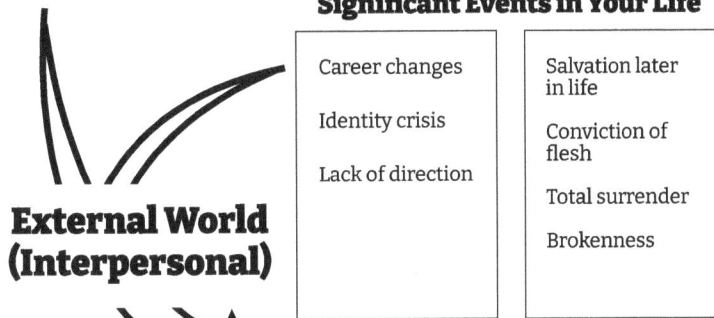

Career changes	Salvation later in life
Identity crisis	Conviction of flesh
Lack of direction	Total surrender
	Brokenness

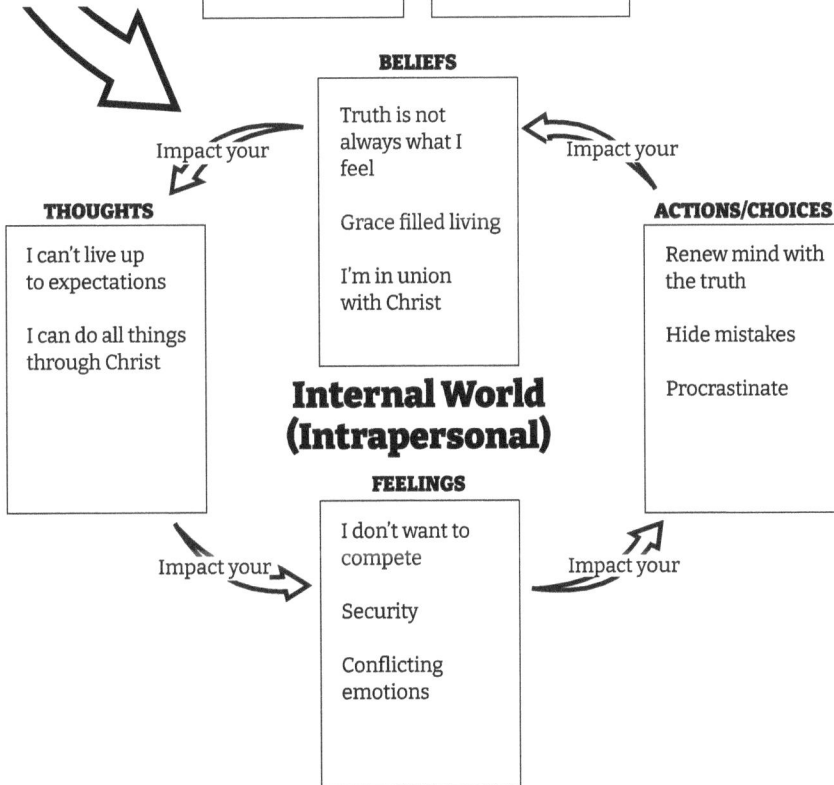

External World (Interpersonal)

BELIEFS

Truth is not always what I feel

Grace filled living

I'm in union with Christ

Impact your

THOUGHTS

I can't live up to expectations

I can do all things through Christ

Internal World (Intrapersonal)

ACTIONS/CHOICES

Renew mind with the truth

Hide mistakes

Procrastinate

Impact your

FEELINGS

I don't want to compete

Security

Conflicting emotions

Impact your

When introducing the **WHO DO YOU THINK YOU ARE?** exercise to the disciplee, the following are facets that he or she must clearly understand:

In the top five boxes, the disciplee will choose the five people who have most influenced their life. These may include parents, grandparents, spouses, or others such as teachers, youth group leaders, employers, or friends. The **MESSAGES** are what that person has communicated *to* them or *about* them, and they may include things they said and/or how the person treated the disciplee. The messages may be positive or negative or a combination of both.

The **SIGNIFICANT EVENTS IN YOUR LIFE** category is subjective. This is asking for an event or events that may or may not *appear* significant but had a strong impact on the disciplee—anything from the divorce of one's parents to a crippling car accident or getting all "A's" on a report card.

Finally, the **EXTERNAL WORLD**, in conjunction with our **INTERNAL WORLD** (our unique God-given chemistry), contributes to our view of the world. This exercise asks, "How did the disciplee learn to see themself?" Are they charming, funny, or not enough? Based on these **BELIEFS**, what kind of **THOUGHT** patterns developed? For example, was it unacceptable to have a bad day or be discouraged? Was there a continual striving to prove themself? Did these thoughts contribute to **FEELING** superior, entitled, or shamed, among others? What did those actions look like once the disciplee's **BELIEFS, THOUGHTS**, and **FEELINGS** fueled their **ACTIONS/CHOICES**?

The discipler may choose to share some or all of the following information when reviewing the **WHO DO YOU THINK YOU ARE?** homework with the disciplee:

- Developing self-awareness is the disciplee's first step in owning their situation.

- When a person is born into the world, they have needs that must be met to survive. The first method we employ to get our needs met is to cry. As we develop, so does our capacity to adapt our behavior to new ways of getting needs met.

- Is the disciplee able to make the connection between the messages they've received, their life experiences, and who they believe they are? What are they believing? Our thoughts stem from our beliefs, and our feelings arise from how we think. If we have shame as a core *belief*, we may *think* we're bad and will *feel* bad. If pride is a core *belief*, we may *think* we're entitled and will *feel* entitled. If our fundamental beliefs are based on a lie, this can leave us with a very false sense of who we are. This, then, is the way we proceed through life. Who we are (or believe we are) drives what we do. Whether true or false, our belief is substantiated when our actions line up with who we think we are.

- The behaviors resulting from messages we receive may follow a pattern or result in a conflict. If we believe we are bad, we may *give up*, choose poor friends, rebel, and do poorly in school. In contrast, we may *try harder* by seeking approval through people-pleasing and perfectionism. It is not unusual to see both types of behavior operating at different times.

Who Do You Think You Are?
Forming Your Identity

Personalize Messages You Received About Yourself from Pivotal People in Your Life

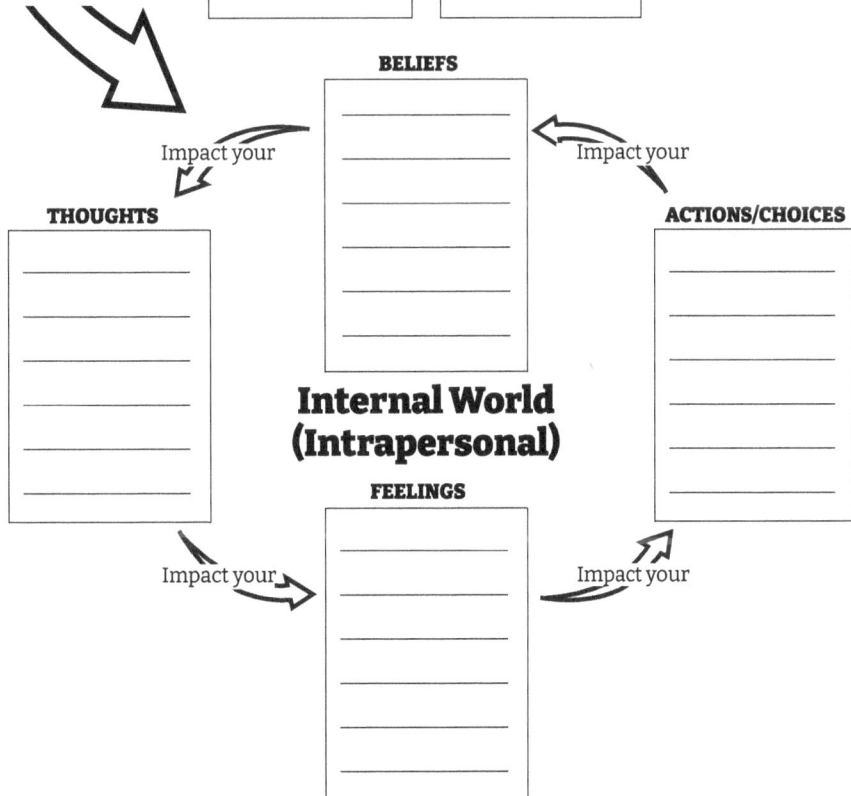

Significant Events in Your Life

External World (Interpersonal)

Internal World (Intrapersonal)

BELIEFS

Impact your

Impact your

THOUGHTS

ACTIONS/CHOICES

Impact your

Impact your

FEELINGS

DISCIPLER'S NOTES

1. We are looking for values, beliefs, and congruity. If a disciplee says appearance is very important, and this is not reflected in their grooming, this indicates inconsistency between beliefs and practice. Would this individual have an objective view of themselves?

2. Many folks are out of touch with their own feelings. The **LIFE EXPERIENCE** survey may produce unexpected emotions if longstanding patterns are recognized for the first time. This new awareness could produce tears or a period of silence. Don't interrupt in either case; demonstrate that you are okay when the disciplee expresses emotions.

3. An example of what might surprise an individual is realizing they have been repeatedly rejected and disappointed. How could this affect their concept of God and ability to trust Him?

4. Sharing intimate details of life with a stranger is difficult. Let the disciplee know that you understand how they might feel. This encourages them to reveal more about themselves as they become increasingly comfortable in the weekly sessions.

CONSIDER THIS: SESSION 1

1. What do you think is reflected through an individual's clothing, personal grooming, and body language? How would you describe your own? What is communicated to others in this way? How important is it?

    _____

    _____

    _____

    _____

2. Did you notice any emotional patterns today as you shared your life story?

    _____

    _____

    _____

    _____

3. Were you surprised by anything you shared about yourself, others, or God in today's session? If so, what were they, and why did they surprise you?

    _____

    _____

    _____

    _____

4. Is it difficult to share details of your life with someone you don't know? Why, or why not?

    _____

    _____

    _____

5. What is the difference between a desire and a goal?

   A. A desire is something an individual may want very badly but may not be able to obtain. Example: a happy marriage.

   B. A goal is something I can take steps to reasonably accomplish through my own sphere of influence. Example: committing to weekly discipleship sessions and prioritizing adequate time for full participation.

   C. Examples of goals for personalized discipleship:

      • Meditate on weekly scripture verses provided in the notebook.

      • Prayerfully personalize the interactive materials and homework.

      • Trust God with my desires.

      • Focus on a growing relationship with Jesus.

6. When filling out the **AN ABUNDANT LIFE** worksheet, we are looking for emotional honesty. What is actually true in a person's thoughts and affections, even if it isn't flattering?

7. Suggest that the disciplee review their answers in the **STRATEGIES AND ATTITUDES** interactive to see if they recognize some behavioral patterns emerging there.

8. Let the disciplee know the **WHO DO YOU THINK YOU ARE?** assignment is an important exercise that will be referred to in upcoming sessions. Encourage prayer and thoughtfulness when personalizing this diagram, and point out that the Holy Spirit may use it to illustrate vital aspects of identity!

5. What is the difference between a desire and a goal? Why is it important to make this distinction? Specifically, what are your goals for personalized discipleship?

A. _____

_____

B. _____

_____

C. _____

_____

6. Fill in (personalize) the **AN ABUNDANT LIFE** worksheet.

7. Complete the **STRATEGIES AND ATTITUDES THAT MIGHT ARISE WHEN I PERCEIVE I HAVE "UNMET NEEDS"** questionnaire.

8. Personalize the **WHO DO YOU THINK YOU ARE?** diagram. Pray before beginning and ask the Lord to guide your responses. Expect to spend at least one hour on this assignment.

What Is the Flesh?

Once we review the disciplee's background and why they have come, we begin a discussion of the flesh. The purpose of **WHAT IS THE FLESH?** is to familiarize the disciplee with the flesh and how it manifests itself in their life. The flesh is most identifiable by its desire to be in control, thus operating independently from God. The flesh is very adaptable in seeking to get what it wants.

Often, a person comes for discipleship because it has become clear to them that life as they know it is no longer working. We address the flesh in the early stage of discipleship to facilitate an awareness of what the disciple *is living out of.* Just as we are convicted of our need for a Savior, we must be convicted of our fleshly living. Revelation of our flesh happens through the Holy Spirit and can be both a point-in-time and a lifelong process.

It can be difficult to disciple someone who doesn't struggle or see a need for change. Once the disciplee sees the fruitless nature of the flesh, they are increasingly motivated to begin living the abundant life God intended for them.

While the **ABUNDANT LIFE, THE STRATEGIES AND ATTITUDES**, and the **RED FLAGS** exercises (as well as Session 4) help the disciplee to understand how their indwelling sin is uniquely manifested in the flesh, there are also fleshly characteristics that apply to every human. These are included here. As the discipler, we may glean further understanding from the notes that follow. As the Spirit leads, we may share this information with the disciplee.

The Flesh is Deceived

As we've seen through the **WHO DO YOU THINK YOU ARE?** exercise, we understand that from birth, the power of sin influences our lives. Because of this, although entirely unaware, we become self-focused in developing our life strategy. We learn to live out of our own resources, with each of us having varying degrees of success. Regardless of how we end up living, we are deceived into believing this is *who we are.* Whether *good* flesh (socially acceptable, well-liked, people-pleaser) or *bad* flesh (depressed, addicted, rebellious), we accept that we are what we are.

The Flesh Despises Powerlessness

Powerlessness is frightening for those who learned early that others would not meet their needs (real or perceived). The flesh does not trust God, nor can it submit to God. Instead, to decrease feelings of powerlessness, the flesh looks for ways to increase its own power.

It is difficult to assign an exact definition of the flesh; however, here are some aspects to consider:

- Although not synonymous with indwelling sin, Romans 8:7-8 tells us that the flesh is *joined with* and enslaved to the power of sin.

- The flesh provides ongoing expression for an individual's response to the power of sin. This response assumes many forms (Galatians 5:19-21).

- Although located in the mortal body, the flesh impacts the soul continually and significantly.

- A constant and persistent *servant* of sin, the flesh produces carnality in the life of the believer.

- Our flesh is always at war with the Holy Spirit (Galatians 5:17).

- The flesh will never be eradicated from our mortal bodies.

UNIVERSAL CHARACTERISTICS OF THE FLESH

The Flesh Is Deceived

The fleshly mind is filled with many distorted perceptions and values. Worldly messaging in education, advertising, social media, and entertainment has profoundly impacted it. Many are convinced that achievement, financial success, and satisfying relationships will provide security and happiness.

Religious flesh believes it is capable of holy living. When *missing the mark* becomes obvious, this variation of the flesh tries harder and is honestly confused by repeated failure (Romans 7:15-24). We develop personal strategies to gratify basic needs (Proverbs 14:12) and avoid pain at all costs. An assumed identity is adopted and adapted to navigate life as smoothly as possible.

The Flesh Despises Powerlessness

The flesh longs to be safe, strong, and satisfied. Those with so-called *good* flesh may establish some sense of these attributes, but a closer look reveals these people are actually being controlled or controlling others. Perhaps family members or colleagues would testify that anger, avoidance,

This attempt at control can take many forms, both offensive and defensive. In many instances, because the flesh can be so deceptive, its actions will not seem controlling.

In **Session 5**, we closely examine what happened at the Cross. If the Spirit leads, now is a good time to encourage the disciplee that God has provided the answer. This encouragement may include a general overview or some level of detail.

The Flesh Assumes a False Identity

Each of us learns to develop our strategy for living based on our own resources. While it may be rare for all of the resources listed to be at our disposal, they may be achievable at different times in our lives. No matter how good these things make us look or feel, or how many accolades we receive, they have no real *life*. For an unbeliever, as a slave to sin (Romans 6:17-18), this is the only life available. As a believer, the good news is that we have a choice to yield to the power of the Holy Spirit.

If we set our mind on these fleshly characteristics instead of the Spirit, we will not be able to please God (Romans 8:8). This self-reliance ignores our true nature of dependence on God for real life and aligns us with the world's values. We become prideful because of how we look and what we've achieved rather than rejoicing in our inherent value as image-bearers of God.

The fleshly identity is inherently corrupt and opposed to God's will and cannot be improved. Even *good flesh* is bad. The only solution for the flesh is to put it to death (Romans 8:13). Jesus accomplished the remedy when He died on the Cross and defeated the power and dominion of sin (Galatians 2:20; Galatians 5:24-25).

The Flesh is Flexible

As stated earlier, the flesh is highly adaptable and easily swayed by different circumstances, worldly standards, cultural norms, fluctuating emotions, and other internal and external influences. It resists the power of the Holy Spirit and clings to old habits, attitudes, and sinful desires.

The flesh is focused on self and making life work, and in keeping with Galatians 5:19-21, it manifests itself in countless sinful actions. Because it cannot trust or depend on the Lord, the flesh will always employ yet one more tactic.

or other forms of manipulation are utilized to maintain control of people and situations.

Blame-shifting, substance abuse, or other self-defeating behaviors may emerge when difficulties arise. While hiding any sign of weakness, there may be a refusal to accept responsibility. The entire focus is now dedicated to minimizing feeling out of control, even though we may not be aware of this agenda.

It becomes evident the believer has little understanding of what happened at the Cross. No true liberty has been appropriated. If prolonged suffering is experienced, anger may be directed towards others, oneself, or God.

The Flesh Assumes a False Identity

- Family of origin
- Human intelligence
- Educational levels
- Physical attractiveness
- Personality/charisma
- Natural talents/abilities
- Financial status
- Achievements/accomplishments
- Vibrant health and fitness

These are lofty aspirations, and it is unlikely that all will be achieved. However, many of us are on a quest for continual self-improvement. There are self-help books (even in our Christian bookstores), New Year's resolutions, and even plastic surgeons. We might switch jobs, move to a new location, and buy a new wardrobe to feel better about ourselves.

Do we understand it is not possible to improve or rehabilitate the flesh? In Romans 8:7, God tells us our flesh is only fit for the Cross. The flesh was condemned at the Cross, but do we really understand what this means?

The Flesh Is Flexible

When we find ourselves in overwhelming circumstances, we discover the remarkable resilience of the flesh. Perhaps our marriage is on the brink of collapse, or one of our children is in serious trouble. We may be facing life-threatening news regarding our health. Our previous efforts to fix these problems have failed, and now we resort to an entirely new repertoire of behaviors.

The mild-mannered person is horrified by their explosive anger and foul language. A responsible, dutiful individual suddenly shuts down and becomes immobilized. Depression and fear sweep over the emotions, and

The Flesh Attempts to Satisfy Needs

As we learned in **THE ABUNDANT LIFE** exercise, feeling loved, secure, and significant are legitimate needs instilled in us by God's design. While people may help, God is the only source who can ultimately meet our needs.

The desire to satisfy our needs is a driving force behind all fleshly behavior. The flesh seeks gratification through illegitimate means to satisfy its wants—indulging in immoral behaviors, relentlessly pursuing possessions, wealth, or status, seeking affirmation and acceptance from others, self-sufficiency, domination, avoidance, emotional highs, or false religion. The flesh attempts to fill the void that can only be filled by God through a relationship with Jesus.

The Flesh Strives to Manage Emotions

By its very nature, the flesh is emotionally immature. It is selfish and self-focused, so it cannot relate to God, others, or its environment in healthy ways. There is no true sense of peace. When its desires are thwarted, the flesh responds in emotionally unhealthy ways, leading to harmful behaviors.

In contrast, when a disciplee experiences a legitimately uncomfortable emotion in response to an actual situation, the desire to regain their comfort and control may cause them to resort to a fleshly response.

Ultimately, when one is walking in the Spirit (with all the fruit of the Spirit at their disposal), a person will display healthy responses in their daily living.

Why Do So Many Christians Continue to Live "According to the Flesh?"

The flesh is both deceived and a deceiver. The mind set on the flesh cannot see what it is living out of, and it cannot cast itself out. It believes it is in control, and even when it feels out of control, it believes it can regain control on its own. A mind set on the flesh alleviates any need to trust in or depend on God.

If I trust God and my suffering continues, what will that do to my faith? Is it *safer* to avoid testing my beliefs to see if the Lord is faithful? We often hear, "The Lord will never give you more than you can handle." Is this true?

bitterness creeps into the heart and mind. For some, debilitating loss and suffering are experienced as never before. At such a time, *life as we know it* falls apart. We realize our new tactics are no better than the old ones. The flesh has no real answers or wisdom to offer.

The Flesh Attempts to Satisfy Needs

Possessions, pursuit of pleasure, and perfect performance do not deliver on their promises. Our essential needs do not go away since they are legitimate and created by God. The problem is believing that we, or others, can satisfy them.

We search for ways to find acceptance if we've been repeatedly rejected. We may become people pleasers, but soon learn this way of relating is hollow and unfulfilling. If we've been betrayed or abandoned, we may discover an inability to forgive those who contributed to our feelings of emptiness. The anger and sadness remain, stealing the very peace we long to experience.

The Flesh Strives to Manage Emotions

Loneliness, anger, anxiety, and fear are not handled well by the flesh. We attempt to eliminate these painful feelings as quickly as possible in various ways. One strategy is compensating by treating ourselves to shopping sprees, expensive vacations, and other "feel good" activities. These may be enjoyable for brief periods but won't provide permanent relief. We will add guilt and worry to our previous struggles if we can't afford these indulgences. In desperation, some may turn to substance abuse or other addictive behaviors. These set into motion a whole new series of problems and painful emotions.

Even activities that are not sinful in themselves can become compulsive and destructive when they are carried to an extreme. What is really going on when we find ourselves spending too many hours preoccupied with social media, television, gaming, or movies? The flesh is a poor steward of our time.

Why Do So Many Christians Continue to Live "According to the Flesh"?

Our fleshly mindset, habits, and goals are often difficult for us to recognize. We've lived this way for so many years and don't realize there is something far better and readily available for believers. How we typically think, choose, and feel are so ingrained that we accept this poor substitute for an abundant life.

Another reason that many believers continue to live according to the flesh is because they don't really understand the provision the Lord has made for us. Do we believe that we have indeed been given *everything* we need for life and godliness (2 Peter 1:3)? If we say we do, why do we continue to behave in ways that belie our words?

This was Paul's dilemma in Romans 7. What happened to him between Chapters 7 and 8, where he exclaims, *"Therefore, there is now no condemnation for those who are in Christ Jesus (Romans 8:1)"*? Perhaps this was the point that motivated his Ephesians 1:17-21 prayer. The eyes of our hearts must be enlightened through the Spirit of God.

The **RED FLAGS INDICATING THE FLESH** exercise is designed to provide additional insight into the disciplee's unique version of the flesh. As the discipler, this exercise will provide additional information as to the disciplee's level of self-awareness. Does the disciplee believe the Lord is revealing something to them? Do they recognize several manifestations of their flesh? It is not unusual for a disciplee to have difficulty identifying all of their fleshly traits.

The disciplee should have an understanding of each of the red flags. The flesh adjusts easily to get what it wants. Just because a behavior doesn't seem applicable today doesn't mean it won't be operating next week or next year.

1 Through Christ and the indwelling Holy Spirit, believers are set free from the power of sin and able to live victoriously. It's a choice of the will.

2 The flesh impacts the body and the soul. To experience union with Christ, the Holy Spirit must communicate the truth of this union to our mind.

3 Legalism allows the flesh to feel a sense of control (through *doing*), while grace requires trust in and dependence on God.

Are there any benefits to fleshly living? The mindset of the flesh believes it is in control and does not need to place much trust in others. We do what we want, when we want—at least to some degree—and avoid suffering at all costs. We are impatient with difficult or needy people and have minimal involvement with them. It's much easier that way; we have busy lives. We attempt to cope with our problems and challenges on our own. Sometimes, we put great effort towards resolving them, and sometimes we give up. Occasionally, we fluctuate between the two in the very same issues. Neither approach is really effective. Even so, asking others for help may not be something we're comfortable considering.

Apart from God's illumination, we will never see our own patterns of fleshly living. The mind set on the flesh establishes fortified areas of unbelief! These become mighty strongholds that can only be displaced by truth. We must ask the Lord to renew our minds during each personalized discipleship session.

RED FLAGS INDICATING THE FLESH

In addition to the universal fleshly characteristics that apply to all humans, each individual develops their own patterns of fleshly behavior. The following red flags indicate we are walking after the flesh instead of walking in the Spirit. Which of these have you experienced consistently in your life?

1. _____ My flesh does not understand victory over sin. Instead, it strives in its own strength. *"There is therefore now no condemnation for those who are in Christ Jesus. For the law of the Spirit of life in Christ has set you free from the law of sin and death"* (Romans 8:1-2). *"For those who are according to the Flesh set their minds on the things of the Flesh, but those who are according to the Spirit, the things of the Spirit"* (Romans 8:5).

2. _____ My flesh cannot testify to the experience of union with Christ. *"The Spirit Himself bears witness with our spirit that we are children of God,"* (Romans 8:16).

3. _____ My flesh tends toward legalism rather than the grace found in knowing Jesus. *"Now I say, as long as the heir is a child, he does not differ at all from a slave, although he is owner of everything … So also we, while we were children, were held in bondage under the elemental things of the world"* (Galatians 4:1,3).

4. Is the disciplee plagued by besetting sin, sinful attitudes, personal attitudes, and lack of time with the Lord? The mind set on the flesh diverts focus from God and puts it on self.

5. How does the disciplee think "renewing of the mind" occurs? Is the disciplee consciously choosing to yield themselves to the leading of the indwelling Holy Spirit?

6. Does the disciplee recognize how fear responds in controlling and/or being controlled by others? Since all flesh wants control, what are some examples of how they personally attempt control? What would it mean if they relinquished control?

7. The Lord must illuminate our union with Christ. John 14:20 is a helpful verse for describing this union. The mind set on the flesh quenches the power we have through the indwelling Holy Spirit.

8. The flesh can always find someone that it looks *better than*. Since the flesh is a pretender and cannot face the truth, it doesn't compare itself to a truly godly man.

9. When the Holy Spirit convicts a believer, he is able to confess and repent of a specific sin. "I told a (specific) lie about you to someone," as opposed to," I did something unkind."

10. Devotion implies a regular habitual practice. Do they "Pray without ceasing?" (2 Thessalonians 5:17). What does that look like to the disciplee? An attitude of thanksgiving maintains a focus on the Lord and His provision rather than our wants and *perceived needs*.

11. Brokenness involves humility and acknowledging our need for and dependence on God. The flesh resists brokenness because it wants what it wants (James 4:1-2).

12. The flesh can imitate *good* works to serve its purpose, but those works have no spiritual value.

4. _____The power of God is not seen in my life. *"...because the mind set on the flesh is hostile toward God; for it does not subject itself to the law of God, for it is not even able to do so ..." (Romans 8:7).*

5. _____ There is no testimony of transformation through a renewed mind. *"And do not be conformed to this world, but be transformed by the renewing of your mind, that you may prove what the will of God is, that which is good and acceptable and perfect" (Romans 12:2).*

6. _____ The flesh is fearful, either controlling others or being controlled—letting circumstances dictate its actions. *"For you have not received a spirit of slavery leading to fear again, but you have received a spirit of adoption as sons by which we cry out, Abba! Father!" (Romans 8:15).*

7. _____ My flesh does not understand the indwelling Holy Spirit, so prays as if God is only external to myself. *"And I will ask the Father, and He will give you another Helper, that He may be with you forever; that is the Spirit of truth, whom the world cannot receive, because it does not behold Him or know Him, but you know Him because He abides with you and will be in you" (John 14:16-17).*

8. _____ My flesh likes to compare itself to others, but not to a godly man. *"But let each one examine his own work, and then he will have reason for boasting in regard to himself alone, and not in regard to another" (Galatians 6:4).*

9. _____ My flesh cannot admit to specific wrongdoing in accordance with conviction of the Holy Spirit. Instead, it minimizes and speaks generally. *"If we say we have no sin, we are deceiving ourselves, and the truth is not in us" (1 John 1:8).*

10. _____ My flesh is not devoted to prayer, nor does it have an attitude of thanksgiving. My flesh prays when it wants something from God or is angry with Him. *"Devote yourselves to prayer, keeping alert in it with an attitude of thanksgiving" (Colossians 4:2).*

11. _____ My flesh resists brokenness when the Lord brings it about. *"For the Flesh sets its desire against the Spirit, and the Spirit against the Flesh; for these are in opposition to one another, so that you may not do the things that you please" (Galatians 5:17).*

12. _____ My flesh imitates the fruit of the Spirit. It is a hypocrite because it is only concerned with outward appearances. *"Woe to you, scribes and Pharisees, hypocrites! For you are like whitewashed tombs, which on the*

13. The flesh relies on itself because it isn't willing to submit to God. It finds no peace in prayer because it doesn't trust and depend on the Lord.

14. The flesh is selfish and self-absorbed and wants what it wants when it wants it.

15. A believer who is confident that God is always good—for themself and others—will not feel sorry for themself in hard circumstances.

16. The flesh can't stand the guilt and shame of sin, so it blames others for its actions. The flesh doesn't understand the role of the Cross in the believer's life.

17. As a believer, Paul experienced in the flesh the persistent influence of sin and his inability to overcome it. Is this all that a believer can reasonably expect?

18. As believers, we belong to God and should desire to live according to His will and purpose. The flesh looks to man for approval and can become enslaved to the thoughts and opinions of others.

19. The flesh understands what a godly person looks like and tries to imitate them. When there is no renewing of the mind, their efforts will always prove unsuccessful.

20. The flesh will do all the right things in order to get right with God because it doesn't understand that our doing is to flow out of who we are in Christ. In the end, this is legalism.

outside appear beautiful, but inside they are full of dead men's bones and all uncleanness" (Matthew 23:27).

13. _____ My flesh experiences anxiety, rather than the peace of God, which comes through Jesus. *"Be anxious for nothing, but in everything by prayer and supplication with thanksgiving let your requests be made known to God. And the peace of God, which surpasses all comprehension, shall guard your hearts and your minds in Christ Jesus" (Philippians 4:6-7).*

14. _____ My flesh gives in to the lust of the eyes, the lust of the flesh and the pride of life. *"Therefore do not let sin reign in your mortal body that you should obey its lusts" (Romans 6:12).*

15. _____ My flesh feels self-pity when it doesn't get what it wants. *"Not that I speak from want; for I have learned to be content in whatever circumstances I am" (Philippians 4:11).*

16. _____ My flesh refuses to take responsibility for sin. It is quick to shift blame to another. *"And the man said, 'The woman who Thou gavest to be with me, she gave me from the tree, and I ate.' Then the Lord God said to the woman, 'What is this you have done?' And the woman said, 'The serpent deceived me and I ate'" (Genesis 3:12-13).*

17. _____ My flesh regularly experiences Paul's frustration expressed in Romans 7. *"For that which I am doing, I do not understand; for I am not practicing what I would like to do, but I am doing the very thing I hate" (Romans 7:15).*

18. _____ My flesh is more concerned about pleasing others than the Lord. *"You were bought with a price; do not become slaves of men" (1 Corinthians 7:23).*

19. _____ My flesh tries to suppress, deny, repress or employ other psychological defenses to avoid the appearance of being conformed to the world. *"And do not be conformed to this world, but be transformed by the renewing of your mind, that you may prove what the will of God is, that which is good and acceptable and perfect" (Romans 12:2).*

20. _____ My flesh tries to be *good enough* by doing good things or being good at things, because it doesn't recognize that we are made righteous in Jesus. *"... and in Him you have been made complete, and He is the head over all rule and authority" (Colossians 2:10).*

21. The flesh is prideful and self-sufficient, not willing to rely on the Lord for true wisdom.

22. The flesh may look down on others to assert (maintain) control, feel a sense of superiority, improve self-esteem, or gain validation of oneself, none of which exhibits spiritual maturity. The flesh doesn't understand that the believer is fully acceptable and accepted in Jesus (Ephesians 1:6 and Colossians 1:12).

23. When we pursue fleshly behavior, even *good* flesh, we look like an unbeliever and bear no fruit for the kingdom apart from the Lord's intervention. We give in to our fleshly thoughts and desires rather than yield to the indwelling Holy Spirit.

24. The flesh doesn't recognize who the believer is in Christ (the new creation) and strives to *do* enough in order to *be* enough.

25. The flesh gives in to the "law of sin and death." I try, I sin, I confess, I try harder. The cycle repeats until I give up. Such a believer lives a defeated life, resigned to failure. The mind set on the things above relinquishes its independence to the new creation life and can live victoriously.

THE GIFT OF EMOTIONS

The **GIFT OF EMOTIONS** material is provided to encourage disciplees that emotions are a normal and natural part of life. Emotions enable us to connect with God and others, reflect our spiritual state, and increase our ability to engage in meaningful worship, among other things.

Most people seeking help or personal growth have emotional struggles that impact their relationships with themselves and others. Some disciplees will have realized that their emotions need to be addressed. Others will have no idea that their emotions are stunted, misdirected, or unhealthy, and should be encouraged to work to develop an awareness of their emotions.

Along with varying degrees of emotional awareness, disciplees will have varying degrees of control over their emotional responses. Allow time in each session to listen to and validate the disciplee's emotions. In order to make progress with a disciplee, they must be able to temporarily set aside their emotions so they can hear, understand and receive God's truths.

21. _____ My flesh is always confident that it is right and does not fear the Lord. *"Do not be wise in your own eyes; Fear the Lord and turn away from evil"* (Proverbs 3:7).

22. _____ My flesh looks down on others. *"Do nothing from selfishness or empty conceit, but with humility of mind let each of you regard one another as more important than himself ...."* (Philippians 2:3).

23. _____ My flesh is very difficult to distinguish from an unbeliever. *"... for you are still fleshly. For since there is jealousy and strife among you, are you not fleshly and are you not walking like mere men?"* (1 Corinthians 3:3).

24. _____ My flesh continually seeks an identity because it doesn't recognize who I am through my union with Christ. *"Therefore if any man is in Christ, he is a new creature; the old things passed away; behold new things have come"* (2 Corinthians 5:17).

25. _____ Because my flesh is unable to relinquish itself to Jesus, it is resigned to its fate. *"... because the mind set on the flesh is hostile toward God; for it does not subject itself to the law of God, for it is not even able to do so ....* (Romans 8:7).

THE GIFT OF EMOTIONS

Emotions. Without them, we are no different than robots. If we allow them to get out of control or make our decisions based on them, we may live with many regrets. Merriam-Webster's Dictionary defines emotions as a "Conscious mental reaction (such as anger or fear) subjectively experienced as a strong feeling, usually directed toward a specific object and typically accompanied by physiological and behavioral changes in the body" (merriamwebster.com).

God has emotions, and because we are created in His image, we are created with emotions, too. Matthew 23:25-32; John 2:13-17; Mark 3:4; Mark 10:14 (anger); Matthew 14:14; Mark 1:41 (compassion); John 11:35 (sorrow); Hebrews 12:2 (joy) are a few examples.

Understanding our emotions and their role is essential to living an abundant life. Because God uniquely created each person, each of us has a unique emotional experience. Emotions are neither right nor wrong in themselves, and we do not need to feel shame for the emotions we experience.

Although the terms *emotions* and *feelings* are often used interchangeably, here we are using more precise definitions. While emotions involve automatic responses, feelings are how we consciously experience our emotions. It's how I *label* the emotion in my mind. This involves subjective interpretations and personal experiences, as we saw in the Who Do You Think You Are? exercise. Feelings can vary widely between individuals, and the expression of both emotions and feelings can vary across cultures. Two people may experience the same emotion and tell themselves entirely different *stories* about what it means.

Due to their involuntary nature, emotions are typically brief and intense. They may be difficult to manage in the moment. Addressing them is important, as suppressing them may make them feel stronger and lead to outbursts. Sometimes, this will involve physical methods to calm physical responses. It may also involve recognizing and naming the emotion. These are learned skills, and each disciplee will have their own work to do.

In contrast, because feelings involve cognitive awareness, we can more easily learn to manage them through understanding the personal nature surrounding them. This enables us to take our thoughts captive and reframe our beliefs to reflect God's truth.

Does the disciplee struggle to control their emotions/feelings? If we are not walking in the Spirit, our emotions both influence and are influenced by the flesh. We return to the cycle seen in the Who Do You Think You Are? exercise, operating out of our fleshly identity rather than who we are in Christ.

The **WHAT DOES IT LOOK LIKE TO ACT ON MY EMOTIONS RATHER THAN WHAT IS TRUE?** example demonstrates how easily we can slip into fleshly thinking and develop false beliefs leading to unbiblical behavior.

How we respond to external stimuli shows what we really believe. When we act on what we believe is true, what doesn't line up with God's truth will lead to fleshly behavior. That's why Romans 12:2 tells us that we are to be transformed by renewing our mind.

In the example on page 65, what am I believing? My friends have gotten together and didn't include me. I *feel* rejected, but am I actually being rejected? Am I unloved because I *feel* unloved? I have no real evidence that my friends don't care for me. To set the mind on the flesh is death (Romans 8:5).

Emotions inform us that something is happening that we need to pay attention to. Emotions based largely on our belief systems cause us to respond to particular stimuli in certain ways. Our response to this stimulus is the critical issue.

Emotions are genuine to the person who experiences them, even if they are not consciously aware of them. Emotions influence our thoughts and motivate our behaviors and can help identify what's in our hearts (see Matthew 12:34). Our feelings are expressions of our core emotions and stem from how we think about specific people or circumstances. These thoughts may be influenced by false beliefs that were formed in our past, stemming from lies about ourselves or about God. When we live according to a lie, our thoughts and emotions will reflect this, and our flesh will look for ways to cope and be more comfortable.

Our emotions respond to what we *believe* is true, so false beliefs hinder us from living God's truth. Unbiblical thinking leads to unbiblical behavior. This is why Philippians 4:8 says, "Finally, brethren, whatever is true, whatever is honorable, whatever is right, whatever is pure, whatever is lovely, whatever is commendable, if there is any excellence and if anything worthy of praise, think about these things." We benefit ourselves and those around us when we experience and express emotions that stem from right thinking (Proverbs 29:11; Ephesians 4:26-27).

When we find that we are unable to live out of Christ's abundance, it is time to examine our thoughts and focus on God's truth. Psalm 42:5-6 asks, "Why are you in despair, O my soul? And why have you become disturbed within me? Hope in God, for I shall again praise Him For the help of His presence. O my God, my soul is in despair within me; Therefore I remember You from the land of the Jordan, And the peaks of Hermon, from Mount Mizar." We must turn our focus and trust to the Lord.

WHAT DOES IT LOOK LIKE TO ACT ON MY EMOTIONS RATHER THAN WHAT IS TRUE?

- I have an experience that leaves me feeling a certain way. For example, I find out a group of friends has gotten together, and I'm not included. I feel rejected and unloved.

Colossians 3:2 tells us to set our minds on things above, not earthly things. In the example, I have set my mind on how I *feel*. What are some appropriate biblical actions that could be taken at this point?

Who am I relying on for the truth? I am not only going by how I feel, but my feelings are affecting my thoughts. Discuss some thoughts that might lead to the behavior described. As a child of God, what biblical truths might have led to biblical behavior? Consider John 6:37, Romans 5:8, and Ephesians 1:6. As I ruminate on my thoughts and feelings of being rejected and unlovable, I begin to consider them as true. I have now formed a belief.

The longer I consider a belief as true (whether true or false), the more my thoughts and behaviors become aligned with it. It may then become a belief system and impact my entire life. In this example, we can assume the time between the initial emotion and the discovery of the surprise birthday party was relatively short. There may have been enough time to develop bitterness or resentment when believing untrue thoughts. Consider the impact of years or even decades of living with false beliefs controlling our decision-making.

How are we to counteract false beliefs that motivate us? We first need to know biblical truth. It is not enough to know the truth; we must also believe it to the point of trusting in it. We then choose to walk in that truth. We have the power to make this choice by the indwelling Holy Spirit. Unfortunately, knowing the truth and being obedient to the truth doesn't immediately change the way we feel. In time, as we walk consistently in biblical truth, the truth permeates our beliefs, thoughts, and behaviors.

What might have happened if I had stopped to consider biblical truth at the outset of my feelings of being rejected and unlovable?

The Lord heals in His way and in His time. Particularly with trauma, 12 weeks will not likely be enough time for physical healing of the brain. Encourage the disciplee that the Lord is faithful, that healing is possible, and that help is available if they need it.

- Because I feel rejected, I act as if I've been rejected. I don't call my friends and avoid being in places where I might run into them.

- Because I don't see them, it confirms to me, and I believe that they have indeed rejected me.

- Because I believe I have been rejected by them, I begin to consider it true that I am indeed an unlovable person.

- I later learn that they had gotten together to plan a surprise party for my birthday and had been very busy putting everything in motion.

What emotions/feelings am I struggling with today? They are real, and my pain is real. Can I trust the God of the universe with my painful thoughts and feelings as I learn to trust Him completely with my life (Psalm 62:8)?

While exhibiting out-of-control emotions may not be acceptable, God already knows what we are feeling. We can acknowledge those feelings, give them to Him, and trust that He has more for us (Ephesians 1:17-21). 2 Corinthians 10:3-5 prompts us to take every thought captive to the obedience of Christ. This is critical when strong, potentially out-of-control emotions plague us.

In Romans 12:2, we are reminded that transformation takes place by the renewing of our minds. Practicing self-awareness can help us grow in exhibiting healthy emotions. We are responsible for displacing our faulty thinking with God's truths, as found in His Word, not our circumstances. To do that, with the prompting of the indwelling Spirit, we must learn to recognize our faulty thoughts in contrast to God's Word. When we faithfully turn to the Lord, He is faithful to renew our minds and emotions.

Trauma, or chronic stress, in various forms, may leave us feeling unsafe or helpless and can impact our emotions and our ability to experience them in a healthy manner. Where there has been trauma, physical changes in our nervous system may prompt us to bury our emotions so deeply that we experience emotional numbness.

In the alternative, we may experience intense feelings of anger, sadness, depression, fear, or shame, to name a few. This does not mean we are not responsible for the resulting behaviors associated with those feelings. Healing from trauma is neither a fast nor easy process and may be aided by the help of a trained professional.

The **EMOTIONS AND THOUGHTS I MAY EXPERIENCE** list aims to prompt the disciplee who has difficulty identifying, understanding, and processing their experiences. For some, their ability to identify their feelings may be limited to a few words. (Here, we are using *emotions* and *feelings* somewhat interchangeably).

This type of list can help develop emotional awareness in the following ways:

1. It can provide a comprehensive range of emotions that a disciplee may not be able to identify on their own, including distinguishing between emotions that are closely related.

2. It can help to identify strategies to manage dysregulated emotions (just the ability to name the emotion can help reduce the intensity).

3. It can deepen our communication with those who want to understand us better and can help us do the same for others.

4. Knowing there is a word to describe what we are feeling can be validating when we wonder if anyone else feels this way.

The disciplee should be encouraged to use the list as necessary to further develop an increased ability to recognize, understand, and manage their emotions. Such knowledge will be useful in personalizing the remainder of the sessions. Draw the disciplee's attention to the **PREACH** steps to forgiveness on page 219.

EMOTIONS AND THOUGHTS I MAY EXPERIENCE

APATHY

Bored	Forgetful	Invisible	Resigned
Can't win	Futile	It's too late	Stuck
Cold	Giving up	Lazy	Too tired
Cutoff	Hardened	Lethargic	Unfeeling
Defeated	Hopeless	Let it wait	Unfocused
Depressed	Humorless	Listless	Useless
Demoralized	I can't	Loser	What's the use?
Discouraged	I don't care	Lost	Why try?
Disillusioned	I don't count	Numb	Worthless
Doomed	Inattentive	Overwhelmed	
Drained	Indecisive	Powerless	
Failure	Indifferent	Preoccupied	

GRIEF

Abandoned	Guilty	Misunderstood	Tormented
Abused	Heartbroken	Mourning	Torn
Anguished	Heartsick	Neglected	Tortured
Ashamed	Helpless	Nobody cares	Unhappy
Betrayed	If only	Nobody loves me	Unloved
Blue	Ignored	Pity	Unwanted
Cheated	Inadequate	Poor me	Vulnerable
Despair	It's not fair	Regret	Why me?
Disappointed	Left out	Rejected	Wounded
Distraught	Longing	Remorse	
Embarrassed	Loss	Sadness	
Forgotten	Melancholy	Sorrow	

FEAR

Alone	Embarrassed	Panic	Terrorized
Anxious	Foreboding	Paralyzed	Threatened
Apprehensive	Frantic	Paranoid	Timid
Confused	Guarded	Scared	Trapped
Cowardice	Hesitant	Secretive	Uncertain
Defensive	Horrified	Shaky	Uneasy
Discomfort	Inhibited	Shame	Unsafe
Distrust	Insecure	Shy	Vulnerable
Doubt	Irrational	Skeptical	Want to escape
Dread	Nervous	Suspicious	Wary
Edgy	Out of control	Tense	Worry

LUST

Abandon	Domineering	Impatient	Ravaging
Anticipation	Driven	Insatiable	Reckless
Callous	Envy	Lascivious	Ruthless
Can't wait	Exploitive	Manipulative	Tempted
Compulsive	Fixated	Miserly	Ugly
Consuming	Forceful	Must have it	Voracious
Controlling	Frenzy	Never enough	Wanton
Cruel	Frustrated	Oblivious	Wicked
Demanding	Gluttonous	Obsessed	
Devious	Greedy	Possessive	
Discontent	Hunger	Predatory	
Disrespectful	I want	Pushy	

ANGER

Abrasive	Frustrated	Merciless	Stern
Aggressive	Furious	Murderous	Stewing
Annoyed	Harsh	Outraged	Stubborn
Argumentative	Hatred	Petulant	Sullen
Bitterness	Hostility	Rage	Vengeful
Brooding	Impatience	Rebellious	Vicious
Caustic	Indignant	Resentment	Vindictive
Defiant	Irate	Resistant	Violent
Disgust	Jealous	Smoldering	Wicked
Explosive	Livid	Spiteful	Willful
Fierce	Mad	Steely	Wrath

PRIDE

Above reproach	Disdain	Overbearing	Special
Aloof	False Dignity	Patronizing	Spoiled
Arrogant	False humility	Pious	Stoic
Bigoted	False virtue	Prejudiced	Stubborn
Boastful	Gloating	Presumptuous	stuck-up
Clever	Haughty	Rigid	Superior
Closed	Hypocritical	Self-absorbed	Uncompromising
Complacent	Isolated	Self-righteous	Unfeeling
Conceited	Judgmental	Self-satisfied	Unforgiving
Contemptuous	Know-it-all	Selfish	Unyielding
Cool	Never wrong	Smug	Vain
Critical	Opinionated	Snobbish	

COURAGEOUSNESS

Adventurous	Confident	I can	Resourceful
Alert	Creative	Independent	Responsive
Alive	Daring	Invincible	Self-sufficient
Amiable	Decisive	Loving	Sharp
Assured	Eager	Lucid	Spontaneous
Aware	Enthusiastic	Motivated	Strong
Capable	Exhilaration	Nonresistant	Supportive
Certain	Explorative	Positive	Tireless
Cheerful	Flexible	Powerful	Valiant
Clarity	Focused	Purposeful	Vigorous
Compassion	Giving	Receptive	Willing
Competent	Honorable	Resilient	

ACCEPTANCE

Appreciative	Friendly	Mellow	Tender
Beautiful	Fullness	Nothing to change	Trusting
Belonging	Gentle	Open	Understanding
Childlike	Gracious	Playful	Validated
Compassion	Harmonious	Radiant	Valued
Considerate	Intuitive	Receptive	Warm
Delight	In tune	Respectful	Welcoming
Elated	Joyful	Responsive	Well-being
Empathy	Kind	Secure	Wonder
Enriched	Loving	Soft	
Everything's okay	Magnanimous		

Do the answers to **CONSIDER THIS** indicate the disciplee has taken the appropriate time to process and understand the materials?

While the flesh is hard to define, does the disciplee understand the difference between the physical body (flesh) and the flesh influenced by and joined with the indwelling sin each believer wrestles with? Review the six bullet points at the beginning of **Session 2** if necessary.

Indwelling sin and the flesh inhabit our mortal bodies but will not exist in our glorified bodies once we are resurrected. In the meantime, indwelling sin and its fleshly counterpart influence our soul as long as we are here on earth. We will consider this truth in the following sessions.

Does the disciplee understand the universal characteristics of the flesh, which apply to every person, as opposed to the unique version of the flesh that each of us develops? Do they understand how this applies to their own lives?

Did the disciplee expose unique patterns of fleshly behavior developed because of their own chemistry and life experiences? No two versions of the flesh look exactly alike. Are they aware of the chameleonlike nature of their flesh and its ability to adapt as necessary?

PEACE

Ageless	Curious	Lighthearted	Satisfied
Amiable	Engaged	Oneness	Serenity
Blissful	Eternal	Optimistic	Soothed
Boundless	Expectant	Patient	Still
Calm	Free	Perfection	Timeless
Carefree	Fulfilled	Pleasant	Tranquility
Centered	Grateful	Pure	Unlimited
Comfortable	Happy	Quiet	Whole
Complete	Hopeful	Relaxed	Worthy
Composed	Inspired	Restful	
Content	Light	Safe	

CONSIDER THIS: SESSION 2

1. Please review **WHAT IS THE FLESH?** and **UNIVERSAL CHARACTERIS-TICS OF THE FLESH**. Jot down any questions or comments in your notebook to discuss next week.

    _____

    _____

    _____

2. Fill in the **RED FLAGS** survey. What were the most surprising aspects of the flesh you recognized? Do you think you may now become more aware of your family and friends' flesh patterns, too?

    _____

    _____

    _____

3. There are several assignments for this week. Does the disciplee have areas they need to clarify? Understanding the **WHO DO YOU THINK YOU ARE?** diagram and the flesh homework (pages 31, 33-39, 57-63) provides the framework for coming sessions, particularly **Session 4**. The disciplee must be thorough.

4. Is the disciplee aware of how their emotional responses affect themselves and others? Do they get along well with others? If not, why not? Does the disciplee recognize when they respond out of heightened emotions—anything from anger to fear to joy? Do they express their emotions fully, or can they control them and express them appropriately in a given situation? Answers to these questions are good indicators of the disciplee's emotional intelligence and self-awareness level.

5. Are there particular circumstances when the disciplee fully expresses themself, whether suitable or not? Do they think they are able to make the choice? Why or why not? Generally speaking, we can learn to communicate our emotions appropriately. The exception to this may be a physical triggering of the autonomic nervous system due to a past or presently occurring trauma. In that case, professional help may be beneficial for the physical healing of the brain.

6. Does the disciplee sense the Holy Spirit moving in their life? Does their sharing allow you to understand what this looks like for them? Encourage them to continue pressing into Him as sessions progress. If not, encourage them that the Lord works in His way, in His time, and that He will honor their commitment to a deeper relationship.

3. Were there any teachings introduced this week that you need more clarity on? If so, please let your discipler know as each new session builds on what was shared the previous week.

4. How do you see your emotions helping and/or hurting you in your daily living? What is your natural response when you experience heightened emotions?

_____

_____

5. Do you need to understand more about why you have a particular response to a circumstance or person?

_____

_____

_____

6. We anticipate the Holy Spirit is honoring your commitment to discipleship and seeks to draw you closer to the Lord. Outside of our session together, has some truth been illuminated for you? Has there been a deeper conviction in some area of your life? Are you seeing and appreciating the depth of God's grace in a fresh way? If so, please share about this in some detail.

_____

_____

_____

_____

_____

_____

The Model of Man

The wheel diagrams on the following four pages are particularly effective for visual learners!

The teaching notes beneath each diagram provide concise descriptions of each part of our being and its specific functions.

Take the time to read through each of these with your disciplee. The notes should be easy to follow, but it is important to verify understanding as you move along in this teaching.

The Bible frequently refers to the terms spirit, soul, body, and heart, and it is helpful to understand their distinctions. This model of man is called *trichotomous*. The heart is not a fourth part of our being but an important aspect that relates to spirit and soul.

If you would like more support for this model biblically and theologically, see our publisher's blog at BiblicalPsychology.net. In rare cases, there will be pushback due to some theologians teaching that spirit and soul are synonymous. If that occurs, ask to use the adjectives *spiritual* and *psychological* since there is consensus that these are different aspects of life.

Pay particular attention to the last paragraph on page 83. It is vital for the disciplee to consider the question, "What is my functional source of life?"

Only when Christ is our source of living do we bear fruit in our daily walk.

The wheel diagram is adapted from *Handbook to Happiness*, by Charles R. Solomon (Tyndale House Publishers, 1971). A video explanation is included in the free online course, *For Me to Live is Christ* (GraceStudyHall.org).

SOUL
Mind
Will
Emotions

SPIRIT
Intuition
Conscience
Communion

Relates to Others

Relates to God

Psychological

Spiritual

BODY
Physiological

1 Thessalonians 5:23
Hebrews 4:12

Relates to Environment

Man: A Tri-Unity

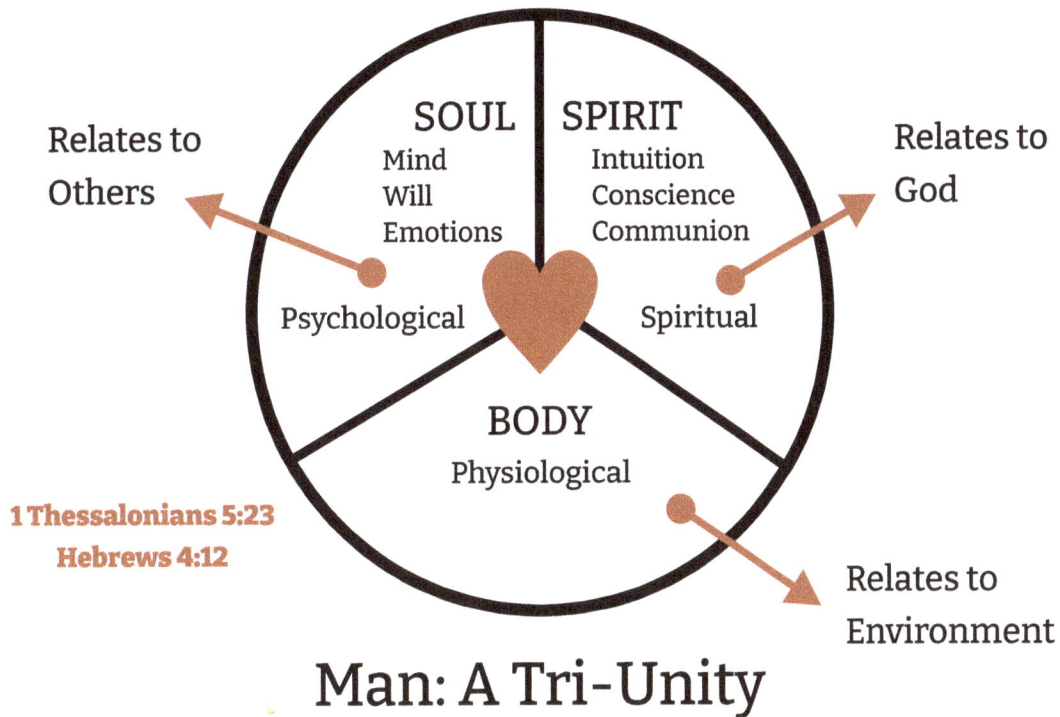

This diagram depicts man as a three-part being consisting of **SPIRIT**, **SOUL**, and **BODY** (I Thessalonians 5:23).

Through our senses, our *body* relates to our material surroundings.

Our *soul* is the seat of our personality and enables us to relate to one another. Our mind, will, and emotions function within our *soul*.

Our *spirit* perceives spiritual realities. The faculties of intuition, conscience (awareness of morality), and communion (the need for a personal relationship with God, who is Spirit) make up our human *spirit*.

We are born into the world as descendants of Adam and partakers of his fallen nature. Our *spirit* is either related to Adam (in Satan's family) or Christ (in God's family). Because of our fallen nature, our *spirit* is initially dead to God (Ephesians 2:1-3; John 8:44). Once salvation occurs, our *spirit* is regenerated through the new birth (John 3:3; Titus 3:5-6).

The heart represents the seat of our reflection, motivations, and affections. The question, "What is my functional source of life?" becomes the essential heart issue.

The diagram on page 85 directs our attention to the spiritual aspect of our being.

The "C" within the red circle illustrates the truth that Christ indwells the spirit of the believer who has received Christ.

Following its description, we see salvation's various benefits. In Christ, we have eternal security and acceptance. We can know without doubt that we have received the gift of salvation. In summary, our union with the indwelling Christ guarantees that our core spiritual needs are satisfied. We are safe, secure, loved, and a new creation!

The last aspect, *identity*, is determined by new birth in our human spirit and union with Christ.

In what part of our being have "old things passed away, and all things become new"? 2 Corinthians 5:17 confirms that this has already taken place in the spirit of every believer.

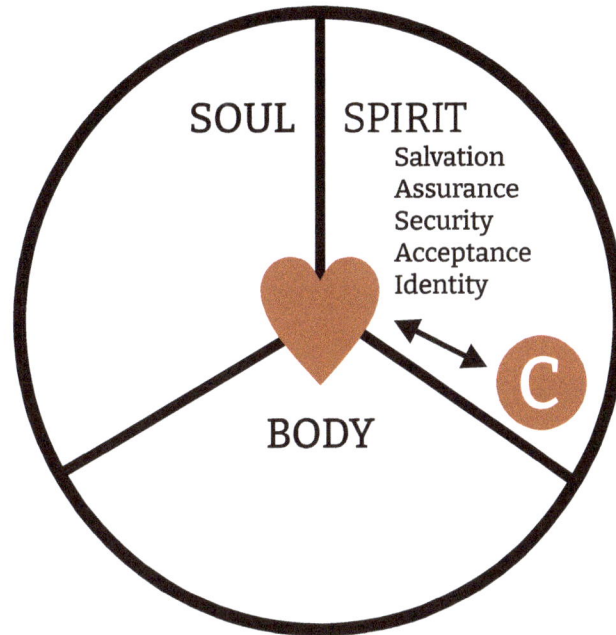

The diagram indicates five blessings for the believer who is born again.

SALVATION: When a person repents and receives Christ Jesus as personal Lord and Savior, they are saved from hell and given the gift of eternal life. Through Christ's finished work on the Cross and His resurrection, the believer is totally pardoned and transferred into God's kingdom (John 1:12; Colossians 1:13,14).

ASSURANCE: Since salvation is by grace through faith, children of God can be assured of salvation. We can know that we have eternal life (John 5:24; 1 John 5:13). Although feelings may vary, God's promises are trustworthy.

SECURITY: The born-again believer can also have security in Christ. This relates to the future. The Lord will never leave or forsake us (Hebrews 13:5). We are sealed by the Holy Spirit (Ephesians 1:13).

ACCEPTANCE: When we are saved, we are welcomed into God's family (1 John 3:1-3). We are accepted in the Beloved (Ephesians 1:6).

IDENTITY: Through regeneration, the believer becomes a new creation. In the spirit, old things have passed away, and all things have become new (2 Corinthians 5:17). Our identity is not based on what others have said or on our own opinions. Instead, our essential identity is based on what God has declared about us since we are "in Christ."

In this wheel diagram, the "S" in the center of the heart illustrates an individual who depends upon their own resources for living.

The Bible describes this self-dependence as "walking after the flesh," and results in the descriptive words listed in the soul area. Thinking, feeling and decision-making are all affected.

The second paragraph illustrates how events and repeated interactions with others affect us over time. Do I respond or react? My reactions may develop into attitudes such as having a "chip on my shoulder,"—also called reactionary sin (pages 211-213).

We compound unresolved hurts from the past with fresh rejections and challenges, creating layers of pain and bitterness. Our souls, operating independently, are unable to cope or compensate for these negative experiences.

The last paragraph shows the various ways we may live out continuous frustration. Hostility, a byproduct of frustration, may be *exported* or *imported*. Some of us tend to take anger out on other people; others attempt to repress or *stuff* these feelings. When anger is directed inward, the mind may seek distraction and relief through fantasy or obsessions.

Rejection

SOUL SPIRIT

Problems:
Family,
Money,
Work ....

Frustration

Inferiority
Insecurity
Inadequacy
Guilt: Real, Imaginary
Worry, Doubts, Fears

Salvation
Assurance
Security
Acceptance
Identity

Hostility

S

C

MIND:
Fantasy
Psychoses
Obsessions
Paranoia

EMOTIONS:
Depression
Anxiety

BODY

Works of the Flesh:
Strife, Wrath,
Deception, Envy ....

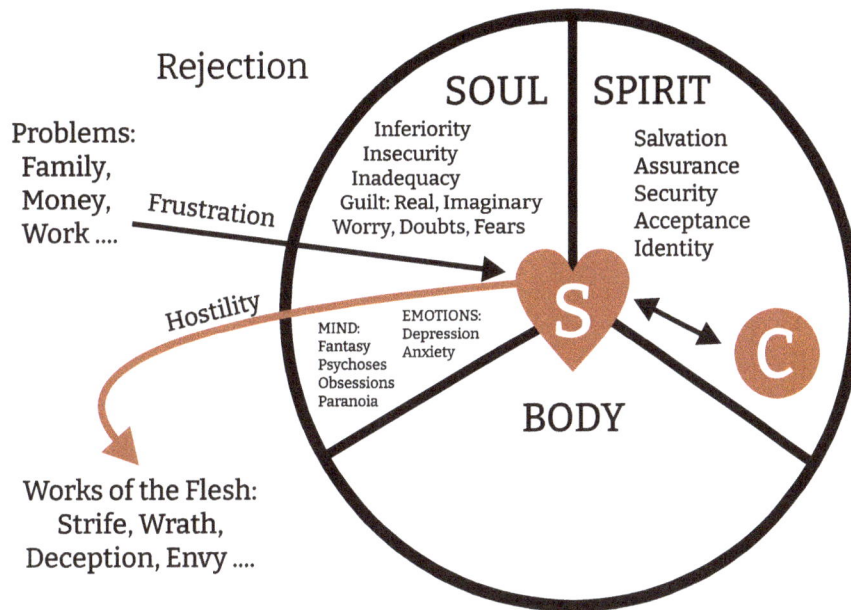

Psychological Symptoms

Carnal describes "walking after the flesh" as depending on oneself to live life with the attempt to be in control (Galatians 5:16,17; James 4:1). The wheel diagram illustrates common symptoms in the soul, whether the person is saved or unsaved. We can simultaneously be new in our human spirit yet miserable in our soul.

Common psychological symptoms can occur due to rejection and other events in this fallen world. Inferiority is the feeling that we don't measure up. Insecurity is the feeling that we are unsafe. Inadequacy is the feeling that we are unable to be successful. When we try to get our needs met independently of God, we sin. This sin violates our conscience and registers emotionally as guilt. Real guilt results from sins of commission or omission. Sometimes, false guilt occurs—a sense of guilt even though innocent.

In addition to baggage from the past, we experience pressures and problems in the present. Family conflicts, financial stress, difficulties at work, and other circumstantial difficulties cause frustration.

The "S" in the center of our diagram represents the fleshly self. Our independent ego becomes frustrated when things don't go our way. This frustration typically results in hostility, vented externally or stuffed internally. Suppressed frustration causes secondary emotional and mental problems. Depression and anxiety worsen, and the mind looks for a way of escape through fantasy. Mental confusion can escalate into psychosis—a break from reality, obsessive thoughts, and paranoia—irrational fears.

We now turn our attention to how carnal living impacts our physical bodies.

It is important to note that not all disorder is caused by sin or soulical distress. Symptoms of physiological damage may be difficult to distinguish from carnal, fleshly living.

Most of us realize that stress takes its toll and contributes to sleeplessness, anxiety, and self-defeating behaviors and that it is not the challenges of life that are to blame, per se.

No one's life circumstances are entirely free of problems or challenges. The issue centers around who it is doing the living to deal with them—our flesh or the Holy Spirit within us.

Sadly, believers in whom Christ dwells still try to harness the flesh to live a holy life. It didn't work for Paul, and it doesn't work for us (Romans 7:15-24).

The carnal disciplee needs to discern that their fleshly self is the root problem. Thankfully, we will explore God's supernatural solution.

Rejection

Problems:
Family,
Money,
Work ....

Frustration

Hostility

SOUL
Inferiority
Insecurity
Inadequacy
Guilt: Real, Imaginary
Worry, Doubts, Fears

SPIRIT
Salvation
Assurance
Security
Acceptance
Identity

S

C

MIND:
Fantasy
Psychoses
Obsessions
Paranoia

EMOTIONS:
Depression
Anxiety

BODY
Tension Headache, Nervous Stomach,
Peptic Ulcer, Hives, Rashes, Asthma,
Some Arthritis, Spastic Colon, Palpitations
of the Heart, Respiratory Ailments,
Compulsive Eating, Fatigue, Insomnia,
Escape in Sleep, Hypertension

Works of the Flesh:
Strife, Wrath,
Deception, Envy ....

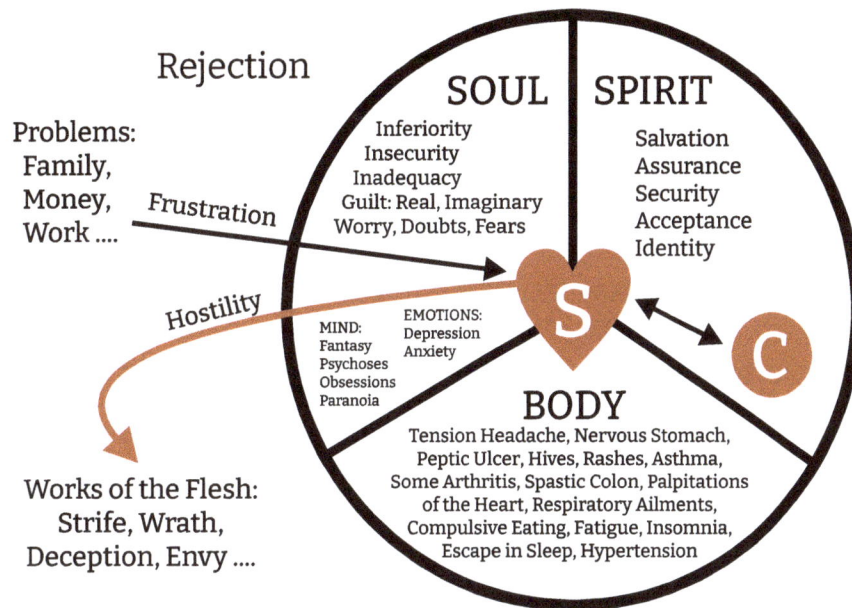

"Doing in Order to Be"
Living Under the Law

Physical Symptoms

The medical community confirms that our mental and emotional condition plays a significant role in our physical condition. The more conflicts in our soul, the more stress-related health problems we experience. This does not mean that all illness is caused by spiritual and psychological conflicts. However, conflicts within our soul usually result in significant factors relating to our physical health.

Our soul, circumstances, and physical problems are not the core issue. Our fleshly self is the core issue. Whether intentionally or unintentionally, if we live as a carnal Christian, our self (flesh) serves as our functional source of life. This does not mean we are unsaved—the natural person (1 Corinthians 2:14), nor that we are a spiritual Christian (1 Corinthians 2:15). It means we are carnal (1 Corinthians 3:1-4).

"What is the nature of a man?" This is an important question.

Are believers half sinner, half saint? Following salvation, do we now possess two natures engaging in a *civil war* within us? Do we *feed the white dog or the black dog* to determine victory? These questions may be helpful to consider and to provide greater clarity on unbiblical thinking.

Scripture tells us we are either "in Adam" or "in Christ."

We must make a distinction when using the term *nature* to describe behavioral patterns versus a Christian's unchanging spiritual nature, established through regeneration. Understanding this precious truth offers profound rest for the child of God.

WHAT IS THE NATURE OF MAN?

When describing an individual, there are two different ways to understand the term *nature*. One is to determine the essential, core components that establish personhood through Scripture. This directs us to the spiritual aspect of our being and differentiates an identity of being "in Adam" or "in Christ." Someone who is "in Adam" is not indwelt by the Holy Spirit and is incapable of walking according to the Spirit (Romans 8:6). They are, by nature, a sinner. Those "in Christ" are believers and, through spiritual birth, are in union with God (Romans 8:9). They are, by nature, righteous (saints) and have the freedom to walk in the Spirit.

The second way to define someone's *nature* is to describe how they typically behave. These tendencies flow out of personal belief systems and influence thoughts, feelings, and choices. Together, they form our habitual patterns of behavior or characteristics. In a strictly behavioral sense, we could even use this definition to refer to animals when we say, "It is the nature of a dog to bark."

Interchanging these two definitions has caused quite a bit of confusion in the discipleship process. It is helpful to realize that our essential identity reflects the condition of the human spirit, established at either our natural or new birth (John 3:3-7).

The second use of the term, *nature*, describes our soulical aspects, which fluctuate. Our souls are intended to express God's life, yet we often walk according to the flesh. We must recognize this tendency and repent when we walk according to the flesh, but our essential nature remains unchanged.

It is important to know who we truly are. Once we realize and receive God's perspective, we can be released from obsessive self-focus. As new creations, we are in union with Christ. This union is the central truth about our identity and a profound reality to appropriate. He is now our focus. We no longer need to obsessively analyze and evaluate our emotions, performance, and experiences. New liberty is available to us as we trust in who God says we are despite how we may feel or what others say about us.

Let's examine what the Scriptures show us about our material and intangible being. We are spirit, soul, and body but one in our *personhood*. Although the human spirit and soul are both intangible and closely associated, there are very significant distinctions between the two. The

We now transition from wheel diagrams to word descriptions outlining the immaterial aspects of our being.

The model of man presented in this notebook supports distinctive aspects of soul and spirit. 1 Thessalonians 5:23 and Hebrews 4:12 most clearly state the unique differences.

Since the discipleship process seeks to understand and encourage growth in grace, it is helpful to note the differences in these two areas.

At the time of salvation, we are sanctified in our spirits, where we are joined in oneness with Christ (1 Corinthians 6:17). Progressive sanctification describes the process taking place in our souls. We examine both aspects of sanctification throughout the personalized discipleship sessions.

To supplement the discussions in our sessions together, we strongly encourage the disciplee to read some of the books included in the bibliography (page 278).

body is material and perhaps the easiest aspect to observe, define, and understand.

Human Spirit

- *Pneuma*—Greek; spiritual life—*Zoe* (Numbers 27:16; Zechariah 12:1)
- The part of man that relates to and has an awareness of God
- Indwelt by the Holy Spirit (1 Corinthians 2:12)
- Regenerated, quickened, and made holy (1 Corinthians 1:2; 6:17)
- Has been sanctified (1 Corinthians 1:30; 2 Peter 1:4)
- Primary means for communion and worship with God (John 17:3; Colossians 1:12)
- Has the capacity to know and receive truth. This knowledge does not arise from the human intellect but is a witness of the Holy Spirit (Romans 8:16; 1 Corinthians 2:14)
- Intended to reign over soul and body (Colossians 1:27)
- Returns to God after physical death (Ecclesiastes 12:7)

Human Soul

- *Psuche*—Greek; psychological life
- Composed of mind, emotions, and will
- Conscious of self and others; intrapersonal and interpersonal awareness
- Progressively being sanctified, primarily through the renewed mind (Romans 8:29; 12:2; Hebrews 12:14)
- Vulnerable to the power of sin; dependent on the Holy Spirit for holy living (Romans 8:2)
- Intended to express spiritual life through my unique personality

Verses Distinguishing Spirit from Soul

"Now may the God of peace Himself sanctify you completely; and may your whole spirit, soul, and body be preserved blameless at the coming of our Lord Jesus Christ" (1 Thessalonians 5:23).

Hebrews 4:12 indicates that God's Word is operative, energizing, and effective. It is also specific! This verse compares details of things that are similar. Soul and spirit are each immaterial aspects of man but are distinct and can be divided or "pierced." In the same way, joints and marrow are each part of bone, yet distinct components.

Thoughts and intentions can be influenced by the flesh or initiated by the Holy Spirit. A believer requires illumination from the Spirit to discern the difference. *Good* ideas can be the enemy of God's *best* for us.

Identifying the distinction between flesh and Spirit determines whether we are walking according to the flesh or walking in the Spirit. The emotions and thoughts I experience may convince me that I'm fighting an internal civil war of coequal *natures.* My tendency to repeat sinful behaviors can indeed cause me to doubt I am truly righteous.

I make sense of this battle by agreeing with Paul (Romans 7:17-20) that it is SIN in me and not me that is causing the problem. Also, I remind myself that God's Word about my identity is true, not what I'm momentarily experiencing.

Galatians 5:17 explains that the real battle for the believer is the flesh versus the Spirit. In other words, who are we depending on to empower a life pleasing to God?

The solution is to recognize that I am once again living independently and not abiding in Christ. Whenever I do this, I experience what Paul describes in the second half of Romans 7.

The aspects of the human body are quite evident and understood, and although my body *houses* sin and the flesh, my soul is definitely and continually affected as well.

My body will not be redeemed until I receive a glorified body where sin and the flesh are no longer present (Romans 8:23).

"For the word of God is living and powerful, and sharper than any two-edged sword, piercing even to the division of soul and spirit, and joints and marrow, and is a discerner of the thoughts and intentions of the heart" (Hebrews 4:12).

1. Why is it important to make this distinction?

2. Has it ever seemed that you are fighting a *civil war* within yourself?

3. Does your propensity to revert to sinful behaviors make you doubt that you are truly righteous?

4. How do you make sense of this experience in light of your new identity?

5. What does Galatians 5:17 tell you about the true conflict for you as a believer?

6. What is the solution?

Human Body

- *Soma*—Greek; *Bios*—Greek; biological life; physiological awareness

- Created to interact with the physical world; equipped with five senses

- Mortal body, location of indwelling sin and the flesh

- Future sanctification, when given a glorified body (Philippians 3:21; 1 Thessalonians 3:13; 5:23; Jude 24)

Encourage the disciplee to take the time to review the wheel diagrams over the next week. Assure them that any questions or need for clarification will be addressed before we move on to Session 4.

Review the two ways we define *nature*. Ask if the disciplee had previously believed their behavior or ungodly thoughts and feelings determined their identity. Since only God has the wisdom and authority to tell us who we are, how has their understanding changed?

Regarding identity in Christ, does the disciplee believe it is helpful to understand the differences between spirit and soul? Reflect on how fluctuating emotions and thoughts affect our knowledge about our true identity. Ask about the implications this has for our daily walk with the Lord.

Understanding Galatians 5:17 is of vital importance for believers. We will continue to look at this verse more closely in the coming weeks to emphasize where our battle really takes place.

CONSIDER THIS: SESSION 3

1. Carefully review the wheel diagrams and notate any questions you have regarding the three parts of man. Do you understand these distinctions and the Scripture verses that verify them? Any questions regarding the trichotomous model of man can be discussed during our next session.

   _____

   _____

2. What had you previously believed about the nature of a believer? Did you describe yourself by your behavioral tendencies or who you are in Christ? Has your thinking changed about this? Who has the knowledge and authority to tell us who we are?

   _____

   _____

3. In **VERSES DISTINGUISHING SPIRIT FROM SOUL**, prayerfully answer questions 1-6. Why is it important to understand the differences in your spirit and soul? Which of these is vulnerable to emotional fluctuations and changing circumstances? Why is understanding the distinctions between spirit and soul significant in your daily walk?

   _____

   _____

   _____

4. How does understanding the Galatians 5:17 description of a believer's true conflict move us from bondage to liberty? Will this important truth create a paradigm shift in your own heart and mind? If so, what will that be like for you?

   _____

   _____

   _____

SESSION 4

Personalizing Our Flesh/ Counterfeit Identity

This diagram illustrates an analogy, comparing the nucleus of a cell to the central dynamic of an individual's version of the flesh.

Hereditary characteristics, carried and stored in the cell nucleus, correspond to family characteristics often established in the flesh.

A hub for information storage in the cell nucleus relates to messages we've received and remembered. These inform and generate belief systems about who we are.

Activity and growth in the cell nucleus are similar to the variable motivations reflected in my thoughts, emotions, and behaviors.

Cell nucleus regulation and control relate to the fortified strongholds in my mind, which may limit and deceive me.

The central part of the cell nucleus is consistent with our understanding of our unique core self. Although it describes a counterfeit identity, it runs the show in our daily lives.

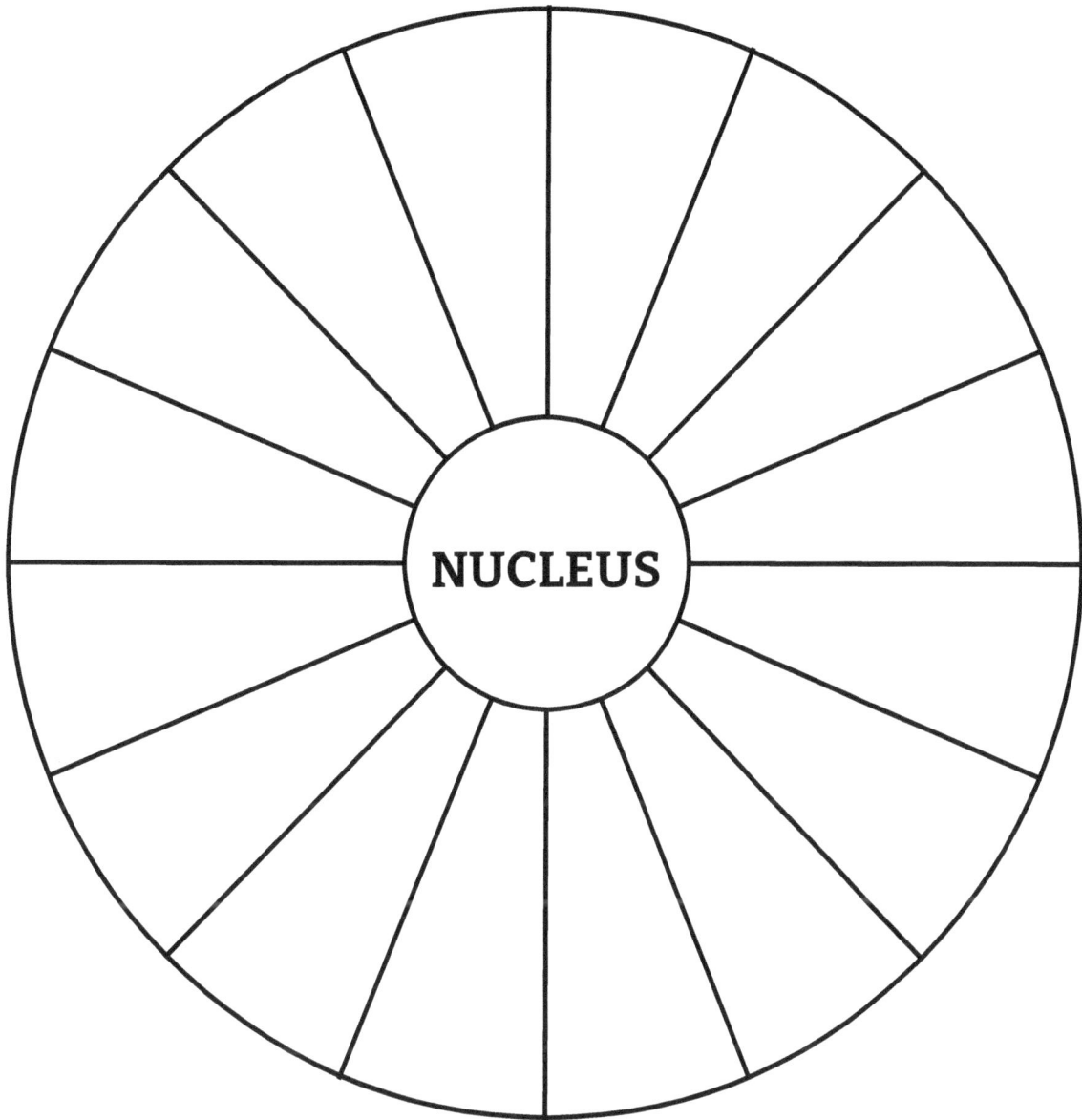

What is a Nucleus?

- That which carries and stores hereditary characteristics
- Headquarters for information storage
- The informing basis for activity and growth
- The aspect that controls and regulates
- The most important, most central part of something

The messages we've received about ourselves from other people can be blindly adopted or vigorously refused!

Ask the disciplee what they thought about the messages they received growing up. Were they encouraged, defeated, or confused by these messages?

Did the disciplee accept the messages communicated to them? Ask if they believed some or most of what they were told directly or indirectly.

Did the disciplee determine the messages they received from significant people in their lives to be untrue, and if so, to what degree?

The identity messages, beliefs/thoughts, feelings, and behaviors listed on the opposite page are taken from the example diagram on page 41. Referring to this page while viewing the messages selected will be beneficial.

Ask the disciplee to read a few of these categories aloud. What do they notice about the descriptions? Note that the descriptions listed under these headings are not always consistent. Some of them may be contradictory.

Take a moment to discuss whether or not these contradictions are typical for most people. If so, ask what could result from such mixed messages.

Because of such confusion about identity, it is no wonder so many people are searching *to find themselves.*

DISPLACING THE NUCLEUS OF THE COUNTERFEIT FLESH

What does your personal version of the flesh look like in the soul? Consider the ways family members communicated to you an *assigned identity.* How did you respond?

Personalize

1. How did you interpret and internalize the messages you received growing up?

2. Did you receive them as an accurate assessment and assume this identity?

3. Did you reject their assessment and adopt another view of who you are?

Bullet-point some beliefs/thoughts, feelings, and behaviors that resulted from this assumed identity. An example is provided from session one's diagram: **WHO DO YOU THINK YOU ARE?**

Identity Messages

- Achievement determines value
- Mistakes are not okay
- You are loved and provided for
- Physical punishment is appropriate discipline
- You are the favorite

Beliefs/Thoughts

- Conflicted about what is best
- Parents are to be feared
- I am valued and loved
- I can't live up to expectations

- I have something special; work hard to be the best

Feelings

- Love is conditional
- Stuff my feelings; not sure how I feel
- I feel confident
- I'm tuned in to what others feel
- I am anxious

Behaviors

- Work very hard; perfectionist
- Hide mistakes and failures
- Chronic procrastination
- Overeating
- Resist authority figures

The disciplee has just read their responses to these same categories on the previous page.

Instruct them to transfer five descriptions from their **WHO DO YOU THINK YOU ARE?** diagram to the corresponding categories.

Ensure the disciplee clearly understands these directions and that this is a part of their homework for next week.

Now, fill in your personalized responses to **WHO DO YOU THINK YOU ARE?**

Identity Messages

- _____
- _____
- _____
- _____
- _____

Beliefs/Thoughts

- _____
- _____
- _____
- _____
- _____

Feelings

- _____
- _____
- _____
- _____
- _____

Behaviors

- _____
- _____
- _____
- _____
- _____

Read the first sentence on the top of page 107 and then turn to the example diagrams on pages 111 and 113 in your own notebook.

Let the disciplee see what an example of a personalized **NUCLEUS OF THE COUNTERFEIT IDENTITY** diagram looks like (page 111). Then, turn to page 113 and ask if they have any questions about how to complete their own diagram. They are simply moving some of their responses listed on page 105 onto the *spokes* of this diagram.

Let the disciplee know that questions 1-3 are to be filled in as part of their **CONSIDER THIS** assignment for next week.

The central paragraph on page 107 is essential; ask the disciplee to read it aloud. Suggest they review the diagram on page 111 in more detail before next week's session. Ask them to imagine what it would be like to live out of that particular identity.

Ask why an individual would strive to reinforce and defend a false identity. Is a false identity, even a poor one, less frightening than no sense of identity at all?

Referencing Matthew 16:24-25, ask what life the disciplee must lose before they can find and save their life. Determine whether or not they understand this verse to contrast a life characterized by the flesh versus the abundant Life.

Write out some of these bullet points on the spokes of the wheel in the **PERSONALIZED NUCLEUS OF THE COUNTERFEIT IDENTITY** Diagram provided.

You may be surprised to notice that some spokes correspond to one another while others are contradictory. This is very typical for many of us.

1. Do you think these contradictions contribute to conflict or confusion in our thoughts, emotions, and choices?

   _____

   _____

2. Is this true for you? If so, give specific examples from your diagram.

   _____

   _____

Despite these inconsistencies, a core assumed identity may come into focus. The center of the circle symbolizes the nucleus of the flesh. All the spokes correspond to this persona, affirming or compensating for it. Once this identity is adopted, we strive to defend and reinforce it. Our example diagram identifies the assumed nucleus of the flesh/counterfeit identity as, "I must be special."

3. Who have you believed yourself to be?

   _____

   _____

   _____

If the Holy Spirit confirms that this is what you have been *living out of,* it will provide a much-needed understanding of Matthew 16:24-25.

> "Then Jesus said to His disciples, 'If anyone desires to come after Me, let him deny himself, and take up his cross, and follow Me. For whoever desires to save his life, will lose it, but whoever loses his life for My sake, will find it'" (Matthew 16:24-25)

Before responding to what Jesus asks of his followers, we must understand what *life* we are to lose. Through the Holy Spirit's illumination, we must see what makes up that life.

The Lord prepares sincere hearts to displace their counterfeit identities and find abundant life. Is it time for you to recognize this assumed identity

Ask the disciplee to read the top paragraph on page 109. Has this brought conviction? If we are honest, we must admit this type of behavior applies to all of us at times.

As we look to identify the nucleus of the counterfeit identity, some questions serve as *clues* to help us understand something about ourselves that is unknown yet powerful.

1. Most of us have pleasant memories of times in our lives when we have been successful. These successes make us feel powerful and in control. However, we are not as mindful of trusting and depending on God during these times. We take a *snapshot* of these strategies and store them away in our minds for easy access.

2. This question is important. If the response is yes, discover what was eliminated and how it was accomplished? If the disciplee ignored that conviction, ask for feedback concerning their decision.

3. The strategies mentioned usually indicate an individual's perceived strengths. However, strongholds of deception may lurk in these perceived strengths, and brokenness needs to occur here.

4. Indicate that this question, in addition to number five, is fundamental and would benefit from prayer before answering. Typically, responses will include loss of love, security, and significance. These core needs are legitimate—instilled by God Himself—and must be met for us to be fulfilled. As the disciplee shares answers next week, ask if they have ultimately trusted Christ to meet those needs. When we say that Christ is our life, we are saying that He is our ultimate provision. Share that we will cover this truth in more detail in Session 7.

Strongly encourage the disciplee to complete questions 1-5 before personalizing the **NUCLEUS OF THE COUNTERFEIT IDENTITY** diagram.

is not who you truly are as a child of God? If so, it will be a great relief for you and those around you! You could now release others from the responsibility of making you feel good about yourself. Instead of manipulating their favorable response, you can rest in Christ. He alone can satisfy your deepest needs and restore your soul (Psalm 23).

CLUES TO DISCERNING THE NUCLEUS OF THE COUNTERFEIT IDENTITY

1. How do you define successful living? Which behavior patterns have produced the most positive outcomes in your memories and experience?

   _____

   _____

   _____

2. Is the Holy Spirit convicting you to eliminate something in your life? If so, how have you responded?

   _____

   _____

   _____

   _____

3. What strategies do you use most often to maintain a sense of control?

   _____

   _____

   _____

4. What would happen if you were to lose control completely?

   _____

   _____

   _____

5. This question often evokes frightening or anxious thoughts and feelings. Maintaining an illusion of control is paramount since we're vulnerable to health, relational, and financial crises. Is God sufficient to provide and protect at these times? Is there any scenario where His grace is not sufficient (2 Corinthians 12:9)?

Our example comprises various identity messages, beliefs/thoughts, feelings, and behaviors selected from the **WHO DO WE THINK WE ARE?** diagram in **Session ONE**. Notice there are sixteen spokes leading into the center of the wheel. Four from each category will be selected to personalize the diagram. **I MUST BE SPECIAL** has been identified as the nucleus in our example diagram. What inner dialogue led to this understanding?

How do I know that I must be special? Well, Mother and Dad both said so, and others did, too. It must be true. Mistakes are not okay, and love is conditional, so this is not just flattery.

It seems I have something special, so I work very hard. Achievement determines value, after all. I'm conflicted about what is best. I procrastinate and hide mistakes or failures when I feel out of control. Sometimes, I do feel confident, and I do know I'm loved. However, I really do need to be special. This perception of being special must be my identity, the truth about who I am.

A helpful way to determine the counterfeit identity is to add the word *so* or *because* between the comments on the spokes and the nucleus definition.

I hide mistakes and failures *because* I must be special. Love is conditional, *so* I must be special. I overeat *because* it is stressful always to be special. Achievement determines value, *so* I must be special.

The adopted identity in our example serves as an explanation and an imperative. *I don't know how I feel plus I have something special*, illustrates an identity that has been informed by what others have said. This individual is *conflicted about what is best* and sometimes feels, *I am not in control.* This is contradictory to other messages such as, *I feel confident* and *work hard to be the best*. Even so, the nucleus of the counterfeit identity seeks to reinforce and defend the illusion that *I must be special*.

5. What core needs would not be met as a result?

_____

_____

_____

NUCLEUS OF THE COUNTERFEIT IDENTITY (EXAMPLE)

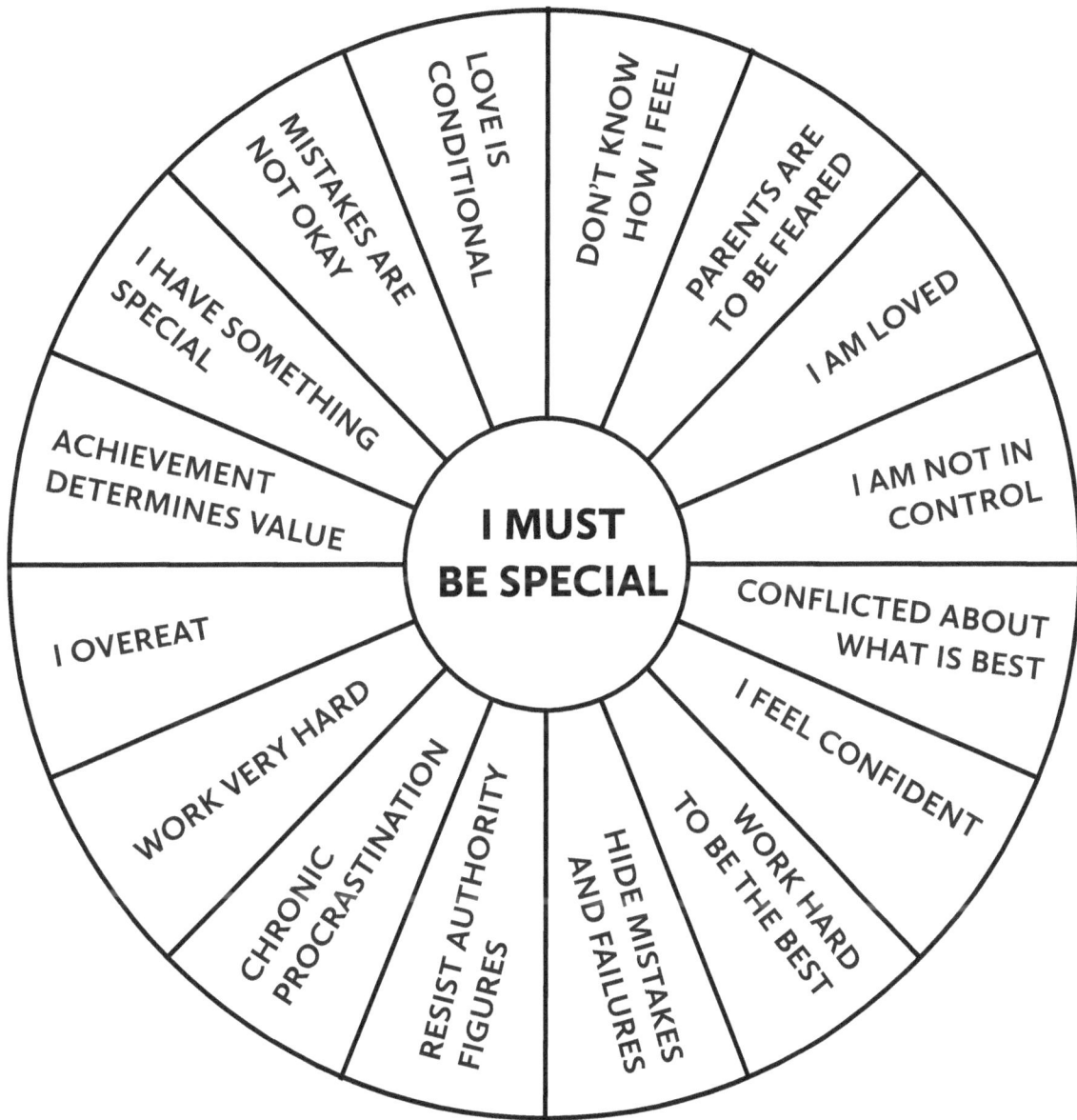

A circular wheel diagram with "I MUST BE SPECIAL" at the center, surrounded by segments reading: LOVE IS CONDITIONAL, DON'T KNOW HOW I FEEL, PARENTS ARE TO BE FEARED, I AM LOVED, I AM NOT IN CONTROL, CONFLICTED ABOUT WHAT IS BEST, I FEEL CONFIDENT, WORK HARD TO BE THE BEST, HIDE MISTAKES AND FAILURES, RESIST AUTHORITY FIGURES, CHRONIC PROCRASTINATION, WORK VERY HARD, I OVEREAT, ACHIEVEMENT DETERMINES VALUE, I HAVE SOMETHING SPECIAL, MISTAKES ARE NOT OKAY.

Ask the disciplee to select four messages from each of the headings in their **WHO DO YOU THINK YOU ARE?** diagram and place them on the spokes of the **PERSONALIZED NUCLEUS OF THE COUNTERFEIT IDENTITY**.

The center, or nucleus of the wheel, can be identified if the disciplee has discovered it..

It may be instructive for the disciplee to solicit feedback from close friends or family members about their wheel's nucleus.

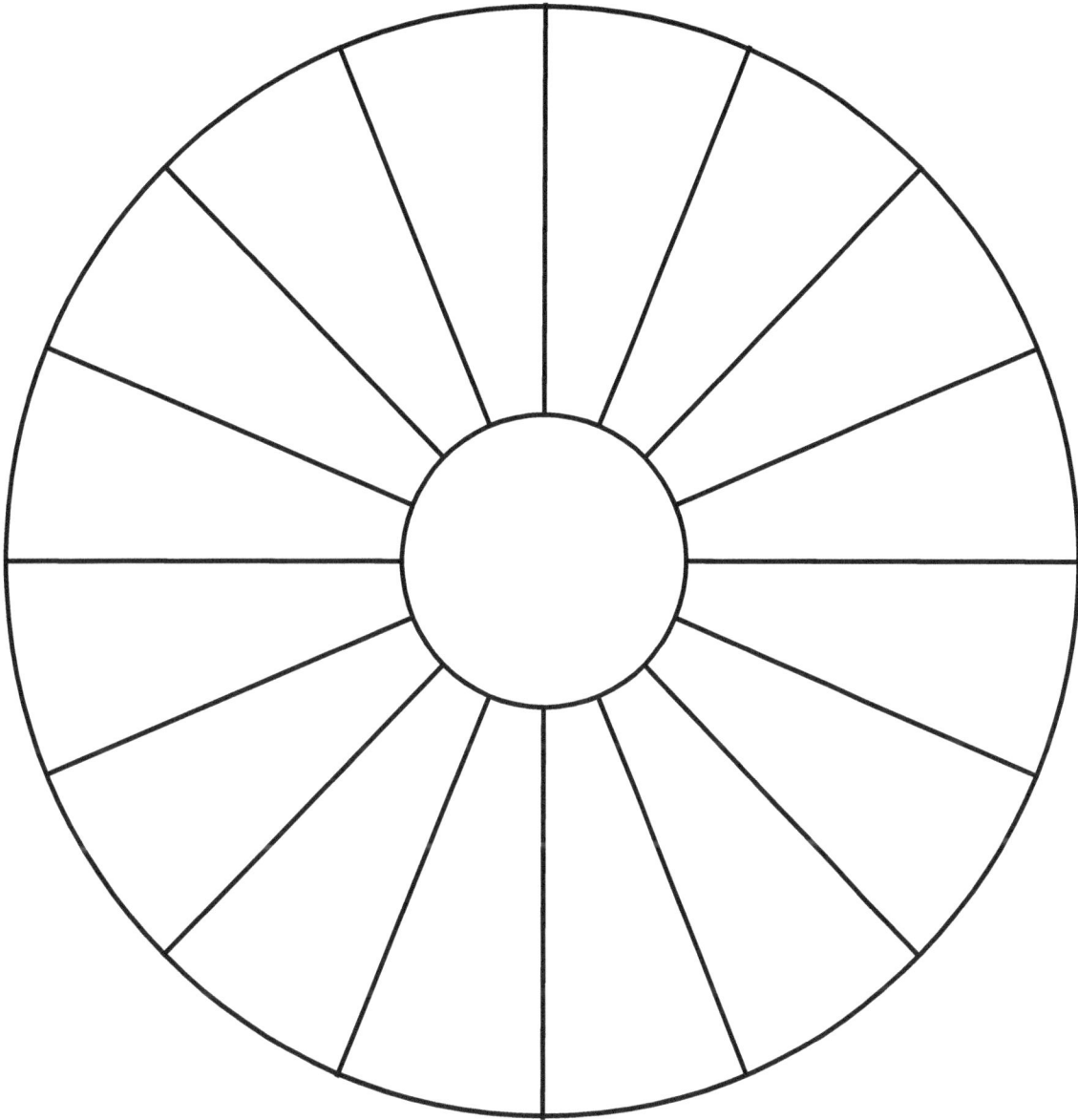

Ask the disciplee if there are any remaining questions regarding the **NUCLEUS OF THE COUNTERFEIT IDENTITY** diagram. Their answers for questions 1-3 should be written on the page opposite the section on **DISPLACING THE NUCLEUS OF THE COUNTERFEIT IDENTITY**, page 102.

The responses to questions 4 and 5 are of particular importance. The emotions we experience and the behaviors we exhibit during these times are clues to the core of the counterfeit identity. When we encounter situations where we feel powerless, we employ specific strategies. We attempt to decrease our sense of powerlessness by increasing *our power*. In essence, this maneuver describes a working definition of the nature of the flesh.

Review the process for personalizing the diagram on page 113. Do not imply that the illuminated nucleus is an essential component of the abundant life. While helpful, this awareness may not occur during the twelve weeks of discipleship. With additional devotion to prayer, we will gain further insight after all sessions have been completed. The Holy Spirit shows us more about our flesh throughout our entire lives.

CONSIDER THIS: SESSION 4

1. Read over the materials we covered in today's session and review the Nucleus of the Counterfeit Identity diagram. Write your answers for 1-3 in the **DISPLACING THE NUCLEUS OF THE COUNTERFEIT IDENTITY** section.

_____

_____

_____

_____

2. In **CLUES TO DISCERNING THE NUCLEUS OF THE COUNTERFEIT IDENTITY**, please answer all the questions and pay particular attention to numbers four and five. Imagine a scenario where all sense of control is lost. Describe what it might be like to believe core needs like safety, love, and significance were jeopardized. What would you feel and do?

_____

_____

_____

_____

3. Fill in your responses to the five bullet points for each of the identity messages, beliefs/thoughts, feelings, and behaviors in the section provided in your notebook. Next, transfer them to the **PERSONALIZED NUCLEUS OF THE COUNTERFEIT IDENTITY** diagram. Refer to the example **NUCLEUS OF THE COUNTERFEIT IDENTITY** diagram to see how this will look. It is not essential, but very helpful, if a Holy Spirit recognition of the hub comes into view!

_____

_____

_____

_____

SESSION 5

God's Provision

The *Personalized Discipleship Notebook* utilizes red to indicate God or God's life.

Blue indicates sin and carnality.

Eternal life describes a unique kind of life that has always existed.

Father, Son, and Holy Spirit are distinct persons, as illustrated by three individual lines. However, each is fully God.

Eternal Life equals the spiritual attributes and life of the Father, the Son, and the Holy Spirit.

ETERNAL LIFE
NO BEGINNING, NO END

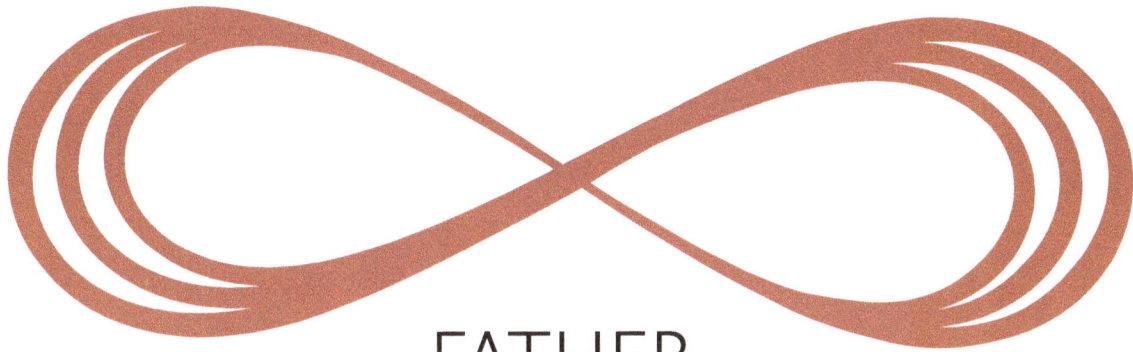

FATHER

SON

HOLY SPIRIT

- Many believers think eternal life is something that begins after they've died and are in heaven with Jesus.

- Ask the question: What is the difference between everlasting life and eternal life?

- All people born physically will continue forever in the future. Hence, their life is everlasting. However, while that life is everlasting, it is not necessarily eternal.

- Eternal life has no beginning; it is outside of time.

- Note that Jesus entered time during His incarnation.

The line diagram is adapted from *Handbook to Happiness*, by Charles R. Solomon (Tyndale House Publishers, 1971). A video explanation is included in the free online course, *For Me to Live is Christ* (GraceStudyHall.org).

Psalm 90:2 ∞ ←————————————————→ ∞ **Hebrews 13:8**

God's Life is Eternal Life

The line diagrams show us the doctrinal basis for the believer's identification with Jesus Christ.

What does the term *eternal life* mean to us? What do we mean when we say God is *eternal*?

Eternal life is actually God's life, with no beginning or end. This truth is symbolized by the horizontal line with an infinity symbol on each end. Eternal life is also above chronological time. Christ declared, "... before Abraham was, I am" (John 8:58). John 6:35; 14:6; 11:25; 1 John 5:11,12 show that Christ's life is eternal. He is the same yesterday, today, and forever (Hebrews 13:8).

- The line diagrams on pages 123-129 provide an overview of God's rescue plan to save a fallen world.

- The incarnation of Jesus, His substitutionary death on the cross, and His return to Heaven are illustrated on the opposite page.

- Take the time to review the diagram with your disciplee.

- Confirm that they understand the description below the diagram—which is a synopsis of the gospel and is usually familiar to most Christians.

The Son of Man came ... to serve, and to give His life a ransom for many (Mark 10:45).

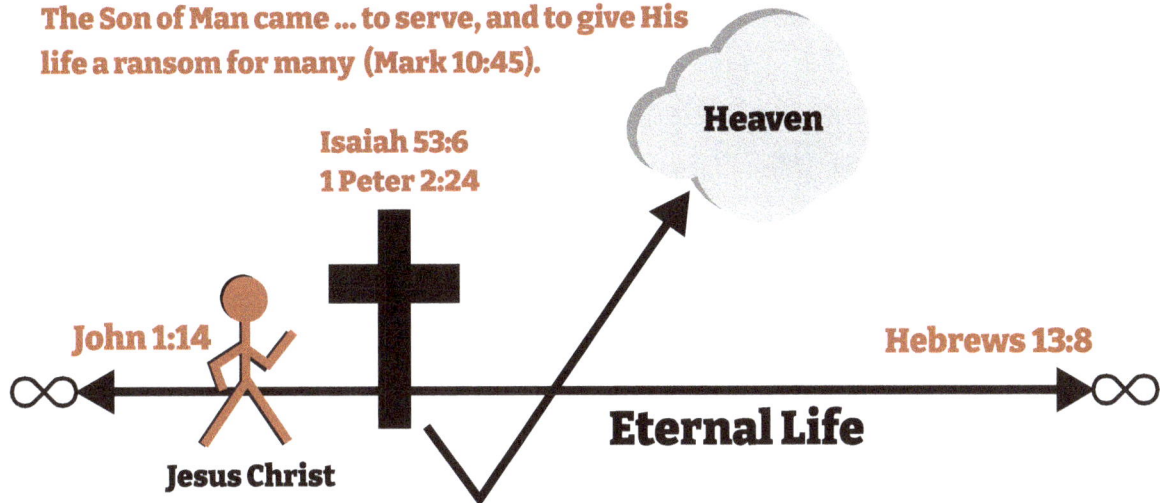

Isaiah 53:6
1 Peter 2:24

Heaven

John 1:14

Hebrews 13:8

Eternal Life

Jesus Christ

The stick figure represents Jesus Christ. He left heaven's glory and clothed Himself in human nature in order to redeem us (Galatians 4:4). He is fully divine (Colossians 1:15-17; Hebrews 1:2,3), yet fully human (John 1:1,14). The Holy Spirit conceived Jesus in the virgin Mary. He came as the Last Adam and did not inherit a sin nature (1 Corinthians 15:45).

Jesus came to die in our place to give His life a ransom for many (Mark 10:45; Isaiah 53:6; 1 Peter 2:24). This depicts His substitutionary death for our salvation. He was buried (the line goes downward), then He was raised and ascended to heaven (the line goes upward).

As believers, we are "...reconciled to God through the death of His Son ...." (Romans 5:10a); "... through the obedience of the One the many will be made righteous" (Romans 5:19b). We gain eternal life by grace through faith in Jesus Christ as Lord and Savior (John 17:3).

- Adam's sin resulted in descendants who were mortal, selfish, and spiritually dead.

- All humans inherited Adam's family tree through physical birth.

- The "In Adam" lifeline begins at physical birth and is destined to an everlasting existence in hell.

- Spiritually dead people are separated from God, the source of life, and are not capable of abundant living.

- God's solution requires spiritual rebirth by grace through faith.

In Adam

The Fall

"Old Man"

Romans 5:12

Eternal Life

Jesus Christ
The Last Adam

Romans 3:23; 6:23

Hell

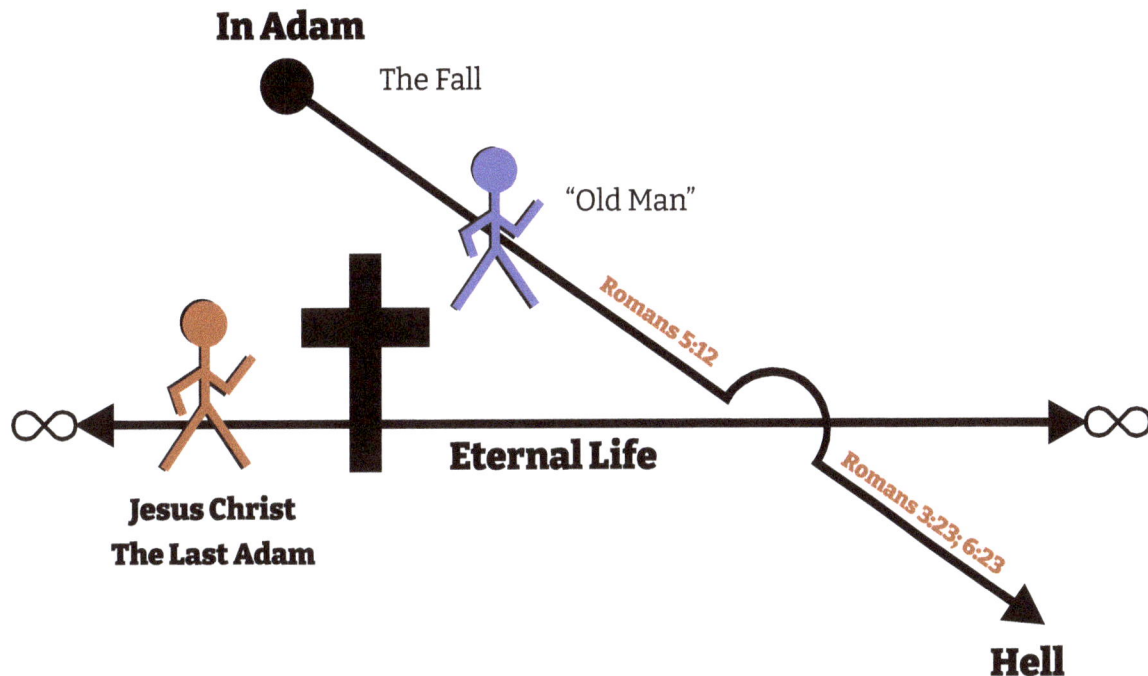

When we were born, we were not born into the eternal lifeline (horizontal line). Instead, we were born into the lineage of Adam (diagonal line). Our natural life (physically, spiritually, and legally) is traced back to Adam, the original man.

From our parents, we inherited physical life (although mortal), psychological life (although self-centered), and spiritual existence (although dead toward God).

When Adam broke the covenant in Eden (Hosea 6:6), he died spiritually that very day (Genesis 2:17). We inherit this spiritual separation from God (Ephesians 2:1) and need rebirth (John 3:3).

We are also legally condemned in Adam, our federal head (Romans 5:12-14, 19).

Unless divinely rescued, we are on the road to hell (Matthew 7:13, 14). We were born into a fallen world where we try to get our ultimate needs met independently of God. So, we are disappointed and looking for fulfillment.

- The IDENTIFIED WITH CHRIST diagram effectively illustrates the believer's union with Christ.

- Ask the disciplee to read through the descriptive paragraphs below this diagram. Read aloud each Bible verse referring to the diagram as you do so.

- This message is simple yet profound!

- The blue stick figure serves as a visual representation of a sinner "In Adam." In Christ, we are transformed into a new creation. The believer is now a saint (purple), in union with Christ. It's important to note that even in this union, a believer does not become divine. Deity is always depicted in red in this notebook.

In Adam

Galatians 2:20

Redemption

1 Corinthians 1:30
2 Corinthians 5:17

Eternal Life

**Jesus Christ
The Last Adam**

Romans 6:3-6

"New Man"

Hell

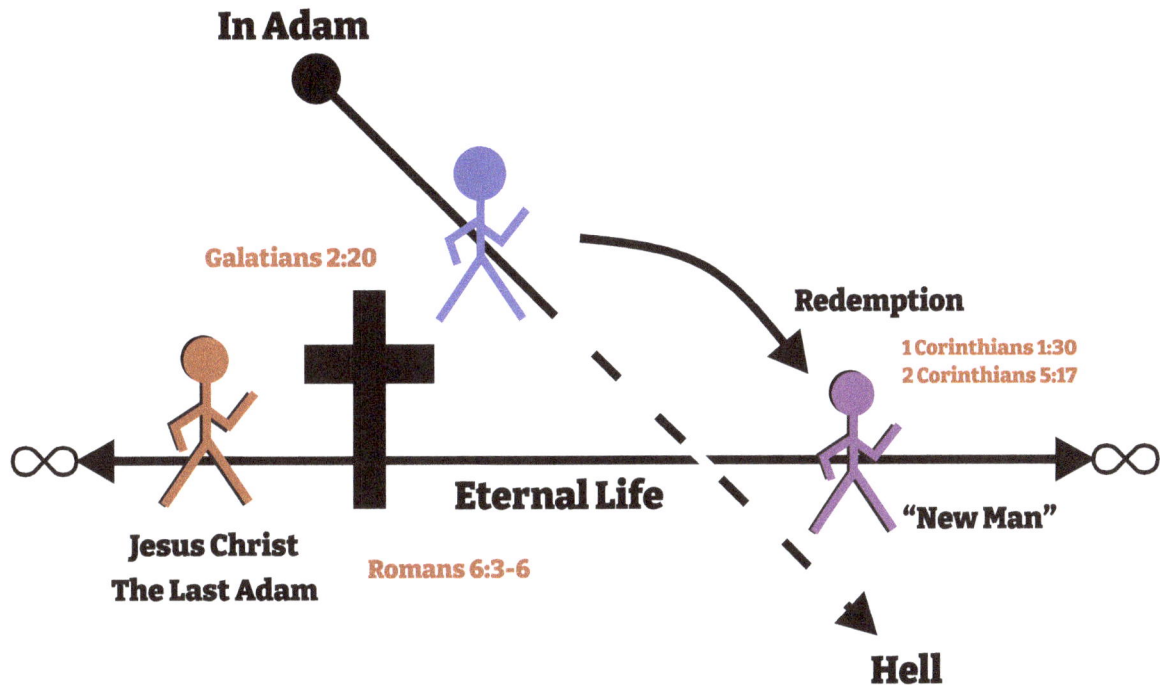

When we received Christ (if we are saved), God took us out of Adam's lineage and grafted us into Christ's life. "But by His doing you are in Christ Jesus, who became to us wisdom from God, and righteousness and sanctification, and redemption …." (1 Corinthians 1:30).

Believers are now IN CHRIST. Instead of being separated from God and spiritually dead, we are now joined to Christ—one spirit with Him, grafted as a branch in the Vine (1 Corinthians 6:17; John 15:1-5).

Therefore if anyone is in Christ, he is a new creature; the old things passed away; behold, new things have come" (2 Corinthians 5:17).

- This diagram illustrates our identification with Christ's death, burial, ascension, and resurrection life. What happened to Jesus physically happened to us spiritually.

- The "old man" is the spiritually dead person we were in Adam. The soul and body of the "old man" were also profoundly impacted by indwelling sin. However, through our identification with Christ, we are liberated from this total depravity and enslavement to the power of sin, experiencing a new spiritual life.

- In Christ, we have a new future and a new spiritual past.

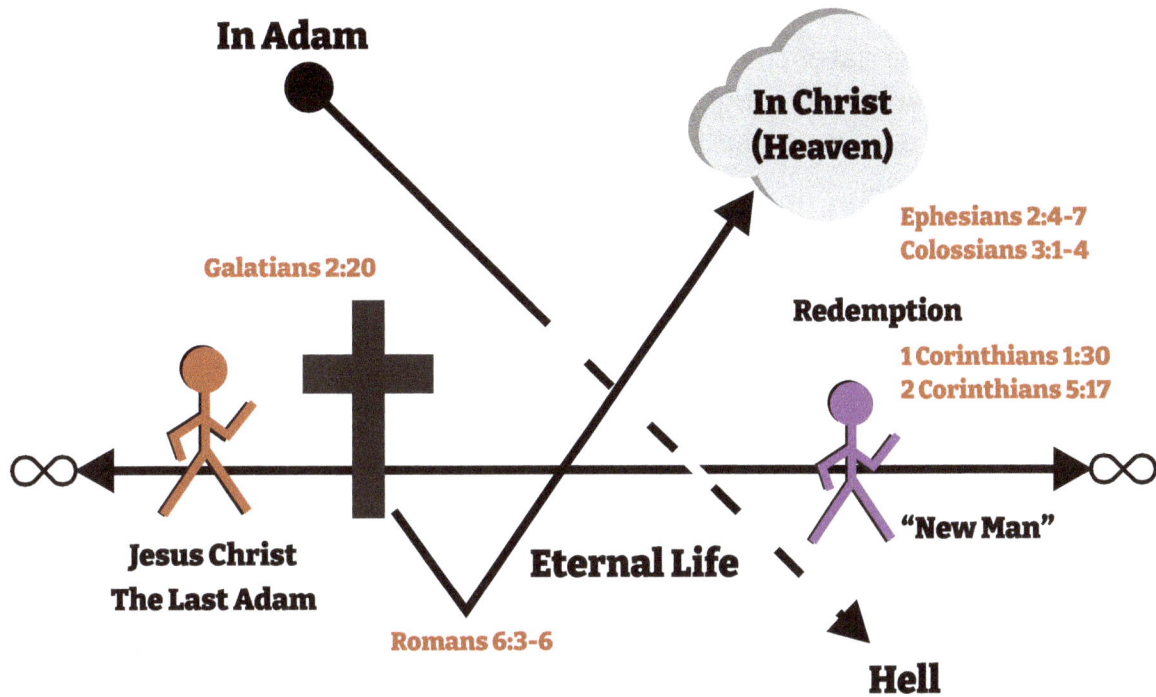

When Christ died on the cross, **our old man** died with Him spiritually and legally (Romans 6:6; Colossians 3:3,9). When Christ was buried, we were also buried (Romans 6:4), symbolized by the line going down. When Christ was raised, **our new man** was raised with Him. We share His resurrection Life (Ephesians 2:4-7; Romans 6:4b; Colossians 3:1). When Christ ascended, our new man ascended with Him (Ephesians 2:4-7), symbolized by the line rising to heaven.

Now, we are represented not by Adam (condemnation) but by Christ (justification). Our sins have been fully paid for and forgiven—past, present, and future (Colossians 2:13,14). Christ's perfect righteousness has been imputed to us, credited to our account (2 Corinthians 5:21). In Christ we get a NEW DESTINY—heaven. In Christ, we also get a NEW PAST. Our spiritual life did not come down through natural generations but is traced back to the cross.

- The UNION WITH CHRIST diagram is a visual depiction of Romans 6:6. Through the Cross our old man was crucified with Christ.

Romans 6:6 also declares that the body of sin is *rendered inoperative* as we abide in Christ. We are no longer slaves of sin. This means we are not compelled to sin and are free to walk in righteousness.

- God the Father, Son, and Holy Spirit now envelop our lives.

- The next two pages focus on multiple verses that identify believers as saints.

UNION WITH CHRIST

Through the Cross, we are baptized into Christ.

"Knowing this, that our old man was crucified with Christ, in order that the body of sin might be done away with, that we would no longer be slaves to sin" (Romans 6:6).

As born-again believers, we are now *in Christ.* Our union with Jesus has made us righteous children of God. Our spirit has been sanctified and is indwelled by the Holy Spirit. Our soul is in the process of sanctification, and our body remains mortal. We have a new identity confirmed throughout Scripture (see verses below).

We are new creations (2 Corinthians 5:17), and the Father, Son, and Holy Spirit now envelop our life.

CHRIST IS NOW MY LIFE

"But by His doing you are in Christ, who became to us wisdom from God, and righteousness and sanctification, and redemption" (1 Corinthians 1:30).

"... just as He chose us in Him before the foundation of the world, that we should be holy and blameless before Him" (Ephesians 1:4).

" ... and raised us up with Him, and seated us with Him in the heavenly places, in Christ Jesus" (Ephesians 2:6).

"Since then you have been raised up with Christ, keep seeking the things above, where Christ is, seated at the right hand of God. Set your mind on the things above, not on the things that are on earth. For you have died and your life is hidden with Christ in God. When

DISCIPLER'S NOTES

- What establishes identity?

- Jesus told Nicodemus he must be born again because that which is born of the flesh is flesh—see scripture verses John 3:3-7 on page 265.

- Identity is determined by birth into a particular family.

- Birth also determines the condition of our spirit.

- In Adam, our spirit is dead to God but alive to sin.

- In Christ, our spirit is dead to sin but alive to God.

- Many verses are referenced to illustrate believers are saints, not sinners. This does not mean saints will achieve sinless perfection while still in their mortal bodies.

Christ, who is our life, is revealed, then you also will be revealed with Him in glory" (Colossians 3:1-4).

"So it is written, "The first man, Adam became a living soul." The last Adam became a life-giving spirit" (1 Corinthians 15:45).

WHO AM I AS A BELIEVER?

My identity is determined by birth, which establishes the condition of my human spirit. I am either *in Christ* or *in Adam*.

New Testament references for believers as saints:

- Acts 9:13, 32, 41; 26:10
- Romans 1:7; 8:27; 12:13; 15:25-26, 31; 16:2, 15
- 1 Corinthians 1:2; 6:1, 2; 14:33; 16:1, 15
- 2 Corinthians 1:1; 8:4; 9:1, 12; 13:13
- Ephesians 1:1, 15, 18; 2:19; 3:8, 18, 4:12; 5:3; 6:18
- Philippians 1:1; 4:21-22
- Colossians 1:2, 4, 12, 26; 3:12
- 1 Thessalonians 3:13; 5:27
- 2 Thessalonians 1:10
- 1 Timothy 5:10
- Philemon 5, 7
- Hebrews 3:1, 6:10, 13:24
- 1 Peter 2:5, 9
- Jude 3, 14
- Revelation 5:8; 8:3-4; 11:18; 13:7, 10; 14:12; 16:6; 17:6; 18:24; 19:8

DISCIPLER'S NOTES

1. Be prepared to review any of the teachings provided in the line diagrams.

2. Body of sin: the human body, which is vulnerable to the power of sin, may be rendered inoperative in believers. The *old man*: who we were in Adam. This person was crucified, died, and buried with Christ. The death of the *old man* is what we are to *know* and *reckon* has taken place in the believer's life.

3. God's wise plan was to baptize us into the very life of Christ so that He becomes our righteousness, sanctification, and redemption. By faith, we appropriate His Life, moment by moment. We will learn more about how this takes place in Session 7.

CONSIDER THIS: SESSION 5

1. The line diagrams shows a considerable amount of biblical truth. What was the most significant new insight they illustrated for you? After carefully reviewing all that was considered today, where may you need further clarification?

_____

_____

_____

_____

2. The UNION WITH CHRIST diagram portrays how my individual life has been baptized into Christ. It is a visual portrait of Romans 6:6. What do you believe happened to the body of sin? What happened to your *old man*?

_____

_____

_____

_____

3. In your own words, summarize 1 Corinthians 1:30. How has Christ become wisdom from God to you? In what way has Jesus become your sanctification?

_____

_____

_____

_____

4. Read all the referenced Scripture verses for Session 5 located at the back of your notebook.

Surrender & Brokenness

A reasonable response to conviction of the flesh is to give up on our self-sufficient manner of living. This critical decision changes the entire direction of our growth in grace.

It is important to distinguish self-effort or willpower from choosing to yield as a reflection of heart obedience. We will examine this further in session seven as we study the **POINT OF YIELDING** diagrams on pages 167 and 169.

If we're walking according to the flesh, we are utterly incapable of knowing or appropriating truth. Obviously, we can't disciple others when we can't even help ourselves.

The flesh is not capable of trusting God, so the surrender process is resisted. A step of faith must be taken if we are to experience the law of the Spirit of life in Christ Jesus, counteracting the law of sin and death. Often, it is sheer desperation that forces us to take that step.

TOTAL SURRENDER AND BROKENNESS

What exactly does it mean to be totally surrendered? Is it the same thing as *Lordship*? What does it mean to be *broken*?

Many Christian leaders refer to believers as *broken people*. Does this mean we're handicapped and therefore incapable in some way? Is there a relationship between surrender and brokenness?

Does my decision to be totally surrendered involve more than my *determination* to submit to the Lordship of Jesus Christ? Wasn't this already true of Paul when he wrote the latter half of Romans chapter 7? Yet, he described his life as defeated and himself as wretched! What more is needed?

In Philippians 3:4-7, Paul tells us he has the best flesh possible. Did he have *religious* flesh? Did Paul believe that his sincere desire for obedience could be carried out in his own strength?

Does total surrender include and require, a Holy Spirit illumination of the bankruptcy of the flesh? Do we need to see that willpower is not sufficient? Our efforts are no match for the power of sin!

Are we convinced of this vital truth? Until that conviction takes place, Paul's Romans chapter 7 experience will be ours too. Why? **Because Romans seven is true whenever the Holy Spirit reveals we are walking according to the flesh.**

In Romans 6, we learn that Paul understood he had died to sin, through his death with Christ at the Cross (Romans 6:6). We also see that he sincerely wanted to live a holy life (Romans 7:17, 20). Paul regards this desire to be a reflection of his most authentic self (Romans 7:22). He knew the behaviors and attitudes he wanted to avoid came from sin and the flesh, which indwelled his mortal body (Romans 7:18).

However, he acknowledges he must still take personal responsibility for his sinful actions (Romans 7:15-16, 19). He is morally liable when he says, "I do that which I don't want to do." No wonder he's feeling miserable and desperate!

When we read Romans 7, do we notice how often Paul refers to "I"?

Does he mention the Holy Spirit, Jesus, or God the Father? What does this illustrate?

Once we are thoroughly convicted of our flesh, we look to another for rescue (Romans 7:24). We need to humble ourselves and be honest about our obvious limitations. This begins an often painful process that leads to brokenness but produces true liberty (Romans 8:1-17).

It is important to emphasize that we frequently return to our own efforts to produce self-control without abiding in Christ.

The *Some May Include* category lists common obstacles that hinder surrender. This list describes a summary overview of fleshly living. For instance, we are often reluctant to place our *insistence on functioning from our soul* on the altar—navigating our life based on what we think, feel, and choose for ourselves instead.

The frequent expectation that others must meet my need for love and acceptance indicates a faulty perception of relationships. God is the ultimate source for satisfying our core needs. All other relationships are resources. This is an important distinction to clarify and discuss in discipleship. Developing healthy relationships and fellowship is important for Christians, but they are intended to be secondary in providing essential needs.

The second category, *I May Be Enabled to Relinquish My Will to His Will in All Areas of My Life*, illustrates that the Holy Spirit must work in me to will and enable the release of *my desires*. Abundant living may—and often does—include rejection, misunderstandings, trials, persecutions, illness, and many other painful experiences that take place without the benefit of an explanation from God. When we resist surrender in these areas for long periods of time, we can become angry with God. It might be wise to ask the disciplee if this has ever been true for them.

A power greater than ourselves is needed, *even though we are new creations in Christ.*

The conflict described in Romans 7 is resolved by giving up on our attempts to live the Christian life through self-effort and self-control. We must discover a better source of living that effectively counteracts the power of sin and the flesh. We must remember, self-control is a fruit of the Spirit!

Seeing the sinfulness of our flesh comes about in many different ways; there is no pattern or formula for everyone. However, there are some commonalities in what typically is yielded or placed on the altar once we have God's perspective.

Some May Include

- My counterfeit identity
- My rejections, bitterness, and pain
- My worldly values and "idols"
- My previous theological perspectives
- My self-focus and self-determination
- My methods of control
- My insistence on functioning from my soul

I May Be Enabled to Relinquish My Will to His Will in All Areas of My Life, Including

- Choosing where I will live, work, or retire
- A particular marital status
- Determining my future hopes, plans, or dreams
- How to spend my leisure or vacation time
- To win versus fail, as I define it
- Financial security
- Self-pity, when I have been despitefully used
- Freedom from trials and persecution
- Release from pain and misunderstandings
- Requiring that others meet my need for love, belonging, or acceptance
- Demanding physical health/healing
- Ministry opportunities
- Requiring an explanation from God regarding my life circumstances

It is helpful to recognize the sinful tendencies and unbiblical thinking that prevent us from total surrender to our Lord.

Underestimating the power of sin can lead to a "New Year's Resolution" mind-set. These resolutions reflect the notion that future improvement of the flesh is still possible.

Another hindrance is believing that what I've experienced or felt is the bed-rock of truth. This may persist in my thinking even when it clearly contradicts God's Word.

Fear of potential suffering or the unknown may erode my decision to trust God completely.

Harboring unforgiveness and bitterness is so universal that we devote the entirety of **Session 10** to address this particular obstacle.

Eventually, I may realize that a life organized around my own plans and carried out with my own efforts is bankrupt.

The conditions for the process of brokenness to begin are now in place. God moves in various ways in my life to conform me to Christ. My faith grows as I cooperate with Him and begin to experience His sufficiency. He is responsible for what is accomplished in and through me. My life takes on an attitude of confidence, rest, and assurance.

Some Common Obstacles to Total Surrender

- Pride
- Fear of the unknown; losing control over what happens to me
- False concepts of God's nature
- Not willing to experience a potential increase in pain or suffering
- Inability to trust
- Unbelief
- Underestimating the power of sin
- Haven't been convicted of the flesh
- No knowledge of God's inerrant Word
- No devotion to prayer
- Unforgiveness and bitterness
- Hidden, unconfessed sin
- I'm trusting in my feelings and experiences to define truth

WHAT GETS BROKEN?

In brokenness, my perception of my own abilities is drastically altered. My flesh is revealed to me, and I am *undone*. I see clearly that my flesh is fueled by sin and utterly incapable of spiritual living.

The process of brokenness can take place in various ways for each of us. God has already prepared the good works He is fashioning us to fulfill (Ephesians 2:10). He is molding and establishing us as His *masterpiece*.

The apostle Paul hungered and thirsted for authentic righteousness but was unable to produce it. We do not know the duration of the turmoil he describes in the second half of Romans 7, but by God's grace, he discovered the way of deliverance (Romans 8:2-17).

The motives of others are not so commendable! The life of Jacob demonstrates a very different pattern of brokenness (Genesis 32:24-31).

It would be difficult to read the Genesis account and believe that Jacob was intent on holy living.

Was Jacob even interested in seeking a relationship with the Lord? He did know that he and his entire family were about to be killed by Esau for his

For Jacob, brokenness took place during a life-and-death crisis event. When he failed to prevail when wrestling with God, Jacob clung to Him and pleaded for a blessing. The request was granted through the conviction of Jacob's flesh; he was shocked to discover what everyone else already knew about him. In addition, a gracious illumination of his true identity as a believer was revealed.

This same sequence of realization takes place for us, too. A decision to surrender wholeheartedly to the Lordship of Christ in our lives is always a crisis event. It may not be an actual life-and-death situation as dramatic as Jacob faced, but it is a significant indication of repentance and a renewing of the mind. Our confidence in the flesh has received a fatal blow!

This doesn't mean that everything will change immediately, but there is a shift from resisting God to cooperating with Him.

previous treachery in stealing the birthright. Jacob wrestled with the Lord in agonizing prayer but still would not *surrender*. Finally, Jacob's thigh was dislocated, and only then did he cling to the Lord and plead for his blessing.

At this point, Jacob could not even run away from Esau and his militia. How did the Lord *break* Jacob after he was physically weakened? The blessing Jacob insisted on came in the form of a question, "What is your name?" (Genesis 32:27). And, in shock of realization, whispering, he said, "Jacob" —*supplanter, schemer, trickster, swindler* (Genesis 32:27 AMP). Is this an example of Holy Spirit conviction and illumination of the flesh?

Could it really be possible that Jacob had not seen himself in this way until then? Could what is obvious to others be unknown to us? The next verse reveals the much-needed blessing—God tells Jacob his true identity is "Israel" (Genesis 32:28). Jacob was made aware that a former, self-serving cheater was now a champion with God.

The Lord is gracious to those who seek Him and those who do not. He oversees each individual's conviction of the flesh, brokenness, and knowledge of union with Him. There may be a dramatic *crisis*, as with Jacob. It could be a gradual, progressive process. Often, it will be a combination of both of these. Brokenness continues to deepen throughout our whole life. There is no finish line where we can say this work has been entirely completed within us (Luke 9:23; Philippians 3:12).

Like Jacob, most of us don't surrender and accept brokenness without considerable resistance. It is common to experience a full array of painful experiences and emotions during this time. We may feel angry and rebellious or frightened and full of shame. We are commonly as *resourceful* as Jacob and determined to live on our own terms. We hate weakness and feeling out of control.

Yet, in time, we understand that brokenness is the gateway to blessing and fruitfulness. When we decide within our own heart to relinquish our independent, soulical (carnal) living, we begin to understand what is involved in total surrender. We will make a conscious choice to trust in God alone for all that we are and all that we have. Only then will we know, experientially, what abundant living can be (John 10:10). When we make this decision, we may begin to understand the Scriptures in a new way.

Gratitude is the primary motivation to offer ourselves to God in view of all His mercies. This is why presenting ourselves as a living sacrifice is a reasonable service. Aligning and submitting ourselves to God is an authentic response; we are holy and acceptable to Him. Romans 12:2 tells us that our surrender will prevent us from conformity to the world and will transform us through a Holy Spirit renewal of our minds. In addition, we are given an understanding of God's perfect will. In any area where we still hold back, we could pray, "Lord, make me willing to be made willing."

Is suffering a means of grace?

Do we learn more about Christ when we participate in persecutions, misunderstandings, and false accusations as He did?

Are we being tested by fire and hope to come forth as gold?

Our high priest can understand what we are going through. He endured the cross for the joy of accomplishing God's purposes through His life. Some people wonder why God doesn't do something about suffering. He did! Sin, death, and the devil were conquered and defeated through the cross.

1. If *self* refers to who I am in Christ, then no. However, if the meaning is the *self-life* or the flesh, then it is to be held in the place of death through the Holy Spirit.

We do not seek out suffering but accept it by grace. Believers are open to the Lord when He directs us away from painful situations or relationships. We don't have to accept everything that can and should be changed. It is okay to ask if *this cup* may pass. However, sometimes the answer may be *no*.

1. What is the primary reason given in Romans 12:1 for presenting myself as a living sacrifice? Does Romans 12:2 provide additional light on the motivation for total surrender?

_____

_____

_____

_____

2. How can we fellowship in the sufferings of Christ (Philippians 3:10-11) and rejoice in our present suffering and trials? (1 Peter 1:3-7).

_____

_____

_____

_____

3. Are we to die to self? Dying to self is a very important consideration!

_____

_____

_____

_____

"No healthy Christian ever chooses to suffer; he chooses God's will, as Jesus did, whether it means suffering or not." —Oswald Chambers, My Utmost for His Highest

What are some indications that brokenness is taking place?

A wholehearted decision to surrender my life to God removes the obstacles to ongoing growth in grace. God honors my choice, and exciting changes are discovered through living and resting in the sufficiency of Christ.

When I begin to feel out of control, I notice a quiet assurance within. Others remark that I now have a teachable spirit. My ability to choose has not been removed. My personality flourishes, more closely resembling the person God created me to be. I experience a marked difference in how I respond to people who ignore, fail to appreciate, or misunderstand me. Through those times, I've come to know *El Roi*, the Hebrew name for the God who sees me. I can afford to let these things go because my most significant relationship is with the Lord. My identity and self-esteem no longer need to be primarily sustained through other people.

I have been given victory over previous sinful habits. As I walk in the Spirit with greater consistency, there is a new freedom and liberty. I begin to know for myself the power of His resurrection in my daily life.

If He directs me to do so, I can attempt new things outside of my own ability, gifting, or previous experience. There is a restful reliance on Christ for everything and a reduction of anxiety and stress. Even so, I am well aware my flesh has not improved; it has just been displaced as abundant life is free to flow. Walking in the Spirit is now typically expressed in my life, and walking according to the flesh becomes the exception.

The specific dynamics the Lord utilizes in the brokenness process will be covered in more depth in **THE MASTERPIECE IN GOD** diagram in **Session 8**.

What Are Some Indications of Brokenness?

When I reflect on the following areas, do I experience increasing and consistent growth—not *sinless perfection*, where one supposedly walks in the spirit 100% of the time, but patterns of growth in grace and knowledge of the Lord (2 Peter 3:18)?

☐ I have presented myself a living sacrifice (Romans 12:1)

As the Lord Directs Me, I Am Willing to Be

☐ Misunderstood or rejected by others

☐ A *failure*, the *loser*

☐ Taught what it means to be humble (Philippians 2:5-8)

☐ Open and honest, even when it is unflattering

☐ Increasingly *teachable*

☐ Assured in the Lord when I feel uncomfortable/out of control

☐ Ignored when I deserve *credit*

I Am Increasingly Aware of the Following

☐ Growth in my understanding of heart obedience (John 14:15)

☐ The total sufficiency of Christ (Philippians 4:13)

☐ Increased desire to build up/honor others

☐ Being content with weakness (2 Corinthians 12:10)

☐ Knowing Christ: increased intimacy in relationship with Him (Philippians 3:10)

☐ Transformation of my priorities and stewardship

☐ Change in focus—thought life (Romans 12:2)

☐ Reduction of anxiety; increase in peace

☐ Rapid conviction when I return to "walking according to the flesh"

☐ Increasing trust/dependence on God in difficult circumstances/relationships

Total surrender is not defeat; it is the result of seeing fleshly living from God's perspective. Brokenness is the gateway to blessing. Ask the one you've come alongside if they are ready for God to do whatever He needs to do in their life.

1. Encourage the disciplee to itemize specific habitual areas of struggle. Recommend that there be at least three examples to share next week.

2. In the second half of Romans 7, Paul describes his experiences of walking according to the flesh. He refers to "I" because he is responsible for his carnality. There is no mention of God because his mind is set on the flesh. There is not a single mention of God the Father, Son, or Holy Spirit.

3. Ask the disciplee to provide several examples of hindrances in their own experience. Placing something on the altar is a recognition of particular areas that need to be offered to God. The Holy Spirit is very specific and clear, showing an individual what needs to be eliminated from their life. Only the enemy is vague and condemning in this area. God wants us to know exactly what the problem is and to trust Him for deliverance.

Notice the term *release* is used. This indicates our inability to decisively deal with these areas through willpower. We must offer to God what needs to be rooted out.

The growing awareness that we're addicted to the flesh is an important realization. How do we feel when we no longer assert ourselves to control a situation? We may be surprised and disappointed that the Lord doesn't move according to our timetable. When we can no longer employ our best strategies, we may feel very vulnerable and weak. Habits we knew were self-defeating and carnal provided a measure of immediate gratification. Now, we don't have that at our disposal.

Ask the disciplee to share some personal examples along these lines.

CONSIDER THIS: SESSION 6

1. Did you previously have a different idea of what total surrender and brokenness looked like in the life of a believer? If so, how has your understanding changed?

    _____

    _____

2. Do you identify with Paul's struggle described in Romans 7:15 - 24? Give some examples of your struggles or challenges.

    _____

    _____

3. In the same section of Romans, why does Paul continuously refer to "I"? Is there any mention of Christ, the Father, or the Holy Spirit?

    _____

    _____

4. There are three sections in the **TOTAL SURRENDER** narrative. These include conviction of what you need to place on the altar, what you need to release, and what common obstacles you may face. Circle the bullet point examples that particularly apply to you. Add two more examples for each section to help you personalize these truths.

    _____

    _____

    _____

    _____

5. After trusting Christ through various trials and illuminations, we begin to experience new freedom for the soul. Some of these challenges continue, yet we walk in the Spirit with greater consistency. We have come to know what liberty means. We are not inactive; we cooperate with the Holy Spirit, yielding to and following Him.

    Old satisfactions have given way to new experiences of what I find truly fulfilling. My habits have changed, and I invest my time, talent, and treasure differently.

6. What gets broken? My confidence in the flesh!

7. There is a tremendous difference between godly and ungodly suffering. The Lord can use godly suffering to bring about brokenness. It is always redemptive. We may not understand the suffering God allows, but it does have a purpose and is motivated by His love for people.

    Ungodly suffering delights the evil one. His methods are to inflict suffering to discourage, frighten, and condemn. His hatred manifests itself in terrible cruelty intended to destroy God's people, making a shipwreck of their faith.

    Discernment is greatly needed to distinguish between these two kinds of suffering. Confusion in this area can serve to perpetuate and hide evil. May the Lord raise up leaders and believers who can protect and advise those who are vulnerable.

5. Do you see a process of brokenness in your own life? Can you describe it?

_____

_____

_____

_____

6. Please answer questions one through three in the section, **WHAT GETS BROKEN**?

7. Is there a difference between godly and ungodly suffering? How would you describe the differences? Why is this an important distinction?

_____

_____

_____

8. Check off the **INDICATIONS OF BROKENNESS** boxes that apply to you.

9. Read all the referenced Scripture verses for Session 6 located at the back of your notebook.

SESSION 7

Appropriation

The biblical sequence in the process of sanctification is clearly laid out for us in Romans 6:6, 11, 13, 14.

1. Realizing the truth is a Holy Spirit recognition of what happened to us spiritually at the cross. Our old man was crucified, releasing us from slavery to sin. Our regenerated human spirit now has the capacity to know truth.

2. To receive the truth, we must personally claim it for ourselves. It is not only a wonderful concept but acknowledgment that I have died to sin and am now alive to God. In salvation, we not only receive something, but we also become someone new.

3. To relinquish in light of the truth means to yield body and soul to the Holy Spirit's direction, depending on His enablement.

4. To remember the truth is to continually set our mind on Christ as our source of living.

5. Moment by moment, our flesh is effectively displaced as we walk in the Spirit.

Trust that God sees our sincere desire to abide in Him and believe the life we now live is fueled by the faith of the Son of God. This life is productive and active without strain or *burnout*. A secondary *baptism in the Spirit* is not required for abundant living. The Christ centered life is also the Spirit filled life (Ephesians 5:18) which involves yielding to His will and empowerment. We are complete in Christ (Colossians 2:10).

PROCESS OF SANCTIFICATION

1. Realize the Truth

"Knowing this, that our old man was crucified with Him, in order that our body of sin might be done away with, so that we would no longer be slaves of sin" (Romans 6:6).

2. Receive the Truth

"Likewise you also, reckon yourselves to be dead indeed to sin, but alive to God, in Christ Jesus our Lord" (Romans 6:11).

3. Relinquish, in Light of the Truth

"Present yourselves to God as those alive from the dead, and your members as instruments of righteous to God" (Romans 6:13).

4. Remember the Truth

"For sin shall not be master over you, for you are not under law but under grace" (Romans 6:14).

5. Respond to the Truth

"But I say, walk by the Spirit, and you will not carry out the desire of the flesh" (Galatians 5:16).

APPROPRIATION

How do we appropriate our union with Christ? Paul proclaims a foundational teaching on sanctification in Galatians 2:20. He realizes his "old man" was crucified with Christ at Calvary. There, he was redeemed from sin's penalty and delivered from sin's power (Romans 5:10; 6:14).

At the Cross, provision was made for the penalty and power of sin. However, our deliverance from sin's power is not automatic. It requires an active choice of heart obedience. "But thanks be to God that though you were slaves of sin, you became obedient from the heart to that form of teaching to which you were committed and having been freed from sin, you became slaves of righteousness" (Romans 6:17-18).

I choose to obey and abide by a continual attitude of yieldedness. I place all my trust in the law of the life of the Spirit to provide the power for my obedience (Romans 8:2). I rest in the faithfulness of God; He enables my walk in the Spirit moment by moment. This life of faith does not require a secondary act of grace or *baptism in the Spirit.* There is "one Lord, one faith, one baptism" (Ephesians 4:5).

John 14:20 is a *life verse* for many believers because it describes our oneness with God in plain language. Some commentators have stated it is one of the most important verses in the New Testament, revealing our union with Christ.

"At that time" refers to historical Pentecost, but there is also a personal application of this truth. *For a believer to see their union with Christ requires an illumination of the Holy Spirit!* When this occurs, an unshakable assurance is established within the soul.

Often, there follows a growing realization that the Spirit is the One to do battle with the power of sin in all its forms. What has been imputed is now imparted as we trust the filling of the Holy Spirit to permeate and govern every area of our lives (Ephesians 5:18).

We may now begin to close the gap between what God's Word declares and what we experience daily. As we worship God in spirit and in truth at our local church, communion and unity are enjoyed corporately with others.

Ask the disciplee if this has been taking place in their own life. If so, encourage them to share one or two examples during your time together.

In Christ's farewell discourse (John 14-17), He prepared His disciples for what was to come. Jesus knew they could not understand why He must be crucified, and He wanted to provide comfort and hope for the days ahead. John 14:20 (AMP) is a key verse in understanding our union with God: "At that time (when that day comes) you will know (for yourselves) that I am in My Father, and you (are) in Me, and I (am) in you." What does this mean for us?

"At that time" refers to the historical Pentecost recorded in Acts 2. The disciples realized on that day that the resurrected Christ was seated at the right hand of the Father in the place of honor and power (Ephesians 1:20-21). They also saw, "He raised us up together with Him, and seated us with Him in the heavenly places, in Christ Jesus" (Ephesians 2:6). And again, it was illuminated that the promised gift of the Holy Spirit had now been given to them by the glorified Lord (John 16:7-15). So, Jesus is in the Father, I am in Jesus, and the Holy Spirit is in Me!

Realizing the truth of our union with Christ and receiving it leads to a personal response. Sanctification by faith becomes progressively true in our souls through our moment-by-moment yieldedness. We continually rely on the faithfulness of the Holy Spirit to counteract and displace the power of sin and the flesh in our daily lives. "But I say, walk by the Spirit, and you will not carry out the desire of the flesh" (Galatians 5:16).

Remember, we are not fighting a civil war. The battle for the believer is between the flesh and the Holy Spirit! "For the flesh sets its desire against the Spirit, and the Spirit against the flesh; for these are in opposition to one another, so that you may not do the things that you please" (Galatians 5:17).

We are not passive. Although we are sealed and indwelled by the Spirit, we must choose to be filled with the Spirit. "Do not get drunk with wine, for that is dissipation, but be filled with the Spirit" (Ephesians 5:18). The verb tense in this verse indicates a continual action; it is stated in the passive voice as a command. In other words, filling is something we receive rather than achieve, provided we maintain an attitude of yieldedness and trust towards the Lord.

In this way, we begin to enjoy communion with the Spirit as He leads us to walk in the Spirit. The verses following Ephesians 5:18 describe the fellowship and joy this filling provides: "... speaking to one another in psalms and hymns and spiritual songs, singing and making melody with your heart to the Lord; always giving thanks for all things, in the name of our Lord Jesus

DISCIPLER'S NOTES

Scripture reveals the beauty of mutual submission between the Father, Son, and Holy Spirit. This is reflected in believers when we are filled with the Spirit and manifest honor and humility toward each other. Being subject to one another is voluntary and doesn't indicate lesser value or individual power-lessness. It's an active choice that displays our union with the Lamb of God and demonstrates His love for people.

We are now under grace, but what difference does this make in our lives? Ask the one you are discipling what this has meant for them personally. Do they know the Lord continually seeks to cultivate a deeper love relationship with them? If so, how has being rooted in the love of Jesus transformed their mind and emotions?

Is there a growing level of trust that Christ will provide all that is needed? Are life events being viewed in a new way? If so, ask the disciplee to share what they've noticed is taking place in their own life and experience.

Christ to God, even the Father; and be subject to one another in the fear of Christ" (Ephesians 5:19-21).

The same truth is reflected in what has been called the High Priestly Prayer of Jesus, "I do not ask on behalf of these alone, but also for those who believe in Me through their word; that they all may be one; even as Thou, Father, art in Me, and I in Thee, that they also may be in Us, so that the world may believe that Thou didst send Me" (John 17:20-23).

While we do not need a *new* doctrine, is there a lack of understanding and appropriation of our riches in Christ? Why is there such a gap between what we have been taught and what we actually live out and experience? Is grace just as ineffective as the law? We know this is false, but do our lives reflect the truth?

Our union with Christ is to be a growing relationship; He continually expands our capacity to know Him. Trusting Christ as our life amid our greatest trials provides a new perspective on their redemptive purposes.

DISCIPLER'S NOTES

The final wheel diagram illustrates a Christ-centered life. Ask your disciplee to read the description below the diagram in its entirety with you.

The cross with the "S" in the soul refers to the self-life or the flesh. The implication is that Christ, as our functional source of living, administers death to carnal, independent living. Since this is a new element in the wheel diagrams, check to see if further clarification is needed.

Our self-life, unlike the old man, has not been crucified. However, when we walk in the Spirit, the flesh is *rendered inoperative* through the counteraction of the Holy Spirit (Galatians 5:16).

The "C" in the center of the red heart shows us that Christ is our Lord and our very life.

CHRIST-CENTERED LIFE

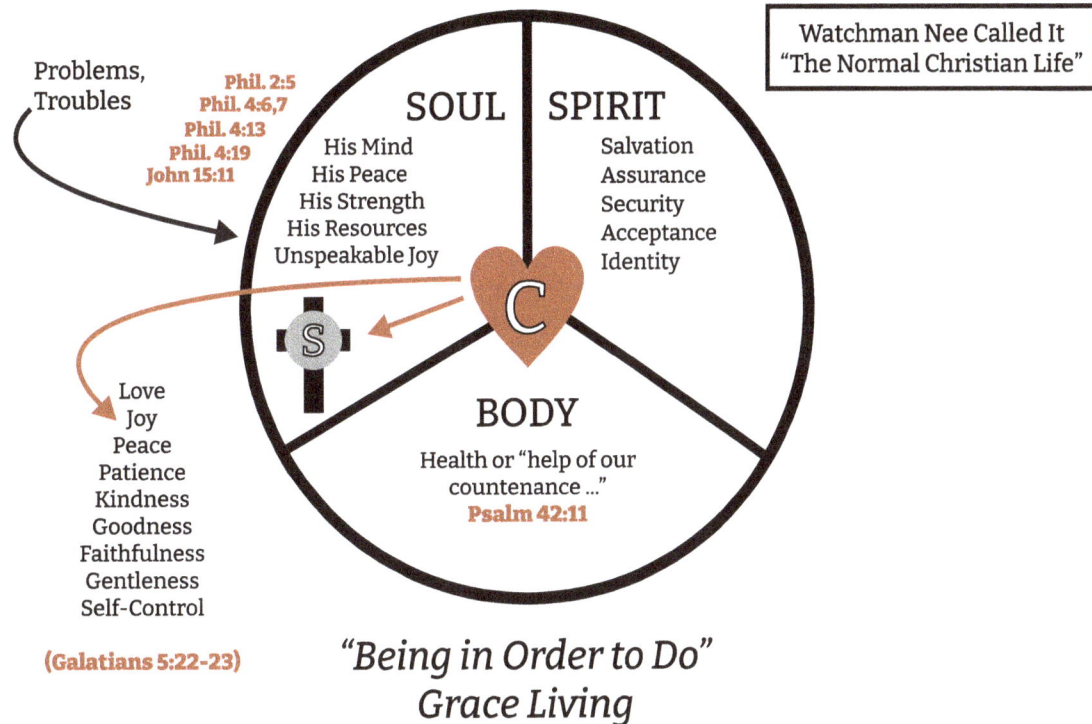

Watchman Nee Called It
"The Normal Christian Life"

Problems, Troubles

Phil. 2:5
Phil. 4:6,7
Phil. 4:13
Phil. 4:19
John 15:11

SOUL
His Mind
His Peace
His Strength
His Resources
Unspeakable Joy

SPIRIT
Salvation
Assurance
Security
Acceptance
Identity

C

S

Love
Joy
Peace
Patience
Kindness
Goodness
Faithfulness
Gentleness
Self-Control

BODY
Health or "help of our countenance ..."
Psalm 42:11

(Galatians 5:22-23)

"Being in Order to Do"
Grace Living

The "Christ-Centered Life" diagram illustrates the importance of the Christ-centered condition. As a believer, we have recognized our carnal condition, repented, surrendered to God, and claimed by faith our identification with Christ (Romans 6:3-14; 12:1,2).

The Holy Spirit then "restores our soul"—suddenly or gradually—as our mind is renewed with truth, our will remains yielded, and our emotions calm down in response to our new source of life. This abiding life is not sinless perfection or a one-time breakthrough. Instead, it is a discovery or return to God's provision for abundant life in Christ (John 10:10).

Positive results of inner restoration include cultivating:

- The mind of Christ (instead of mental confusion)
- The peace of Christ (instead of emotional turmoil)
- The strength of Christ (instead of inadequacy)
- The resources of Christ (instead of self-effort)
- The joy of Christ (instead of depression)

The "S" on the cross represents appropriating the revelation of Galatians 2:20, "I have been crucified with Christ, and it is no longer I who live, but Christ lives in me; and the life which I now live in the flesh I live by faith in the Son of God, who loved me and gave Himself up for me."

The "C" in the center symbolizes the believer abiding in Christ, yielding to Him, and trusting in Him as our source of living (John 15:4,5; Colossians 3:4; Ephesians 5:18; Matthew 11:28-30).

DISCIPLER'S NOTES

The introduction to **CHRIST IS LIFE** provides an overview of the diagram on page 167.

The key theme is that our souls were intended to express God's life through our individual personalities. Much biblical discipleship is devoted to teaching and exhorting believers in *what* they are to do. This diagram illustrates the dynamics of *how* they are to do it.

The last paragraph defines the flesh in a slightly different way. It is helpful to offer varying words and phrases to facilitate a broader understanding of the truths we share.

A wise discipler cannot overemphasize the fleshly tendency to believe that our previous experiences and emotions are the ultimate reality. However, only God's Word illuminates the bedrock of truth.

CHRIST IS LIFE

This section is an introduction and explanation for personalizing the diagrams provided on the following two pages. All are adaptations from materials written and devised by Paul Travis.

> "Now may the God of peace Himself sanctify you entirely and may your spirit and soul and body be preserved, complete without blame at the coming of our Lord Jesus Christ" (1 Thessalonians 5:23).

God's purpose is to make us more and more conformed to the image of Christ (Romans 8:28-29). We are the temple of the Holy Spirit with Christ living within (1 Corinthians 6:19-20; Galatians 2:20; Colossians 3:4; 1 John 5:11-12; Galatians 4:19).

Believers are joined to God in Christ. Through this union, we are a new creation (2 Corinthians 5:17), with the imputed righteousness of Christ. In our new identity, we desire to please God in our spirit. As indicated by the red highlights, God wants to live His life in and through us. This happens as we yield in heart obedience to the indwelling Holy Spirit, allowing His life in our spirit to flow into our soul, which results in our experiencing the fruit of the Spirit (peace in our mind, joy in our emotions, and love in our will). Remember that this yielding is a choice of our will, trusting in the empowerment of the Holy Spirit.

Not only can we experience His life internally, but He also wants to express His life through us (see statements in boxes). God has made our spirit new (past); we are to allow His TRUTH to renew our mind (present) (Romans 12:12). As we experience His life in our soul and His truth in our mind, we will express His life through our personality. One day, we will enjoy a new body (future).

Our flesh is the remaining corruption in the mortal body conditioned by living independently of God. Satan uses the world system, the flesh, and indwelling sin to feed us lies (in our minds), impacting our decision-making. We must choose, moment by moment, to yield (in heart obedience) to what we know to be the TRUTH of God's Word, or we will act instead on the lies we have come to believe because of our emotions or past experiences.

The diagram on the opposite page clearly portrays the dynamics of walking in the Spirit. Red illustrates the movement and impact of the Holy Spirit through our human spirit to our soul when we yield in heart obedience to His leading.

As a result, we can know for ourselves the fruit of the Spirit.

"If you love me, you will keep and obey my commandments" (John 14:15). My love for Christ motivates me to yield my will in heart obedience and enjoy communion and fellowship with Him.

"I have told you these things so that my joy and delight may be in you and that your joy may be made full and complete and overflowing" (John 15:11 AMP). Joy fills my emotions, even amid challenging circumstances.

"My perfect peace I give to you; not as the world gives do I give to you. Do not let your heart be troubled, nor let it be afraid" (John 14:27). My mind is quieted and spiritually sustained, even when I encounter unsettling events.

The decision to yield and trust results in a renewed mind that directs our actions. As I walk in the Spirit, others are ministered to and nourished through me. This encourages unity and fellowship among believers.

POINT OF YIELDING

HEART OBEDIENCE

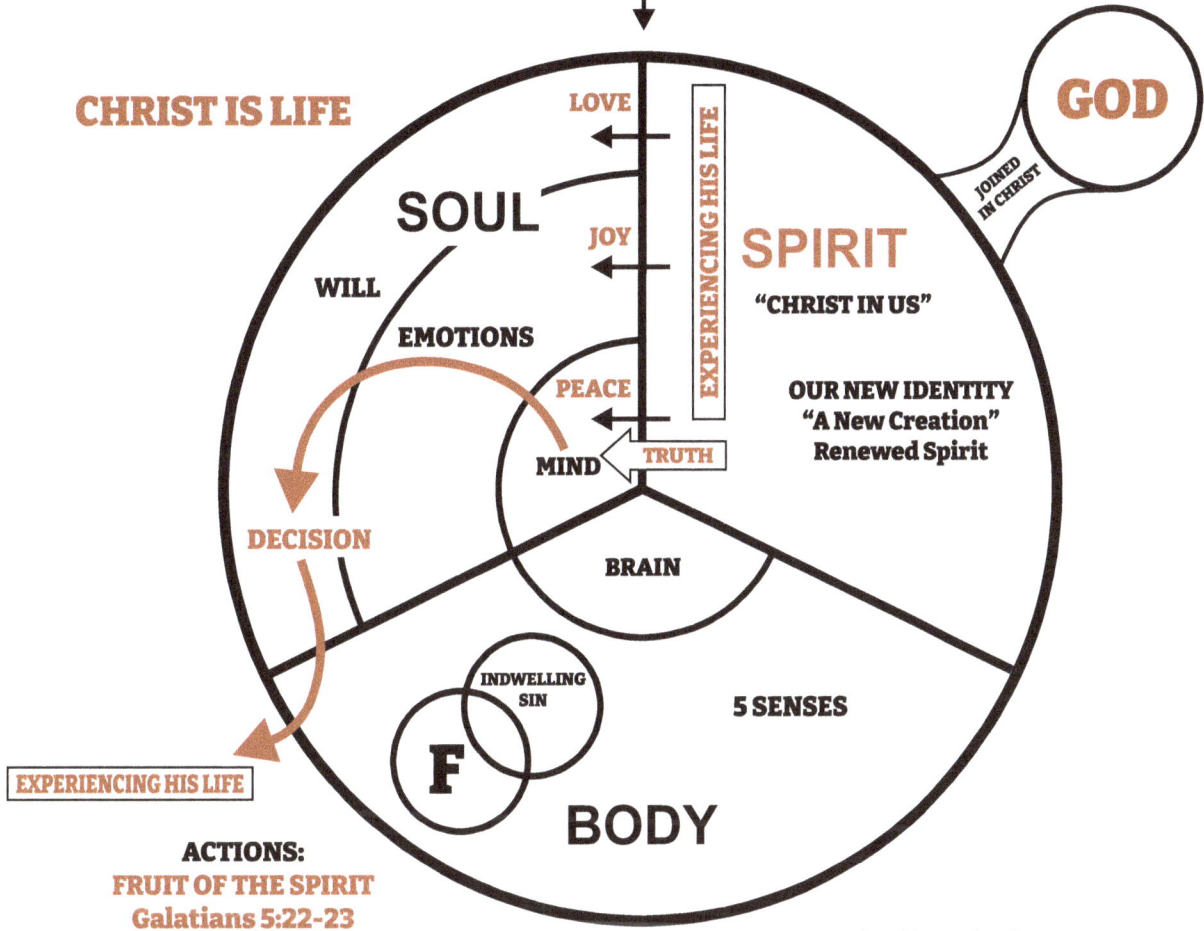

CHRIST IS LIFE

SOUL

LOVE

JOY

SPIRIT

"CHRIST IN US"

EXPERIENCING HIS LIFE

WILL

EMOTIONS

PEACE

OUR NEW IDENTITY
"A New Creation"
Renewed Spirit

MIND

TRUTH

DECISION

BRAIN

INDWELLING SIN

F

5 SENSES

BODY

EXPERIENCING HIS LIFE

ACTIONS:
FRUIT OF THE SPIRIT
Galatians 5:22-23

GOD

JOINED IN CHRIST

Adapted from Paul Travis 2021
Used by Permission

This diagram contrasts with the one on the previous page, showing us the dynamics of walking according to the flesh (blue).

In the context of this list of works of the flesh in Galatians 5:19-21, the apostle warns, " ... that those who practice such things will not inherit the kingdom of God" (Galatians 5:21). Works of the flesh characterize the unsaved. However, redeemed ones are also prone to walking after the flesh (Galatians 5:17; Romans 7:14-24). 1 Corinthians 3:1-4 rebukes believers who have lapsed into this carnal condition.

If we walk after the flesh, Christ is still our life, but we are not appropriating Him. The soul functions out of its own capacity to think, choose, and operate independently. Spiritual life is ignored through an unyielded heart. This choice results in the mind falling prey to the power of sin, offering up lies through Satan, worldly influences, and fleshly strongholds. These are yielded to, and the Spirit's fruit is forfeited. Instead, the works of the flesh become evident through thought, word, and deed.

The Holy Spirit has no testimony in our lives when we are unyielded. It may be helpful to cover the spirit/Spirit portion on the diagram with our hand to demonstrate the lack of empowerment when we walk according to the flesh.

Does the disciplee understand the importance of the **POINT OF YIELDING** in their daily walk? Ask them to share what insight they received after studying these diagrams.

POINT OF YIELDING

UNYIELDED HEART

CHRIST IS LIFE

GOD

JOINED IN CHRIST

SOUL

LOVE

JOY

PEACE

EXPERIENCING HIS LIFE

SPIRIT

"CHRIST IN US"

OUR NEW IDENTITY
"A New Creation"
Renewed Spirit

WILL

EMOTIONS

LIVING INDEPENDENTLY OF GOD

LIES

TRUTH

MIND

FLESHLY PATTERNS

DECISION

BRAIN

5 SENSES

BODY

INDWELLING SIN

F

ACTIONS:

WORKS OF THE FLESH
Galatians 5:19-20

SATAN

WORLD SYSTEM

Adapted from Paul Travis 2021
Used by Permission

Previously, we have written about how to appropriate Christ as our life in daily living.

The interactive exercises on pages 173 and 175 will show us how we may experience this in our own lives.

Another benefit of the assignment is learning the difference between *responding* to people instead of *reacting to* them. This practice promotes discernment as we trust the Lord's guidance and avoid falling prey to reactionary sin.

It is wise to seek out the counsel of mature believers who have our best interests at heart. We need to fellowship and pray with others for encouragement and accountability. Often this is comforting and edifying. At other times, people can be well-meaning yet uninformed about the true nature of our situation. Only the Good Shepherd can be relied upon to direct us perfectly.

KNOWING JESUS AS MY LIFE

Trusting Jesus as our life is a conscious yielding to the Lord's sovereignty and will. Moment by moment, we are able to choose a godly response to what happens to us. There will be those around us who will not choose to act in a godly way. How do we respond to these people?

While we may accept that we are in a particular situation or feeling a certain way, this does not necessarily mean the Lord wants us to remain there. We can go to Him with our cares and concerns.

Many people will give us their opinions on how we should think, feel, or act. While we may seek counsel from others who are wise, we have been given the Holy Spirit so Jesus can live His life in and through us. In John 10:27, Jesus tells the Jews that His sheep hear His voice. If we abide in Him (John 15:4), He will lead and guide us in our responses.

The chart on the opposite page takes us through a sequence of steps initiated by a particular event or life circumstance.

Many examples are provided, but let's look closely at the first one, betrayal by a friend. Three areas of response follow this experience.

The first is a willingness to relinquish being accepted by my friend. This does not rule out pursuing reconciliation if the Lord leads me to do so, but another's acceptance is not something I'm entitled to.

Next, I must honestly acknowledge the emotional pain this betrayal has caused me. Often this step is omitted, but it is important to include it.

Finally, I focus on my primary relationship with Christ as the ultimate source of acceptance.

EVENT OR LIFE CIRCUMSTANCE	KNOWING JESUS AS MY LIFE MEANS THAT MOMENT BY MOMENT, I AM FREE TO CHOOSE TO		
	RELINQUISH MY DESIRE TO BE:	ACCEPT THAT I MAY BE OR FEEL:	LOOK TO JESUS AS MY:
Betrayal by friend	Accepted	Rejected	Friend
Don't make the team	Acceptable	Unacceptable	Identity
Wrongly accused	Understood	Misunderstood	Friend
Cancer diagnosis	In control	Out of control	Savior
Mess up at work	Perfect	Make mistakes	Adequacy
Don't get the job	Successful	Fail	Identity
Don't get promotion	Seen as a success	Seen as a failure	Reputation
Loss of a parent	Strong	Weak	Protector
Receive rude comment	Angry/hold a grudge	Forgive	Judge/Redeemer
Left by spouse	Loved	Unloved	Security
Incorrect answer	Smart	Dumb	Wisdom
Have dirty house	Admired	Scorned	Reputation
Develop chronic illness	Healthy	Sick	Strength/peace
Someone cuts in line	Treated fairly	Mistreated	Protector
Friend won't listen	Right	Wrong	Wisdom
Injury	Comfortable	In pain	Strength/peace
Car breaks down	Rescued	Abandoned	Protector
Try to apologize	Listened to	Ignored	Wisdom
Try something new	Encouraged	Put down/criticized	Strength/peace
Make extra effort	Noticed	Ignored	Protector
Go beyond the norm	Appreciated	Taken for granted	Friend
Say something foolish	Respected	Made insignificant	Confidence
Falsely accused	Trusted	Viewed with suspicion	Security
Broken engagement	Married	Single	Reputation
Unexpected illness	Financially stable	Financially stretched	Confidence

Now it's time for the disciplee to personalize these steps for themselves.

Three events will be selected and written on page 175 each day. Those listed in the chart on the previous page are examples of what could be included. Other life circumstances will likely be chosen in place of some of these examples since each of us is unique.

Begin by selecting three events that took place on a particular day. A brief explanation or description is sufficient.

The second column describes the *desires* that we are willing to relinquish. Sometimes, what we place on the altar will not need to be sacrificed, but the attitude is one of willingness.

The third column describes the emotional cost of what has taken place. It is essential not to minimize how these events may impact us emotionally.

Finally, identify how Jesus provides for our needs. As we focus and trust in His sufficiency, healing takes place in His way and time.

We need to come to know Him as Jehovah Jireh—*the Lord will provide.*

KNOWING JESUS AS MY LIFE MEANS THAT
MOMENT BY MOMENT, I AM FREE TO CHOOSE TO

EVENT OR LIFE CIRCUMSTANCE	RELINQUISH MY DESIRE TO BE	ACCEPT THAT I MAY BE OR FEEL	LOOK TO JESUS AS MY

1. Sanctification by faith is the means to appropriate our riches in Christ. Christ IS our sanctification, and we must have the eyes of our heart opened to see this truth. Does your disciplee question whether or not sanctification is by faith? If so, ask what the alternative would be. The only other option is that sanctification takes place by works or a combination of works plus faith. They will discover that only sanctification by faith leads to experiential sanctification.

2. The human spirit is where the Holy Spirit indwells us, but the soul is where the Holy Spirit fills us (Ephesians 5:18). This filling takes place through our choice of yieldedness. He then empowers our decision.

3. Throughout the week, 21 examples have been documented. Some who have finished the first week of this discipleship interactive have chosen to continue journaling along these lines.

   What does this process prepare us to do?

   Walk in the Spirit!

CONSIDER THIS: SESSION 7

1. What is sanctification by faith? To walk in an understanding that sanctification is by faith, our mind must be renewed through God's Word (Galatians 3:1-3). "... Christ in you, the hope of glory ...." (Colossians 1:25-27). Christ's indwelling is not a *secret* but a *mystery* that has been clearly revealed in Scripture. How has your understanding of union with Christ grown during your discipleship sessions?

   _____

   _____

   _____

2. The Paul Travis diagrams beautifully illustrate how it is possible to walk in the Spirit versus walking according to the flesh. Where does the filling of the Spirit take place? How does it take place? Where does the Holy Spirit indwell us? Be prepared to discuss these two diagrams next week.

   _____

   _____

   _____

3. The section, Knowing Jesus as My Life Means That Moment by Moment, I Am Free to Choose To, may prove to be a very informative exercise! Record your responses to the four columns (examples and forms are provided). Every day, write out three examples for each of the lines, including *Event, Be Willing to Relinquish, Be Willing to Be or Feel*, and *What I Trust Jesus to Provide.* You will have several examples to share by next week's session. What do you think this process prepares you to do?

   _____

   _____

   _____

A Masterpiece of God

The disciplee may have concerns that yielding to Christ, and the process of brokenness, may lead them to be passive. Nothing could be further from the truth, as last week's interactive assignments should have proven. God's initiative never cancels our ability to freely choose a response.

Walking in the Spirit requires active volition; I must choose to cooperate through a maintained attitude of yielding and trusting. This is not an automatic process. I willingly participate.

Ask your disciplee if they believe God is controlling. This is a very important question that reflects their concept of God. Do controlling people allow others to freely make their own choices?

When we fail to walk in the light and make poor choices, are we afraid God will respond harshly towards us? There may be consequences or loss, but He is faithful to convict and redirect us.

We can trust that God sees our heart and does not abandon us when we fail to abide. His steadfast love seeks to lift us up and restore our fellowship with Him. Receiving His grace after times of failure sustains and encourages us.

IS LIFE IN CHRIST PASSIVE?

Does walking in the Spirit mean I don't do anything? Is my heart attitude, "Holy Ghost, go ahead and push me around"? Should I just say, "Let go, and let God"?

I am in union with Christ, yet I am a distinct person with a unique personality. I have the ability and responsibility to make choices. God does not eradicate my soulical capabilities. I have the freedom to abide in Christ, and when I do, I receive His sufficiency and fullness.

I must choose to cooperate and participate in the indwelling life of Christ. For example, if I am a discipler, I will study and prepare for opportunities to minister (2 Timothy 2:15). While meeting with an individual, I am open and sensitive to the Lord redirecting what I had planned to share. There is only one Wonderful Counselor!

God is sovereign and in control, but is He controlling? The answer to this question is an important distinction to consider in our walk with the Lord. Does He *drive* us, or does He *lead* us?

When I fail to abide and find myself walking according to the flesh, do I believe my momentary failure is greater than God's grace? I do need to earnestly repent, confess my sin, and thank God for his forgiveness. Sin is not to be minimized or ignored and may result in consequences for me and others. Opportunities that may have been available could be temporarily forfeited. Still, we may approach the Lord with confidence, knowing His mercies are new every morning (Lamentations 3: 22-24).

Am I paralyzed, continually *waiting* on the Lord for every small decision? Or do I trust that He is able to safeguard and accomplish the purposes He has for me (Ephesians 2:10)? Is He faithful to provide necessary course corrections when I need them? How will He do this?

Do I panic if I temporarily *violate* something I had previously surrendered? Does victory depend on my ability to maintain an attitude of surrender perfectly?

God sees the heart and knows if my desire to obey Him is genuine. He will continue to be active in my life (Philippians 2:13). Growing in grace and knowing Christ more intimately is my primary goal (2 Peter 3:18).

Will I emotionally collapse and shut down when unexpected suffering or loss comes my way? Can adverse circumstances help me recognize what

Ask the disciplee to consider if their daily walk is *upside down*, referring to the headings on the opposite page.

Living out of emotions characterizes a life that is driven by feelings. Shame, guilt, and inadequacy strongly inform and influence many of us. Sadly, our behavior often reflects these emotional wounds and contaminates relationships with others. As a result, people may view us as unhealthy and avoid our attempts to connect with them. When this happens, we tell ourselves, "See, I knew I would be rejected!" Each time we repeat this pattern, we reinforce a poor self-image.

As Christians, our daily walk should reflect the truth. We know who we are in Christ and have reckoned it to be true for us personally. Union with Christ can be reflected in our behavior and relationships with increasing consistency. Although we may experience rejection and disappointment, we trust Christ to bring healing in the way He chooses.

What you know will eventually change what you feel!

As God renews the mind with truth, healing gradually occurs and new behaviors emerge.

Through our walk in the Spirit, we discover our heart's true desires. The fruit of the Spirit is ours to enjoy and express to others.

We have already been given victory over self-defeating habits and behaviors. Our union with Christ does not mean we won't be tempted or experience cravings. Sin is not dead, and we will feel the pull to indulge in various unhealthy ways. However, we have died to sin's authority. This means we may freely choose to rely on the Holy Spirit's power over any temptation.

my source of life is? Do my choices and actions at these times display my union with Christ?

In practical terms, is my daily walk *upside down*?

Living Out of My Emotions

- I feel *bad* (sad, shame, guilt, inadequate, rejected).
- My behaviors flow out of the emotions I am experiencing.
- Others respond accordingly and add to my poor self-image.
- The lies that hold me captive are now reinforced!

Living in the Light of the Truth

- I realize what is true.
- I receive it personally (know it is true for me).
- I choose to respond to the truth and trust the Spirit to empower my behavior, moment by moment.
- I trust Christ for my emotional healing and well-being when and how He provides it.

Am I required merely to ignore everything I want? If those desires originate from my flesh, are they authentically mine? Do they reflect my true identity, a new creation defined by union with Christ? When we walk in the Spirit, is there any lack of joy, peace, or fulfillment? Isn't that what I yearn to experience?

Must I "wait on the Lord" to deliver me from self-defeating, unhealthy habits such as overeating? Do I doubt I've died to sin because I continue to experience powerful food cravings? What if I occasionally succumb to these temptations? Does appropriating victory in this area depend on the removal of cravings? Why or why not?

INTRODUCTION: A MASTERPIECE OF GOD describes how crisis and process are incorporated to progressively sanctify believers.

God works in various ways and at different seasons of life to conform us to Christ. We may struggle and become discouraged when facing trials and suffering. At those times we can trust that the Lord is faithful to establish our growth in grace. He accomplishes His workmanship through discipline, conviction, Holy Spirit illumination of Scripture, and answered prayer.

The diagram on page 186 gives us a *bird's eye view* of God's transformative work in the lives of believers. Understanding how sanctification is accomplished redeems our perspective on past events. As we pray and reflect on our circumstances and relationships, we discover fresh evidence of God's love and purposes.

The following scriptures point to the goal of this process:

"And we know that God causes all things to work together for good to those who love God, to those who are called according to His purpose. For those whom He foreknew, He also predestined to become conformed to the image of His Son" (Romans 8:28,29).

"My children, with whom I am again in labor until Christ is formed in you..." (Galatians 4:19).

INTRODUCTION: A MASTERPIECE OF GOD

The diagram on the following page is from Dr. Charles Solomon's book, *The Ins and Out of Rejection*. We have adapted his illustration and writings contained on pages 110-112.

An important emphasis in this section is to reassure believers that God is always at work in our lives. Beginning with our physical birth and continuing after our spiritual birth, He actively shepherds our growth in grace.

When we trust Him with our entire lives, God is faithful to *hedge us in* through various means. Our circumstances, relationships, sufferings, and blessings all serve to direct us to the center of His will. We are convicted and sometimes disciplined when we choose a course that pulls us away from His ultimate plan. Prayer and Holy Spirit illumination of the Scriptures renew our minds and reveal our union with Christ (Romans 12:1-2).

It is vitally important to know that God is always intervening for our greatest good. When we are struggling or discouraged, and there is no evidence of this, we must trust in His ways and His perfect timing.

Sometimes, the overall growth process is easier to recognize when we're older and look back on our life. The events and relationships that seemed random or even negative at the time may now be viewed as significant means of transformation.

Personalizing the diagram **A MASTERPIECE OF GOD** will be an encouraging reflection that testifies to the Lord's steadfast care for us.

How do we become a masterpiece of God? He is Jehovah-Mekodishkem—*the Lord Who sanctifies you.*

The **MASTERPIECE OF GOD** diagram illustrates God's perfect will for us by the red line extending from the triangle's apex to the physical birth bullet point. It is labeled **IN THE CENTER OF HIS WILL**.

To begin sharing this diagram with your disciplee, you will start at the bottom.

We are born physically in accordance with God's will. As the Father draws us, we are convicted of sin, righteousness, and judgment and receive Jesus as our Savior. Although reconciled to God, we are convicted of living independently and walking according to the flesh. This leads to a total surrender of our former manner of living and a dependence on Christ alone.

Next, the Sanctifier opens the eyes of our understanding to see our death, burial, resurrection, and ascension with Christ through our union with Him (identification).

We are more likely to cooperate with the Lord's direction after this, but sometimes we run ahead of Him or try to *help out.* In doing so, we veer away from His will for us (illustrated by the curved blue lines moving towards the sides of the triangle). He guides us to return and abide in Him, often through difficult relationships and circumstances. As we continue to surrender and trust during times of trial, we find liberty to draw closer to the Lord. We may experience painful emotions, but we now appropriate and experience God's resources in responding to them.

As we grow in grace, the Lord works more directly through our times of prayer and meditation on His Word. Our minds are given clear direction to keep in step with the Spirit. By His enabling, we stay closer to the center of His will, often with a greater understanding of God's purposes for us.

There is no set formula for how God moves in the lives of His children. It is possible to receive Christ as Savior, Lord, and Life simultaneously at initial salvation. Our diagram illustrates a typical sequence of progressive sanctification. There is no *end game* for growth in grace during our earthly lives.

A MASTERPIECE OF GOD

HOW A DECISION OF TOTAL SURRENDER BECOMES TRUE IN US

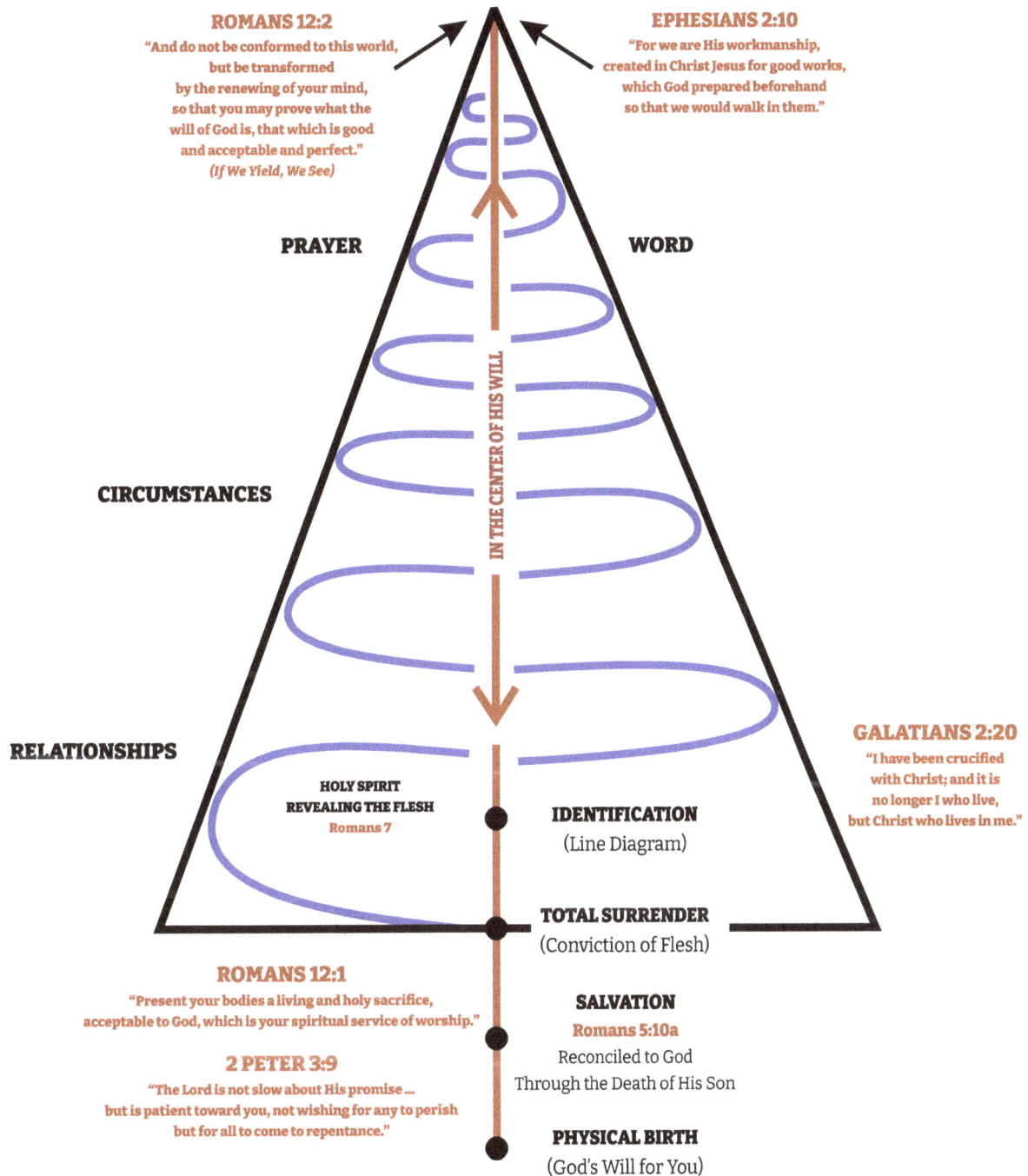

ROMANS 12:2
"And do not be conformed to this world,
but be transformed
by the renewing of your mind,
so that you may prove what the
will of God is, that which is good
and acceptable and perfect."
(If We Yield, We See)

EPHESIANS 2:10
"For we are His workmanship,
created in Christ Jesus for good works,
which God prepared beforehand
so that we would walk in them."

PRAYER

WORD

IN THE CENTER OF HIS WILL

CIRCUMSTANCES

RELATIONSHIPS

GALATIANS 2:20
"I have been crucified
with Christ; and it is
no longer I who live,
but Christ who lives in me."

**HOLY SPIRIT
REVEALING THE FLESH**
Romans 7

IDENTIFICATION
(Line Diagram)

TOTAL SURRENDER
(Conviction of Flesh)

ROMANS 12:1
"Present your bodies a living and holy sacrifice,
acceptable to God, which is your spiritual service of worship."

SALVATION
Romans 5:10a
Reconciled to God
Through the Death of His Son

2 PETER 3:9
"The Lord is not slow about His promise ...
but is patient toward you, not wishing for any to perish
but for all to come to repentance."

PHYSICAL BIRTH
(God's Will for You)

1. Encourage the disciplee to carefully study the examples that contrast living out of emotions versus living out of the truth. Which is true for them? Our daily walk is often a combination of the two, but take the opportunity to discuss this in some detail. Emotional wounds can create deep strongholds that remain undetected in our lives. When these are not recognized, they may steal our best intentions. Having Christ as my life does not promise I will be anesthetized from hurt and disappointment.

2. Does the disciplee understand that total surrender is a starting point in progressive sanctification and one that will deepen throughout their lives? Suggest that a personal example be given for a circumstance, a relational issue, an answered prayer, and an illumination of God's word.

3. Ask the disciplee to describe one consequence of discipline they received from the Lord. Were they angry with Him or led quickly to repentance? Suggest they write about this in detail, including whether it created an opportunity to discover something new about their flesh.

4. To personalize this diagram, it may be helpful to place dates at various points in the diagram. Birth and salvation are usually easy to designate, but what about total surrender or identification? Were there milestones in relationships or circumstances? Hopefully, there will be an increasing awareness of undesirable patterns that have become less prominent or have been eliminated. Trials and revelations tend to be the most trans-formative events. Ask your disciplee to describe the most significant challenge they have faced and the greatest blessing they received. Where would they place them on the diagram?

CONSIDER THIS: SESSION 8

1. Read **IS LIFE IN CHRIST PASSIVE?** and fill in your responses for each of the bullet point paragraphs. Pay special attention to the section that asks if your daily walk is *upside down*. Does this seem like what you experience in your daily living?

   _____

   _____

2. Please allow time this week to prayerfully consider the diagram, **A MASTERPIECE OF GOD**. What is your understanding of the relationship between total surrender and knowing the indwelling life of Christ? Share specifically how the Lord used a pivotal circumstance or relationship, answered prayer, or directed you through His Word. In what ways did these people or events draw you closer to the center of His will?

   _____

   _____

3. Have you experienced consequences or discipline in your life? If so, did you discover more about your flesh at that time? What did you learn from the way you responded to the Lord's chastening?

   _____

   _____

4. When you personalize **A MASTERPIECE OF GOD**, where do you notice the most significant challenges taking place in your life? What has proven to be the greatest blessing?

   _____

   _____

5. What is your current understanding of Ephesians 2:10?

   _____

Belief Systems

Awareness of our belief systems is important for our mental and emotional health and our ability to appropriate God's truths. If we hold beliefs that are inconsistent with or contrary to biblical truths, they can hinder our relationship with God or others.

The necessary knowledge and understanding should now be in place for the disciplee to make a total surrender of heart obedience to the Lord. If there is still hesitation, looking more closely at their underlying beliefs may be necessary. The information on the following pages and the **WHO DO YOU THINK YOU ARE?** exercise on page 43 helps the disciplee dig more deeply.

Ask clarifying questions of the disciplee. However, the Lord will have to reveal any existing strongholds. Examples of belief systems that interfere with an ability to surrender to God include:

- A belief that one should not have to suffer

- A belief that God might ask you to do or give up something that you highly value, such as relationships or comforts

- A belief system that highly values intellectual excellence

- A belief system built on the need for independence and self-sufficiency

- A belief that everything must be *provable* by evidence

- A belief that security comes through wealth or status

Personal experiences can influence belief systems. Trauma, loss, or disappointment may promote beliefs that the world is not a safe place, and God may be uncaring or even punitive.

Listen to the disciplee. What they believe influences how they interpret their experiences. If I have a prodigal child who hasn't contacted me in a year, what am I believing if I ask the Lord what I've done to deserve this and beg for mercy? Do I believe that God is good (Psalm 100:5; Nahum 1:7; 1 Peter 2:3)? Do I believe that He is working all things together for good (Romans 8:28)? If I really believe that, might I believe there is something for me to learn in this season and thank Him that I can trust Him with my prodigal?

BELIEF SYSTEMS

What Are Belief Systems?

Belief systems form the basis for how we understand the world around us. They are basic assumptions that we form about ourselves and life. We consider these assumptions to be *facts* and hold *truth* to be what we have experienced in life so far. They include but are not limited to what is right and wrong, how to relate to others, how to get our needs met, and how to avoid being hurt.

Belief systems are based on a cluster of interrelated ideas that are dependent on each other and thus form an entire system. If we change one belief, it will affect the system as a whole, especially if it is a core belief. We are often completely unaware of our beliefs, though they become ingrained in our thinking and affect our decisions, how we react to events, and how we see and communicate with others.

We like to think that what we believe is true. Therefore, we guard our beliefs carefully, and our minds will subconsciously look for proof (evidence) to support and validate them. If new information (objective truth) tries to penetrate, we will *spit it out* if it doesn't line up with our own experience or emotions. What we believe is acted out in our behavior.

A healthy individual will test their own beliefs to see if they are justified or just assumed. The truth can withstand scrutiny.

Where Do We Get Our Beliefs?

We generally form our beliefs by a combination of our experiences and/or by accepting what others tell us to be true. We receive many of our core beliefs from our *family heritage*. These beliefs then operate like a *set of rules* that may remain with us the rest of our lives.

Other sources for our beliefs can include:

- Religion
- Community, made up of extended family
- Friends or teachers
- Culture/media
- Power of sin
- Books
- Life experiences

Satan can use any or all of these to establish fortresses of deception. Who we trust and what we believe is critical.

How Do Belief Systems Work?

Life's circumstances affect us profoundly, with no explanation for our reactions. We are not to simply brush off such responses. Psalm 139:23-24 is a template for approaching God to walk us through these times. The diagram on page 195 helps the disciplee process painful emotions and poor self-worth.

An event occurs in our life that prompts a response from us. Many of us have false beliefs we rely on when reacting to our experiences (see page 65-66). Event: my friends get together without me. I assume they don't want to be with me. I feel rejected and unloved. My emotions cause me to act ungodly, avoiding friends or lashing out at them.

What false belief leads me to my deceptive thinking, making me feel rejected and unloved? It could be, "I'm a loser. My friends must not really like me." *I must choose to bring God's truth about me to mind* in order to displace the false belief. Some examples are found in John 1:12, John 15:15-16, Rom. 8:17; 2 Corinthians 5:17; Galatians 3:26, Ephesians 1:1, Colossians 3:3, Colossians 3:12, and 1 John 3:12. This choice brings my focus from a false belief to God's truth. Now, instead of an ungodly response, I choose a God-honoring way to respond.

Examining our thoughts doesn't come naturally. If this is new to the disciplee, it may benefit them to practice this. See number 9 on page 207.

In time, the disciplee may recognize the false assumption and move directly from it to God's truth without having to experience the associated false belief.

What Are Strongholds?

While both a false belief and a stronghold influence thoughts, emotions, and behavior, a false belief can change with new information. Example: a person I'm supposed to meet for coffee doesn't arrive on time or call to say they will be late. I believe they are disrespectful of my time. In reality, they had an accident and couldn't call. When I find out the truth, the false belief is replaced with understanding and concern.

How Do Belief Systems Work?

A situation occurs, prompting us to think and feel something. We generally act on these thoughts and feelings based on what we believe.

However, just because we believe something does not make it true.

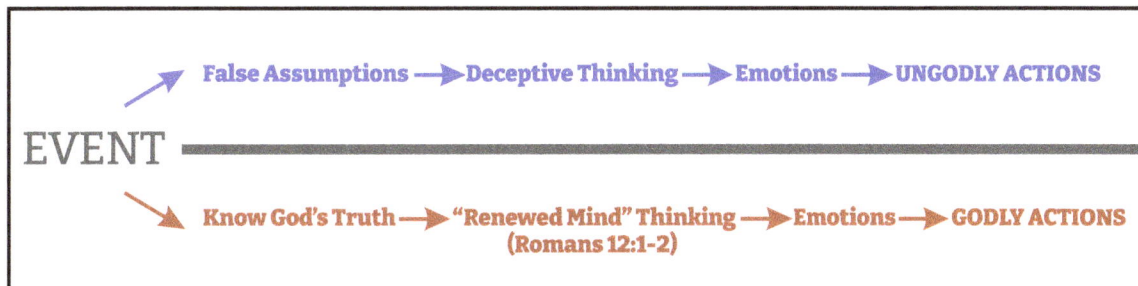

```
                    False Assumptions ──▶ Deceptive Thinking ──▶ Emotions ──▶ UNGODLY ACTIONS

EVENT  ──────────────────────────────────────────────────────────────────────────

                    Know God's Truth ──▶ "Renewed Mind" Thinking ──▶ Emotions ──▶ GODLY ACTIONS
                                          (Romans 12:1-2)
```

*Adapted from *The Search for Significance* by Robert S. McGee.

My response is not about what actually happened to me, but what is the significance to me? Example: Would I feel inadequate if I tried out for and did not make an NFL team? What if I homeschooled my child, and they did not make it into any of the colleges they applied to?

What Are Strongholds?

New Oxford American Dictionary defines a stronghold as, "A place that has been fortified to protect it against attack; a place where a particular cause or belief is strongly defended or upheld."

A stronghold may stem from a false belief, often starting with an early experience that leaves us hurt or disappointed. We are then left vulnerable and open to lies that are planted by Satan. These may include distorted perceptions of God, of ourselves, and of others. False beliefs about ourselves and God can become limiting beliefs, preventing us from becoming who God created us to be.

- ❧ I am not smart enough to ....
- ❧ God could never use someone like me.
- ❧ I've made too big a mess of my life.

Sometimes, our false beliefs are partially true. As an example, *"People who fail get what they deserve."* All behavior has consequences, but a small amount of truth in a false belief increases its impact. Sometimes, even accurate thinking leads to a false belief—*I feel bad, therefore I am bad.*

Our core beliefs form in early relationships and continue through social and cultural influences (see page 43). We may unknowingly reinforce belief patterns, making them strongholds which control our mind and are resistant to change.

At an early age a caregiver may be unwilling or unable to meet our needs. We take this personally and don't feel loved. We become *self-sufficient*, watching out for ourselves, never entering into genuine relationships. Ultimately, self-reliance apart from God confirms our belief.

False beliefs lead to behaviors that sabotage well-being. I may become guarded to avoid rejection. Because I don't interact with other children, they think I'm *stuck-up* and avoid me. This *set-up* confirms I'm unlovable. By the time I'm old enough to date, I've formed a stronghold of shame. I'm afraid my spouse will find out who I really am and reject me—eventually ending my marriage and confirming I was unlovable.

Some strongholds are difficult to detect as they are ingrained in our thinking and may feel *normal.* Others, such as addiction, may be easier to see—at least for others. Whether we are aware of them or not, strongholds keep us from doing what is best.

Because the Lord is the answer to all true freedom, an unbeliever cannot experience the breaking of a stronghold.

Identifying Strongholds

Is the disciplee aware of any persistent sin patterns? Do they engage in negative thought patterns? Do they have occasions when emotional responses are disproportionate to circumstances confronting them? Are there destructive behaviors or broken relationships in their life? Do you think you see something the disciplee is unaware of?

Is the disciplee aware of any unhealthy thought patterns or emotional responses? Listen carefully to the disciplee. Is there rigidity in their thinking? Are they unable or unwilling to consider alternative viewpoints or truth from Scripture? Is there a behavior they are unable to break free from?

Is the disciplee spiritually defeated and lacking in growth? Are they trying to overcome these areas through fleshly means? Is their behavior inconsistent with what the disciplee claims to believe?

God created us for relationship. Dysfunction occurs when our relationships are damaged or lost. This can lead a person to becoming self-sufficient and thinking, "I am on my own!"

Self-sufficiency often leads to the thinking that we cannot trust others. This conclusion may be true concerning some people in our lives, but it certainly is not true of all people.

We reinforce false beliefs through *set-ups* when we behave in such a way that the anticipated result occurs. It then becomes a self-fulfilling prophecy.

When we buy into the lies of our false beliefs, repeatedly failing to reject them (2 Corinthians 10:5), they become an area that Satan retains a hold over—a stronghold.

Strongholds may keep us stuck or in bondage, impacting our emotions and decisions. This false thinking will resist any attempt to displace it and causes us to deny truth. People trapped in strongholds may know what to do, but their recurring destructive habits continually get the best of them.

Examples of strongholds include but aren't limited to:

- Addiction
- Anger
- Anxiety
- Arrogance
- Bitterness
- Depression
- Fear
- Laziness
- Lying
- Manipulation
- Poor self-esteem
- Pride
- Sexual sin
- Shame
- Stubbornness
- Unforgiveness

Unbelief is an initial stronghold that is necessary to overcome.

Identifying Strongholds

1. Is there an area in my life where I have ongoing struggle?

2. Do I have an unhealthy thought pattern or habit that I deal with regularly?

3. Is there an area in my life where I want to prove I am worthy, secure, and valued, that is tied to one of these habits or patterns?

Detecting strongholds is the first step to addressing them. Our self-reflection and feedback from others we trust may cause us to examine our beliefs. The weapons of our warfare cannot be of the flesh but are divinely powerful (2 Corinthians 10:4).

Following are some key spiritual weapons:

- We must examine our beliefs in light of biblical truth (Ephesians 6:17).

- The blood represents the victory that Jesus has won (Revelation 12:11).

- Believers can call upon the name of Jesus for authority (Philippians 2:10).

- We approach God for protection, strength, wisdom, and revelation of our strongholds (Ephesians 6:18).

- At the Cross, our co-crucifixion and co-resurrection with Jesus gives us the power of the indwelling Holy Spirit to break our strongholds (Galatians 2:20).

Belief Systems and Emotions

Our ideas, values, and assumptions influence our emotions. What does the disciplee believe about the world? Is it dangerous, causing fear and anxiety, or generally safe, bringing good feelings? What expectations have we developed? Unmet expectations can bring disappointment, frustration, or even anger. Strong emotional responses can reinforce beliefs that triggered them in the first place.

When emotions conflict with beliefs, we are uncomfortable. This can be a head/heart split, leading us to change our beliefs or reinterpret the experience to restore harmony. If we change our beliefs, our emotions change.

To bring about healthier responses, we must reshape false beliefs in light of God's Word. Conversely, paying attention to unhealthy emotional responses provides insight into underlying beliefs.

Belief Systems and the Flesh

Just as belief systems influence emotions, they also influence the flesh, and vice versa. Beliefs that align with worldly values justify pride, selfishness, or immorality and strengthen the flesh. In contrast, a belief system rooted in biblical truth helps us resist fleshly temptations. Unfortunately, the flesh fights against biblical principles and the Spirit (Galatians 5:17). Where the flesh can influence our thought patterns, it may confirm and strengthen self-centered beliefs.

The concepts on pages 199 and 201 clarify displacement and are key to overcoming false beliefs. Does the disciplee focus on the truth to displace false beliefs?

Strongholds may prevent us from finding peace and joy. We usually cannot see our own strongholds, although others may see them clearly. If we are consistently exposed to thoughts and beliefs contrary to our own, we may start to question them. The Lord must reveal a stronghold for us to overcome it. It often takes a personal crisis for us to become desperate enough to want to replace the lies with God's truth.

Renewing the mind is essential to displacing the lies and replacing them with God's truth (Romans 12:1-2; 2 Corinthians 10:5). We no longer have to live by our fleshly thoughts. We have the mind of Christ (1 Corinthians 2:16). If we walk according to the Truth, the lies will fall away. We must fight with spiritual weapons.

Belief Systems and Emotions

Because we are created in God's image, we have the same emotions He does. Unfortunately, as humans, we are afflicted with a certain measure of false beliefs that impact how we feel. Our emotions reside in our soul and are being sanctified as we are. We can learn to steward our emotions in a God-honoring way.

2 Corinthians 10:3-5 prompts us to take every thought captive to the obedience of Christ. To do that, we must become aware enough to know what we are thinking and feeling and be able to consider why. If the why is based on a lie, we can displace that lie with truth.

Belief Systems and the Flesh

We are born spiritually dead, and our flesh seeks a way to feel alive rather than facing its reality. Depending on our unique version of the flesh, specific effects of false beliefs vary from person to person. In addition to control, our flesh always seeks comfort. Our memory banks retain *snapshots* of how we use our fleshly behaviors to successfully meet our needs—both in the moment and out of our own resources. In the case of *good flesh*, there may be many such memories, creating deep strongholds that hold us captive.

When we walk in the Spirit (Galatians 5:16), we see a pattern of *displacement.*

- We cannot focus on two things at once. If we focus our mind on the Truth, false beliefs are displaced. This is not an attempt to suppress the thoughts.

When we experience unhealthy thoughts and feelings, we must become aware and take our thoughts captive. If we don't see our problem but others we trust see it, we must be willing to pray that the Lord will reveal the truth.

We saw on page 165 and the resulting diagrams that as we yield to the indwelling Spirit, His Truth renews our minds. We then see our lives in light of Scripture and respond in heart obedience. We can also see our past hurts and experiences through the lens of truth, changing our perception and promoting spiritual growth.

To heal and grow, we must deal with our past. Particularly where there has been trauma, while we cannot dwell on it, we cannot pretend it didn't happen.

STEPS TO DISPLACING FALSE BELIEFS

This is God's work. It will happen in His way and in His time. He is always good and always good for each of us. We pray that God will act on behalf of the disciplee and trust and accept the outcome.

1. Realize the Truth

- The Holy Spirit illuminates (*rhema*) truth to our spirit. This personal word for the believer differs from *logos*, which is general biblical truth.

- God is the initiator.

- This truth is revealed. We can't merely *discover* it.

2. Receive the Truth

- The truth illumined by the Holy Spirit is believed in our minds.

- We personalize the truth. "This is true for me. I know that I know."

3. Relinquish in Light of the Truth

- I am an instrument of righteousness.

- I yield to Christ as a decision of my will. This is my act of worship (Romans 12:1). It is done out of heart obedience, but the Lord brings the outcome.

- As the Spirit acts in and through me, I will walk in obedience to the truth.

4. Remember the Truth

- My righteousness is not earned but comes from Christ.

- I keep my attention on illumined truth.

- I look to Christ as my source for all things.

- I live from a heart transformed by grace and not as a legal obligation.

5. Respond to the Truth

- As I choose to set my mind on Jesus, I walk according to the Spirit's leading, and my fleshly desires are displaced.

- As I walk by the Spirit, in His time, my feelings align with what I know to be true.

- As I live according to the Spirit, the moral law is naturally fulfilled.

🌿 Renewing our mind (Romans 12:1-2) involves both different responses in the present and a different perception of past hurts/experiences.

If we want to grow, we must be prepared to walk through the pain rather than avoid it. As we experience the emotions that accompany such growth, we turn to God for peace, comfort, strength, and healing.

STEPS TO DISPLACING FALSE BELIEFS

Any attempt to tear down strongholds must begin with God.

1. Realize the Truth

🌿 The Spirit bears witness to our spirit (Romans 8:16; Romans 9:1; Hebrews 10:15).

🌿 Consider it as a fact.

2. Receive the Truth

🌿 Our mind understands.

🌿 We believe by faith (Romans 6:10-11).

3. Relinquish in Light of the Truth

🌿 Make a decision of the will, as a result of heart obedience (Romans 6:17).

🌿 There is a change in our behavior, as a result of what we believe (James 2:17).

4. Remember the Truth

🌿 We are no longer under law but under grace (Romans 6:14).

🌿 Therefore, sin will not be master over us.

5. Respond to the Truth

🌿 If we live by the Spirit, let us also walk by the Spirit (Galatians 5:25).

🌿 But I say walk by the Spirit and you will not carry out the desire of the flesh (Galatians 5:16).

APPROPRIATING GOD'S TRUTHS

God is my ultimate source of security, significance, strength, and refuge. I can rely on Him in every aspect of life.

A negative stronghold based on false beliefs is a fortified area of unbelief that can wreak havoc in our lives and relationships. Because of our distorted perception of reality, our thoughts and emotions may cause us to reject truth and objective reasoning.

Knowing Christ as my life provides me with a positive and reliable stronghold, a fortified area of belief, and an indwelling place of safety against enemy attacks. This includes victory over temptations, doubts, and fears.

When the Lord is my stronghold, I have unshakable trust in Him as my source. While people are resources that the Lord may provide for fellowship and relationship, the Lord is my ultimate source of security, significance, and love.

As I trust in the Lord to lead me in His truth, I can rely on the Spirit of God to personally quicken the Word of God in my need. Having the Word quickened in this way assures me that God sees my situation, increasing my faith and trust.

A belief system built on the Lord (who He is and my union with Him) will ultimately lead to transformation in my life through the renewing of my mind. As His truth speaks to me, my behavior and emotions will align with that truth.

Does the disciplee believe they have placed faith in the Lord as their positive stronghold and that He has broken any negative strongholds operating in their life? Are you seeing the disciplee exhibit trust and peace in keeping with the Lord as their stronghold?

Do you need to revisit what total surrender means? Does the disciplee understand that total surrender is accomplished through the Lord, and our part is to have a heart's desire to surrender?

Prayer, trust, and patience are essential as the disciplee walks in the Spirit moment by moment.

APPROPRIATING GOD'S TRUTHS

Vigorously Protected Spiritual Realities

When false beliefs have been displaced, and I am believing and living out God's truths,

- the Lord is my stronghold;

- I am getting my deepest needs met by Jesus;

- as the power source for God's truth, the Spirit of God personally quickens the Word of God (Rhema versus Logos);

- what I know will eventually change how I feel.

    "The Lord also will be a stronghold for the oppressed, A stronghold in times of trouble" (Psalm 9:9). "Because of his strength I will watch for You, For God is my stronghold" (Psalm 59:9). "But the Lord has been my stronghold, And my God the rock of my refuge" (Psalm 94:22).

Becoming aware of my beliefs and how they affect my emotions and resulting behavior, and intentionally working to renew my mind, will result in changed behavior over time.

The **CONSIDER THIS: Session 9** questions are designed to prompt the disciplee to self-examination leading to self-awareness. Leading into **UNDERSTANDING FORGIVENESS: Session 10** and the remaining sessions, it is important that the disciplee has a heart attitude of surrender.

It is helpful if the disciplee was previously aware of the concept and operation of belief systems. When this concept is new to us, recognizing false beliefs and strongholds can be particularly hard. They have generally been a part of who we are for a long time and acknowledging them as false may disrupt our sense of who we are.

1. People may think they are more self-aware than they actually are. By their nature, false beliefs and strongholds often operate subconsciously and can elicit very strong emotions. Even if they have strong emotional reactions, a person may want to justify and defend their behavior.

2. This will indicate what the disciplee thinks about their openness to new information. Do they see themselves as willing to consider another perspective? Is it in line with what you see? Is the disciplee open to hearing what you see, if it differs from their thinking? Remember to ask questions. As a discipler, we want the Lord to do the convicting, not us.

3. Is the disciplee aware of problem areas? Some areas may be easier to identify than others, although denial is a very powerful coping/defense mechanism.

4. Does the disciplee identify with any of the strongholds? Past or present? If past, does the disciplee believe they have been broken? Is that consistent with what you see? If present, review the steps to displacing false beliefs.

CONSIDER THIS: SESSION 9

1. Have you spent any time before now considering your belief systems? What have you learned?

_____

_____

_____

2. How would you describe your level of self-awareness concerning your emotional responses?

_____

_____

_____

3. How do you respond when someone questions your thinking?

_____

_____

_____

4. Were you able to name any areas in your life where you have ongoing struggles? Examples: difficulty with authority, relationship problems with the opposite sex, same sex, people pleasing, anger, anxiety, etc.

_____

_____

_____

5. Did any of the listed strongholds resonate with you?

_____

_____

_____

_____

6. A limiting belief is a deeply held conviction or assumption that typically restricts a person's views of who they are or what they are capable of. As with many beliefs, they may begin early in life and impact a person throughout their entire life. If the disciplee experiences limiting beliefs, it is important that those beliefs and resulting thoughts and feelings be displaced with who they are in Christ.

7. The disciplee's answer to this will indicate their flesh patterns. Are they making progress in mastering these since beginning their discipleship sessions? If not, can they identify the problem?

8. Is the disciplee aware of their emotions and the thinking they stem from? Hopefully, at this point, they will have an increasing ability to recognize and manage unhealthy emotional patterns.

9. If the disciplee continues to struggle with their emotions, it may be beneficial for them to jot down instances when they've had trouble throughout the week. Things to consider might include:

   - What happened?

   - What am I thinking? As a result of my thoughts, what am I feeling?

   - Is it true? (Sometimes you will be able to know, but not always).

   - What does God say is true about me in this situation? See John 1:12, John 15:15-16, Romans 8:17, 2 Corinthians 5:17, Galatians 3:26, Ephesians 1:1, Colossians 3:3, 3:12, and 1 John 3:12. Look up more verses if necessary.

   - If I count this as true, how do I feel now? (Eventually, my feelings will line up with what I know to be true about myself).

6. Where have you seen limiting beliefs impact you?

_____

_____

_____

7. What thought patterns do you consistently have to _take captive_?

_____

_____

_____

8. What emotions, if any, do you have trouble managing? Why do you think this is?

_____

_____

_____

9. Pay attention to your emotions this week. If you find yourself experiencing strong emotions, stop to consider what they are and where they are coming from. Is there a lie that needs to be displaced? Jot down each instance.

_____

_____

_____

10. Read all the referenced Scripture verses in Session 9 at the back of your notebook, paying particular attention to the **STEPS TO DISPLACING FALSE BELIEFS** on page 201.

_____

_____

_____

_____

Understanding Forgiveness

We have reached the point in the discipleship process when it is time to "practice these things" (Philippians 4:9).

We have addressed the disciplee's unique version of the flesh. We have seen God's provision for us as believers to win the flesh versus spirit battle. The disciplee should have at least an intellectual understanding of what it is to totally surrender to the Lord and appropriate life in Christ through the indwelling Holy Spirit.

We looked at belief systems to help ascertain whether there is anything that would prohibit a heart desire on the disciplee's part to be obedient to the Lord in all things.

If the disciplee has indeed arrived at this place, it would be appropriate for them to want to resolve any lingering unforgiveness that may inhibit their growing in the grace of our Lord.

Knowing Christ as our life doesn't mean we won't experience emotional hurt or feelings of anger. These may be triggered by past trauma, which can occur with no warning. While we may be caught off guard and need to calm or settle ourselves, we still have the power to choose our response.

We may also feel hurt and anger from treatment we receive in the present moment. In this case, we have security in who we are in Christ and peace that allows us to surrender and trust in the Lord to bring justice and healing for wrongs committed against us. Again, we have the power to choose our response.

Do you see the evidence of this change in the disciplee's perspective? Is there a heart's desire to respond in grace to those who cause harm? Are they both liberated and empowered by the truth that the Holy Spirit is to be their source of living? If you are unsure, this may be an appropriate time to discuss these questions. A decision not powered by the Holy Spirit but made out of our will can become legalism.

How do we respond when we are hurt or offended by someone?

What is Emotional Hurt?

Emotional hurt often stems from rejection. This can be outright rejection, when we've been told we are not acceptable, or implicit rejection, leaving us *feeling* rejected whether or not this is the case. A feeling of rejection may also originate from an underlying false set of beliefs. Unfortunately, false beliefs give rise to genuine emotions, which may do unnecessary harm.

Once we perceive we have been rejected, we may feel unloved, threatened, insecure, powerless, vulnerable, ashamed, sad, confused, or any number of other emotions. We each experience a unique set of emotions in response to a set of circumstances. When hurt feelings remain unaddressed or invalidated, those feelings may escalate to anger.

What is Anger?

Anger is a strong, natural, unpleasant feeling (emotion) of upset. Since anger is an emotion God has given us, it is normal and healthy as long as it does not get out of control. Ephesians 4:26-27 tells us, "Be angry and do not sin; do not let the sun go down on your anger, and give no opportunity to the devil." This passage indicates that there is an anger that is not sinful. We know God Himself cannot sin, yet the Bible clearly tells us He is a God of wrath.

Anger is typically a secondary emotion following the experience of another emotion that makes us feel vulnerable, such as fear, sadness, anxiety, insecurity, worry, disappointment, discouragement, guilt, jealousy, or loneliness. This vulnerability causes us to feel out of control and uncomfortable. Our feelings may shift from hurt to anger, increasing our sense of power and control.

Anger may also arise in response to something we feel entitled to that is being denied us. This can be anything from unmet basic needs to simply feeling we should not be subjected to life's normal inconveniences. "What causes quarrels, and what causes fights among you? Is it not this that your passions are at war within you? You desire and do not have, so you murder. You covet and cannot obtain, so you fight and quarrel" (James 4:1-2).

When you are hurt or feel there is nothing you can do about a certain situation, how has an anger response changed your perception of the situation?

While there are physiological changes to the brain that may impact our responses, managing anger is a learned skill. A healthy response to anger

What is the proper response in the face of mistreatment by another? Because the Holy Spirit indwells us, we have the fruit of the Spirit at our disposal. We always have a choice, and as we yield to His will, we respond in a godly manner.

WHAT DOES ALL THIS HAVE TO DO WITH FORGIVENESS?

Living in a fallen world and being in a relationship with people who sin, we will certainly be hurt or offended, which may lead to feelings of anger. Forgiveness includes acknowledging and addressing these feelings. They have to be dealt with. It never works to ignore our feelings or pretend an incident never happened.

Forgiveness will typically follow a hurt from a specific source, resulting in lack of trust due to feelings of disrespect, disappointment or something else.

Forgiveness will not always be tied to a serious wrong. When resulting from minor grievances or unintentional harm, it may still help us let go of lingering emotions that may limit us.

We must also be self-aware. Most anger is not righteous. Can we admit when we have overreacted or are simply wrong? Are there any such instances in the disciplee's life?

Why Should We Forgive?

Forgiveness is both a command and a reflection of the character of God. As such, forgiveness will promote personal healing, reconciliation, and fellowship with God. The Lord would not call us to forgive without providing the means to do so. We are of little use if we live in our own sin of unforgiveness.

is to be assertive—to stand up for our needs, values, and beliefs without harming, depreciating, or devaluing another person. If anger escalates, a person may go beyond assertiveness and enter into reactionary sin. This can result in violent outbursts, sarcasm, venting, overreaction, an attempt at revenge, or an array of covert behaviors. This is why it is critical for believers to practice 2 Corinthians 10:5, "We are destroying speculations and every lofty thing raised up against the knowledge of God, and we are taking every thought captive to the obedience of Christ."

Emotional distress is related to ever-present thoughts and can be more harmful than physical pain over the long term. When a person has experienced the effects of long-term oppression, what appears as reactionary sin is often a self-defense response and may require a different approach.

WHAT DOES ALL THIS HAVE TO DO WITH FORGIVENESS?

Regardless of how we deal with feelings of hurt or anger, they do not resolve by themselves. Appropriate anger may relieve tension, but the source of the offense is not necessarily removed or resolved. Living with unresolved anger leads to bitterness and an attitude of unforgiveness.

Does this mean we "just get over it" as if the injustice had never happened? Real forgiveness is best achieved after experiencing the righteous anger that accompanies injustice. There are also times when anger is unjustified. We must then be able to examine the motives and desires that may have caused our anger.

Why Should We Forgive?

There are many reasons to forgive, all of which ultimately benefit the forgiving person. God calls us to forgive (Matthew 6:14-15; 18:21-22; Ephesians 4:32; Hebrews 12:14-15). It is always in a believer's best interest to obey God's word.

Unresolved anger takes a physical and emotional toll on our bodies. If we practice forgiveness, we are able to move forward with a clear conscience, focus on the Lord, and live out His plan and purpose.

HOW PRIDE CAN HINDER FORGIVENESS

The need to be right can cause us to refuse to acknowledge the value of others' viewpoints. We may become defensive or dismissive, possibly out of fear that being wrong diminishes our self-worth. In contrast, minimizing others' beliefs and opinions gives us a false sense of superiority and can prohibit compromise necessary for conflict resolution.

Insistence on an apology makes forgiveness dependent on the offender's actions when it is an individual's heart obedience that matters. The focus is on ourselves and that we are *owed* something. It puts us in the position of deciding whether someone is remorseful enough.

A person who withholds forgiveness often experiences a sense of moral superiority, making them feel more in control of the situation. Unforgiveness may be a form of punishment against the offending party and an attempt to manipulate through a guilt trip.

Revenge may be an attempt to restore wounded pride. Not taking revenge may feel like it diminishes the degree of the offense. Revenge turns from potential healing and peace to protecting our ego and self-worth.

An unwillingness to accept responsibility for our feelings maintains the focus on the offender and the offense, keeping the offended in the victim role. Pride holds on to anger, a more controlled emotion.

If the offended person believes they are entitled to anger or resentment, forgiveness changes from an act of grace to something that is earned, potentially through the offender receiving a consequence.

Pride may cause a person to be unwilling to suffer hurt again. Unforgiveness allows the offended party to create emotional barriers for self-protection.

In conjunction with the fear of being hurt again, withholding forgiveness can operate as a defense mechanism to avoid vulnerability. A person with an inflated sense of self would suffer a blow to their image if they were to admit personal weakness.

Through denial, minimizing, or rationalizing, we will blame others if we can't acknowledge our own sin.

We've all heard different opinions about what forgiveness looks like. The true-false questions on the following pages should help clarify areas of struggle.

A believer is indwelled by the Holy Spirit. As a new creation, it is in our nature to forgive through the power of the Holy Spirit. Not to forgive is contrary to our identity in Christ.

What Might Hinder Us from Forgiving?

Pride is the original sin man committed when severing his communion with the Lord (Matthew 7:2-5). According to Proverbs 6, the Lord hates pride.

Pride can manifest itself in the following ways:

- Our need to be right
- Our insistence that the offender apologize
- Retaining a sense of power and control by withholding forgiveness
- Our need to exact revenge
- Our unwillingness to take responsibility for our feelings
- Our sense of entitlement
- Our fear of being hurt again
- Our fear of looking or being weak
- Our inability to acknowledge our sin

We may lack an understanding of the true meaning of forgiveness.

What has hindered you from forgiving someone in the past? Be specific.

_____

_____

_____

F   Sin is sin. While we may forgive a sin against us, we should never call it anything other than *sin*.

F   Address the wrong directly. Forgiveness is an intentional act (Matthew 18:15).

T   We forgive because God forgave us, not because of the level of damage caused (Ephesians 4:32). As we mature spiritually, our ability to forgive should become easier.

F   A healthy believer won't suffer just for the sake of it. The prudent person protects himself from danger. It may happen, but we have a choice in how we respond.

F   Forgiveness is a decision of the will. I may choose to forgive even if I don't feel like it. If I do forgive and act accordingly, my feelings will eventually line up.

F   We may experience uncomfortable or painful emotions long after an offense. Choosing forgiveness means I choose not to act according to my emotions. I may both forgive and put healthy boundaries in place.

F   Seeking justice and accountability for the offender is a healthy response, particularly if it brings about repentance. Enabling sin serves no good purpose.

F   We are wise to remember the offense, so we don't allow it to repeat itself. If it comes to mind, we remind ourselves that we have made the choice to forgive. Once the offender has repented and made appropriate changes, we DO NOT keep bringing it up.

F   Trust is earned. If the offender repents and bears fruit in keeping with repentance, trust may be restored in time.

F   While I understand that trauma or other life circumstances may strongly influence sinful behavior, there is no justification for sin. Our behavior is always a choice.

F   Forgiveness is a decision of the will out of heart obedience. It does not mean you will never think of the incident again nor feel emotions in keeping with the harm done. You can remind yourself that you have already made the decision to forgive.

T   We don't have to *feel* like forgiving. We are called to forgive. As with other acts of obedience, we aren't told we can choose when to be obedient. We have the power to forgive because of our identity in Christ, through the power of the Holy Spirit.

F   Our need to forgive may apply to people who are no longer in our lives, whether through death or other circumstances.

F   Just as I choose to forgive, I am free to choose the nature of any ongoing relationship.

T   Forgiveness is a transaction between me and the Lord. I am letting the person "off the hook" with me, but they are "on the hook" with God.

WHAT IS FORGIVENESS?

Forgiveness means that I condone the behavior or offense (Isaiah 5:20).　　TRUE　FALSE

Forgiveness means that I pretend the harm never occurred (2 Samuel 12:9-13).　　TRUE　FALSE

Forgiveness has nothing to do with the *size* of the wrong.　　TRUE　FALSE

Forgiveness means that I must allow the same thing to happen again (Proverbs 22:3).　　TRUE　FALSE

Forgiveness is something I must feel in order for it to be true forgiveness.　　TRUE　FALSE

Forgiveness means I will no longer feel hurt, anger, or emotional pain from what happened to me.　　TRUE　FALSE

Forgiveness means I no longer desire to see justice done (Hebrews 10:30-31).　　TRUE　FALSE

Forgiveness means I completely forget the incident, and I need to be concerned that if it comes to mind, I really have not forgiven.　　TRUE　FALSE

Forgiveness means I now regain trust and confidence in the person who has hurt or offended me.　　TRUE　FALSE

Forgiveness means I can understand and justify the offender's behavior.　　TRUE　FALSE

Forgiveness is something I may need to do several times if the incident keeps coming to my mind.　　TRUE　FALSE

Forgiveness is something I choose to do as an act of my will.　　TRUE　FALSE

Forgiveness only truly releases me if I tell the other person I have forgiven them.　　TRUE　FALSE

Forgiving others means I will become a doormat.　　TRUE　FALSE

Forgiveness does not depend on the other party's changing their ways or repenting.　　TRUE　FALSE

F We forgive unconditionally because God commands it. There may be consequences to the offender's actions which prevent an ongoing relationship with them. That remains to be seen.

F In union with Christ, I am a forgiving person through my new nature. Choosing not to forgive makes me a hypocrite, not operating in line with who I am.

F Forgiveness does not mean the offending person is without consequences. We are not called to enable sinful behavior. This will be between you and the Lord.

T The Lord dispenses perfect justice; He knows exactly what the offender needs. We can pray for good for the offender in keeping with the Lord's perfect wisdom and holiness.

T As a saint, in union with Christ, I am forgiving by my very nature.

T Forgiveness is a personal act of releasing someone from a moral debt or sin debt (Matthew 6:14-15). At the same time, justice and/or compensation may be appropriate on a societal level. The focus is on the heart attitude.

F A person can and should set appropriate boundaries to maintain a safe and healthy relationship.

HOW DO WE GO ABOUT FORGIVING SOMEONE?

P We should always begin the forgiveness process with prayer. We may be aware of people we need to forgive, but there may be times when we harbor deep-seated resentment at our subconscious level. Denial may play a part. The Lord may bring these people to mind. There may be times when professional help is appropriate to uncover past traumas. If we know Christ as our Life, we can trust Him—the Ultimate Forgiver— to express the process of forgiving others through us.

R It is important to understand the nature and severity of the offense and its impact on us. Every individual has different experiences.

E The Lord gave us our emotions and our unique personality. Give yourself permission to feel all of your emotions as you work through them with the Lord. There is no *should* or *should not* to what you feel. The list of emotions on pages 69-77 may help you identify your emotions.

A We cannot force anyone to change. If a person tells us who they are, whether through words or actions, it is best that we believe them. Based on what we know, we can decide whether to continue in a relationship with them and what that will look like.

C This is the cancelling of the moral and spiritual debt. God is the judge and will deal justly with the offender. Compensation and consequences may still be appropriate.

H While I may choose to forgive as an act of my will through the power of the Holy Spirit, it doesn't mean that my feelings will immediately line up with my choice. I can and should choose to act according to who I am in Christ and my decision to forgive as I move forward. If the thoughts and feelings resurface, I may have to remind myself of the decision. This doesn't mean I have failed to forgive.

Unconditional forgiveness results in an unconditional relationship.	TRUE	FALSE
If I forgive when I don't feel forgiving, I will be a hypocrite.	TRUE	FALSE
Forgiveness means I give up any claim for compensation.	TRUE	FALSE
Forgiveness means I wish the offender good rather than harm.	TRUE	FALSE
Forgiveness is easier for people who are forgiving by nature.	TRUE	FALSE
Forgiveness means canceling the offender's debt (Colossians 2:13-14; Matthew 18:23-35).	TRUE	FALSE
Forgiveness means I will not set boundaries with the offender.	TRUE	FALSE

HOW DO WE GO ABOUT FORGIVING SOMEONE?

Pray that the Lord will reveal any unforgiveness toward people in my life (Psalm 139:23-24).

Recall the harm that the other party did to me. Be objective about the severity of the offense. Recall what happened and what it cost me.

Experience the emotions that are associated with the hurtful experience. Bring them before the Lord, and work through the pain (refer back to the list of emotions if it is helpful).

Accept the offender unconditionally for who they are; acknowledge they may never change, and the relationship may never be restored.

Cancel the debt, and consider it done.

Honor the Lord in how I move forward with the offender regardless of my feelings.

Release

Releasing a person from their sin or moral debt does not necessarily release them from the obligation to make restitution for the damage they've caused. Note the example of Zaccheus in Luke 19:8. Both forgiveness and justice can coexist, with forgiveness being a heart attitude and justice and restitution fulfilling a societal order.

The Bible addresses forgiveness of debt as an act of grace and restitution as the fruit of repentance. The details of different circumstances are beyond the scope of this writing. This is why, in union with Christ, we can look to and trust the Lord to guide us in what canceling the debt looks like. We can always forgive the sin debt but may or may not choose to forego the consequences of the sin. Out of a loving heart, it may be the kindest thing we can do to allow the consequences to be brought about. Forgiveness does not require enabling sin to continue against us, which is good neither for us nor the offender.

Does the disciplee understand that forgiveness is an action taken on our part and requires only a heart attitude of obedience to the Lord? Do they know they don't have to *feel it*? Is there anyone the disciplee still feels they are unable to forgive?

Reconciliation

While forgiveness opens the door to reconciliation, it will not always lead to reconciliation. Reconciliation is a process that involves both parties and requires more than forgiveness. One party offers forgiveness for the offense and is open to growing in trust of the offender. The offending party repents, which includes acknowledging the wrong committed and sincerely attempting to turn from their behavior (2 Corinthians 7:10). This does not mean that everything is fully healed or back to its original state. Attempting to turn from the behavior may not provide a safe enough environment for the offended person. Some people may not be capable of the behaviors necessary to re-establish connection.

Sometimes complete reconciliation hinges on whether or not the door is open to potential restoration (see page 223). True reconciliation is impossible if the offender doesn't truly repent. Only saying they are sorry is not enough. Not addressing the harm or pretending it didn't happen is not enough to produce reconciliation. Trust cannot be *restored* under such circumstances. The offended party is the one to determine whether they can trust the offender. What appears to be true repentance may not be a sustained heart change.

Does the disciplee have any relationships in this condition? Do they understand and have a plan for their next steps? Are they comfortable with where things are? What might help them be more comfortable? Does the disciplee understand that they cannot force a heart change or behavior change from the offender?

WE CHOOSE TO FORGIVE, NOW WHAT?

We may hesitate to forgive because we are under the false assumption that unconditional forgiveness means unconditional relationship.

Release

When we choose to forgive, we are choosing to release the debt owed by the person who has wronged us (Romans 12:17). We make this choice before the Lord, as we are by nature a forgiving person in Christ. Our choice to release them does not mean they are *off the hook* with God. Through this choice, we eventually experience freedom from our painful emotions.

We accept that there may be ongoing negative consequences due to the offender's behavior. As was the case with Jesus, we decide to forgive, knowing we cannot force the offender into a particular response. We protect ourselves from further harm by instituting healthy boundaries and choosing to love them as an enemy (Matthew 5:44).

While we can still desire justice for the offender, we release our desire or attempts to carry out that justice ourselves. As fellow image bearers, we can pray for this person and want the best for them—that they would know the Lord and totally surrender to Him.

Reconcile

A choice to forgive opens the door to reconciliation. Unlike forgiveness, which is a vertical transaction between the believer and the Lord, reconciliation requires action on the offender's part.

Jesus died on the Cross so that all who repent and place their trust in Him can spend eternity in heaven with Him. If there is no repentance, there can be no relationship with Jesus. A repentant sinner is reconciled to Jesus (Luke 17:4; Acts 2:38; Acts 3:19), but the relationship that occurs at this point (salvation), while eternally secure (1 Corinthians 3:15), is generally not deep and abiding but develops over time.

A similar change of mind must occur in the offender before true reconciliation can happen in a relationship. Even when repentance occurs and the relationship is reconciled, it doesn't necessarily mean the relationship will be deep and intimate. The offended person may not feel safe with or be able to trust the offender at this time. It is wise to maintain healthy boundaries until new relationship patterns are established.

Restore

While reconciliation may remove hostility and restore civil relations, broken trust requires time.

An offender who has not experienced a true heart change will not be able to maintain a change in behavior.

On occasion, the original relationship may have been unhealthy and not built on a firm, or even reasonable foundation. In such a case, *restoration* of the *relationship* might look like something entirely new. On the other hand, this might be a time when restoration is impossible because there is nothing to restore.

As was discussed, reconciliation comes through repentance and opens the door to a repaired relationship, just as repentance and turning to Jesus removes the sin barrier with God. At that point, we are a new creation in Christ, but that doesn't necessarily mean we are fully surrendered to Him. Sanctification is a journey in learning to trust the Lord and yield to His indwelling Holy Spirit. Paul says in Galatians 2:20, "It is no longer I who live, but Christ who lives in me." While this may be true in our spirit, it doesn't automatically become true in our soul. This is where progressive sanctification occurs.

Several scenarios may play out, but starting with forgiveness is always the proper response. The level of harm may play a part in how we move forward. These are examples and are not exclusive.

We can forgive and still avoid a relationship with the person. This may happen if the behavior has been an ongoing issue, and the person has made no effort to change despite our requests they do so. Lack of hostility does not necessarily mean civil relations are a safe possibility. In this case, no contact with the offender may be the best option.

We can forgive and reconcile yet change our expectations of the offender. If the offender doesn't repent and make efforts to change and make amends for their behavior, real trust can't occur. Proper boundaries may allow us to participate in a ministerial or contractual relationship, but real intimacy is impossible.

We can forgive and adopt a wait and see approach. If the offender repents and takes responsibility for their behavior, through continued work and personal growth, time will tell whether they are a safe and trustworthy person for potential restoration. During this process, each party will determine whether they are willing to move forward in their efforts.

Restore

A damaged relationship may be restored if both parties are willing to put in the effort. This requires a safe environment in which to work on healthy communication so that trust may be restored. Bringing about restoration means that the offending party takes the necessary steps toward repairing the damage that has been done. However, there may still be long-term consequences that result from the offense (James 1:2-3).

Only time will tell if a human connection can be restored to a deep and mutually satisfying level. Sometimes, the wounds may be too deep to overcome. Even in restored relationships, healthy boundaries remain appropriate for maintaining harmony.

As in human relationships, our intimacy with the Lord grows only as we invest time and energy into building it (John 15:13-15). Time in prayer and fasting, as well as the Word, brings our *relationship* with the Lord to a deep and abiding *fellowship* with the Lord.

1. While our personal makeup contributes to our emotional responses, other factors are also involved. These may include past wounds or trauma, low self-esteem/fragile self-image, fear of rejection or abandonment, unrealistic or high expectations of others, emotional insecurity, poor attachment style, lack of boundaries, and over-analyzing or overthinking, among others. Self-reflection, self-awareness, and possibly professional help will be important factors in understanding this.

2. Is the disciplee self-aware? If they have struggled with anger, do they see a pattern that may help them understand where it's originating? Are there questions you might ask to help?

3. Can the disciplee assume responsibility for their angry thoughts, feelings, and behavior? Are they able to cite an example?

4. Does the disciplee recognize that they have a choice in how they respond to others and that acting on anger is a choice? Will a review of the WHEEL AND LINE diagrams help them see that they can yield to the indwelling Holy Spirit for their response?

5. Look for an understanding that as a new creation in Christ, we are indeed forgiving by our nature. We can choose to forgive by the power of the indwelling Holy Spirit.

6. Does the disciplee believe they can choose to forgive and move forward regardless of what the offender chooses? Do they recognize that all true Christian obedience comes from the power of the Holy Spirit?

7. Does the disciplee understand the steps in the forgiveness process? While the process is personal, can the disciplee share enough to demonstrate a working knowledge of the steps?

CONSIDER THIS: SESSION 10

1. Are you easily hurt in your personal or professional relationships? Describe. Where do you think this hurt is coming from?

_____

_____

2. When have you struggled with unresolved anger?

_____

_____

3. How have you handled it in the past? Give at least one example.

_____

_____

4. How will you handle it differently now?

_____

_____

5. Did you learn anything about forgiveness that is contrary to your prior understanding?

_____

_____

6. How will it impact your ability to forgive moving forward?

_____

_____

7. Review the forgiveness process. Ask God to reveal any unforgiveness in your heart. Does anyone come to mind? If yes, work through the process. Do so with each person the Lord brings to your mind.

Living a Life That Overcomes

The remaining two sessions are an opportunity to wrap up the truths covered to this point, clarify any questions the disciplee may have, and encourage the disciplee as these biblical truths become a part of their moment-by-moment sanctification process.

Through the discipleship process, the disciplee has hopefully tasted what the abundant life in Christ is like. As in the entirety of the Christian walk, the work is the Lord's. This is why it's important to understand Paul's prayer in Ephesians 1. Just as the Father is responsible for drawing people to Himself (John 6:44), we look to the Father to give us the spirit of wisdom and revelation in the knowledge of Him. We have been praying that the disciplee receive spiritual illumination through the Holy Spirit, revealing their union with Christ. This occurs in His way and in His time.

Does the disciplee report that they have *realized* the truth of their union with Christ? Do they believe they operate from a place of victory in Christ? Has this influenced their thoughts and behaviors? Are they able to share specific examples?

Brokenness as a Blessing

What is the disciplee's attitude about brokenness? Have they expressed an experience of brokenness in their life? How did it change things for them?

If the disciplee doesn't report an experience of brokenness, have they expressed a heartfelt attitude of total surrender? Do they understand that as long as we have any trust in our own capabilities, we will never be wholly surrendered to the Lord? Are they willing for the Lord to bring it about? You may review *Some Common Obstacles to Total Surrender* on page 143 if they are still hesitant.

So, what does this abundant life that Jesus spoke of in John 10:10 look like? For many, the Christian life consists of practicing Christian disciplines regularly. These include studying the word of God, meditating on and memorizing Scripture, prayer and fasting, witnessing to others, and attending church regularly. These are all excellent practices and can be a powerful outflow of the Holy Spirit in a believer's life. Unfortunately, a person may be engaged in all these practices and still feel defeated in their Christian life.

In Ephesians 1:17-20, Paul prays, "That the God of our Lord Jesus Christ, the Father of glory, may give you a spirit of wisdom and of revelation in the knowledge of Him. I pray that the eyes of your heart may be enlightened, so that you may know the hope of His calling, what are the riches of the glory of his inheritance in the saints, and what is the surpassing power toward us who believe. These are in accordance with the working of the strength of His might which He brought about in Christ, when He raised Him from the dead, and seated Him at His right hand in the heavenly places."

To live a life that overcomes, we need a revelation that only God Himself can provide. We need a revelation that we are a sinner in need of a Savior (John 6:65). We also need a revelation of the fleshly persona that we have been living out of and so easily revert to (Romans 8:7-8). While our "old man" was crucified with Christ (Galatians 2:20), this fleshly persona must die daily in the battle between flesh and Spirit (Galatians 5:17).

Finally, as Paul prays, we need a revelation of the power that believers have been given as an inheritance. This is the revelation of who we are in Christ and who Christ is in us.

Brokenness as a Blessing

Unconditional surrender requires brokenness, which brings us to a place where we agree with God that we cannot live our Christian life in our own strength. Aloneness generally accompanies brokenness and brings us to complete dependence on God.

Has the Lord brought the people or circumstances into your life that have brought you to this point? Would it be a bad thing if He did? If not, do you want the Lord to bring you to that point? Let's look at brokenness through the analogy of the breaking of a horse.

An unbroken horse is powerful—sometimes frightening. Because of his size and stature, the horse usually does what he pleases. Yet, his stubborn behavior is likely to be unproductive.

As the discipler, having walked with the disciplee for roughly 10 weeks, you may see where the Lord is working to grow their faith. Perhaps they have become more accepting and at peace with difficult circumstances in their life. Can you encourage the disciplee with areas where you see this growth?

It may be beneficial to revisit the difference between resignation and relinquishment. Are there circumstances in their life that are difficult and beyond their control? How do they feel about them?

Take the example that my mother is dying of cancer. She has been through all the available treatments, and the doctors tell us there is nothing more they can do. I know that there is nothing that I personally can do to restore my mother's health. What is my heart attitude? Do I accept it and tell myself I will just have to deal with it since I have no choice? Or, do I come humbly before the Lord and prayerfully offer my mother up to Him, knowing that His timing and will are perfect and I can trust Him? Does the disciplee see the difference between these two attitudes? Do they knowingly choose relinquishment?

How does the disciplee respond to the questions about their flesh versus Spirit battle? It is very difficult to see our own flesh, particularly *good flesh.* Are they open to your insights and input?

How does the disciplee respond to the question, "What needs to be broken?" Do they understand self-sufficiency interferes with their surrender?

The Surrendered (Broken) Life

What does it look like to lead a surrendered life? We will not make it through this life without ever being disobedient. Does that mean we aren't surrendered? No. We need to confess, make it right if we've sinned against someone else, and put our focus back on the Lord. We don't want to be distracted into taking our eyes off the Lord. If our focus is on ourselves and our sin, we do not have our eyes set on the things above.

Unless the trainer approaches him in a specific way, the horse resists all attempts at being broken. Step by step, the trainer gently seeks to win the horse over. Finally, the trainer mounts the horse. At first, the trainer meets with resistance because the horse has no idea of the potential relationship available to him. He discovers it is much easier and more pleasant if he yields to the trainer's commands.

While the breaking process may be painful, is the horse better off before or after the trainer gets through to him? Once broken, is he to be pitied because of his miserable state, or is he now stronger, more focused, and single-minded? What has been broken?

Does this sound familiar? Might our Heavenly Father approach you in this manner? Are you at the place where you have stopped resisting? In Acts 7:51, Stephen accuses unbelieving Jews of being "stiff-necked and uncircumcised in heart and ears ... always resisting the Holy Spirit ...."

Are you losing the flesh versus Spirit battle more often than not? Do you lack signs of complete surrender to the Lord? Do you worry about circumstances out of your control? Do you feel sorry for yourself when your relationships or circumstances do not meet your approval? Do you still seek the approval of others to gain assurance of your value?

How many times a day do you think about yourself and what you want, as opposed to the power of the indwelling Holy Spirit and what He can do in and through you? The answers to these questions will help determine whether the flesh is in control. Sometimes, even the most noble-looking behaviors are merely an attempt to manipulate others to get what we want. Is there breaking that needs to take place in your life? If so, what areas still need to be broken?

The breaking process can be confusing and painful. No one likes to lose *perceived* control. But our God is loving and works all things together for our good if we love Him and are called according to His purpose (Romans 8:28).

The Surrendered (Broken) Life

What might surrender look like in the example of our horse and trainer? The horse is now broken and is accustomed to the bridle, bit, saddle, and rider. He has learned that life is better when he obeys the trainer, but does he always obey? What if something spooks him, a burr under his saddle causes him discomfort, or he doesn't want to be ridden one day. He may

The horse will always do its best when it is submitted to the trainer's will. The same is true of us, as we trust the Lord to bring about surrender in our lives.

To live the abundant life, our walk with the Lord requires that we deny ourselves. I pick up my cross daily because I am prepared to die to my self-life when my will does not match the Lord's will. This doesn't always feel like sacrifice, although sometimes it will. But it always involves putting the Lord's will above our own. Sometimes, the choice will be clear, as when I desire something that is obviously sinful. Other times, discerning God's will may be more difficult, especially for those with *good* flesh.

The answer remains the same. Moment by moment, I totally surrender my choices to the Lord and move forward with a heart attitude of obedience, relying on the Holy Spirit to direct my steps. This is a life-long process, and the Lord is always faithful to His followers.

Because believers are already surrendered in their spirit (through our union with Christ), fleshly soulical living needs to be denied. How does this happen? As was discussed in **Session 7**, what we know in our spirit has to be *received* in our mind.

What is God's Truth About Me?

Discuss with the disciplee what this would look like for them. Have they put this into practice? Can they name specific negative, self-centered, or anxious thoughts that plague them? Are they dealing with false beliefs and belief systems that are contrary to what the Lord says is true about them?

Which of the noted Scriptures help them to dispute their own fleshly thinking? Are there others that they are able to rely on? As they set their mind on the things above, the Holy Spirit will affirm the truth of what has been received.

Does the disciplee recognize and acknowledge their choice in their thinking? They can't control what thoughts come into their mind, but they can choose what they do with them.

engage in any manner of behaviors to avoid the trainer's commands—including bucking him off entirely.

The same can be true in our flesh versus Spirit battle. In Luke 9:23, Jesus says, "If anyone wishes to come after Me, let him deny himself, and take up his cross daily, and follow Me." Is our cross whatever circumstance is currently giving us trouble? We have learned that the Cross is an instrument of death. However, it is also the means by which we receive new life in Christ. Through our daily death to the self-life, Christ can live His life in and through us.

A believer is already surrendered to the Lord in his spirit. "For you have died and your life is hidden with Christ in God" (Colossians 3:3). We have already risen with Christ, but in our souls, we make moment-by-moment decisions to surrender or not.

This surrender includes my *mind.* Am I willing to be transformed by the renewing of my mind, as described in Romans 12:2? Thoughts of all kinds bombard me continually. Am I willing and able to stop and examine those thoughts and identify their origin? If my thoughts do not align with God's word, will I take them captive and replace them with God's truth? (2 Corinthians 10:5).

What is God's Truth About Me?

- I am a new creation in Christ (2 Corinthians 5:17).

- By His doing I am in Christ Jesus, who became to me wisdom from God, and righteousness and sanctification and redemption (1 Corinthians 1:30).

- I am chosen in Him before the foundation of the world, and I am holy and blameless before Him (Ephesians 1:4).

- I am seated with Christ in heavenly places (Ephesians 2:6).

- I am now able to consider myself dead to sin but alive to God in Christ Jesus (Romans 6:11).

I am in Christ and I am to set my mind on the things above (Colossians 3:2).

This is a choice I make—a truth that must permeate my mind. If I am in Jesus and Jesus is in the Father, I am perfectly protected spiritually. Since my Father is sovereign, having supreme authority and absolute power (Jeremiah 32:17; Matthew 19:26), nothing can reach me without the Father

As I receive God's truths into my mind, knowing who I am in Christ, who He is in me, and the power I now have for right living, I choose to surrender my will to His purposes for my life. This would be appropriate worship for the One Who has given me everything. What does this mean for me? As I set my eyes on the things above, my circumstances and my own desires take a back seat to the Lord's will. Does the disciplee exhibit a deepening trust in the Lord?

What Is God's Will for Me?

As my mind experiences an intellectual understanding of the truth the Holy Spirit reveals, I *relinquish* my will in heart obedience. I present myself as a sacrifice and say, as Jesus did, "... yet not My will, but Yours be done" (Luke 22:42).

I choose to cooperate with the indwelling Holy Spirit to accomplish what the Lord has for me. As I yield, the Holy Spirit will fill my soul, changing my behavior as a result of the truth I believe. This happens in His way and in His time.

As the Holy Spirit has more control over my life, we see the truth of Romans 8:29 coming to pass, as I am conformed to Christlikeness. As Paul proclaims in Galatians 2:20, "I have been crucified with Christ; and it is no longer I who live, but Christ lives in me; and the *life* which I now live in the flesh I live by faith in the Son of God, who loved me and gave Himself up for me."

Is the disciplee experiencing the Christ-centered life described on page 163? Would those closest to them attest to a change in their daily walk?

Emotions Have a Place in Our Lives

We have discussed and dealt with the disciplee's emotions. They should now understand that emotions have good purposes yet can cause significant damage in our daily lives if they aren't surrendered to the Lord, along with our minds and will.

How does this happen? Our minds and emotions work together to execute informed decision-making by our will. It is important to have a balance of both.

knowing about it and allowing it. I accept this truth by faith, thank God for His grace, and walk it out in my life (2 Corinthians 5:7).

Moment by moment, I must be willing to surrender my *will* to His will (Matthew 26:39). Am I willing to let go of my fleshly desires and behaviors, even the ones that look good to others?

What is God's Will for Me?

- That I present myself as a living and holy sacrifice (Romans 12:1).

- That I not be conformed to the world, but that I'm transformed by the renewing of my mind (Romans 12:2).

- My body is a temple of the Holy Spirit, whom the Lord has given me. I am not my own, therefore, I am to glorify God in my body (1 Corinthians 6:19-20).

- I can humble myself under God's mighty hand, and He will exalt me at the proper time (1 Peter 5:6; James 4:10).

- The world is passing away, and also its lusts; but the one who does the will of God abides forever (1 John 2:17).

- I am predestined to be conformed to the image of His Son (Romans 8:29).

Christ is in me in the form of the indwelling Holy Spirit. What is true of Jesus now becomes true of me. His life and His resources are mine. I can do all things through Christ who gives me strength (Philippians 4:13). Paul prays we will see this truth through spiritual eyes in Ephesians 1:17-20. I accept this truth by faith, thank God for His grace, and walk it out in my life (2 Corinthians 5:7).

Our emotions may threaten to derail our complete surrender to the truth about who we are in Christ and the power we have for daily living. We must be willing to surrender them to the will of God.

Emotions Have a Place in Our Lives

We value certain emotions—happy, hopeful, pleased, curious, optimistic—while we want other emotions—anger, guilt, shame, resentment, envy—to disappear. Emotions are an indicator of something in us that needs attention. We cannot simply ignore them and expect everything to be alright. Nor can we let them be our primary decision-makers.

Sometimes, it feels as though we have no choice but to succumb to our overwhelming emotions. Because they can be so strong, it can be easy to mistake my feelings for *truth*.

What is God's Will Regarding My Emotions?

As Ephesians 4:26 and James 1:19-20 indicate, in Christ, we have the capability to honor the Lord in how we conduct our lives. How do we go from feeling out of control to having the peace of God, which surpasses all comprehension (Philippians 4:7)?

We intentionally surrender our emotions to the Lord in the same way we surrender our minds and will.

- I recognize and name my emotions, which can reduce their intensity (Psalm 139:23-24).

- I lift up my emotions in prayer, trusting God to bring me peace (Psalm 62:8).

- I renew my mind with God's truth, replacing overwhelming thoughts and emotions (Romans 12:2; 2 Corinthians 10:5; Philippians 4:13).

- I can *remember* the truth and praise God that sin is no longer master over me (Romans 6:14).

- To manage recurring, painful emotions, I may seek help from others.

We must bring our emotions before the Lord and acknowledge we need His Spirit and guidance in dealing with them.

God has designed us with our own unique set of emotions, influenced by our family of origin and the belief systems we have developed throughout our lives. Emotions stemming from faulty belief systems result in unbiblical thinking and lead us to unbiblical behavior.

In Christ, we have been granted power for everything pertaining to life and godliness (2 Peter 1:3). As we set our minds and focus on Jesus, we can appropriate God's truth and Jesus's resources in walking in faith, despite our emotions.

What is God's Will Regarding My Emotions?

- I am to grow in walking out Christ's life through the strength of the indwelling Holy Spirit (2 Peter 1:5-9; Ephesians 5:15).

- I am to have self-control (Proverbs 25:28; Proverbs 16:32).

- I am to let the peace of Christ rule in my heart (Colossians 3:15).

- I can look to the Lord to supply all my needs in Christ (Philippians 4:19).

- I am to cast all my anxiety on Him because He cares for me (1 Peter 5:7).

- I am to think about whatever is true, whatever is honorable, whatever is right, whatever is pure, whatever is lovely, whatever is of good repute, and any excellence and anything worthy of praise (Philippians 4:8).

I thank God for all He has given me in Christ, and by faith I trust Him to work out His will in my life. "For whatever is born of God overcomes the world; and this is the victory that has overcome the world—our faith" (1 John 5:4).

Being a new creation in Christ does not mean we will never experience physical maladies. When a person undergoes trauma, it physically changes both the body and brain. Depending on their life experience, there will be times when a person chooses to seek professional help in dealing with persistent, painful emotions. Does this mean they are not a *good enough* Christian? No! Just as we seek a doctor's help healing an external wound, a professional can also help heal internal damage to the brain and central nervous system.

Broken To Be Free

Does the disciplee recognize that the breaking process will continue as a means to sanctification?

If not, are they ready to surrender all to the Lord, prepared to face the circumstances the Lord brings into their life?

Does the disciplee understand that as they *respond* to the truth, they will not carry out the desires of the flesh?

Broken to Be Free

Returning to our horse and trainer illustration, the horse eventually learns to trust his trainer, for the trainer does the horse good and not harm. As their relationship deepens, the trainer and horse develop a greater knowledge and trust in one another. We may have been privileged to watch a horse and rider working together for years. They move as one, with the horse knowing each movement of the trainer and responding in the way he knows will please his trainer. There is no longer a need for the bit and bridle. The trainer knows how the horse will respond to the trainer's every move and can trust his horse to do his bidding. A horse who does his trainer's bidding is more useful, and at this point, as the trainer continues his work, the horse experiences the rewards of his brokenness.

In the same way, once I have fully surrendered myself to God's will, through the power of the indwelling Holy Spirit, I am now free to daily pick up my cross, so that I may die to my self-life and all the self-centered thoughts and behaviors I may engage in. I willingly relinquish all aspects of my life to Him, rather than being resigned to those circumstances that are beyond my control. I now have the opportunity to live out Christ's life in me.

DISCIPLER'S NOTES

1. Does the disciplee describe an experience where they have personally had their union with Christ illuminated? If not, do they look forward to having the eyes of their heart enlightened in God's timing? Will they wait in patient surrender until that time?

2. What is the disciplee's understanding of "take up your cross daily?" Do they recognize a moment-by-moment death to their self life is accomplished through a decision of their will and the power of the Holy Spirit?

3. How has the disciplee applied this truth to their life? Do they have examples?

4. Emotions are a God-given part of us that gives us the capacity to relate to Him, ourselves, and others. They are key to all relationships and are reflective of the condition of our souls. Our emotions should be guided by God's truth under the power of the Holy Spirit and not the driver of our decision-making. If a disciplee continues to feel overwhelmed by their emotions at this point, there may be a need for further help.

5. Does the disciplee articulate an understanding of the connection between their unique fleshly persona, their union with Christ as a born-again believer, a heart desire for total surrender, and the ability to choose obedience as a decision of the will?

CONSIDER THIS: SESSION 11

1. What does the Ephesians 1:17-20 prayer mean to you personally?

   _____

   _____

   _____

2. Does the meaning of "take up your cross daily" line up with your previous understanding of that verse. How is it the same or different? (Matthew 16:24-25).

   _____

   _____

   _____

   _____

3. What does it mean for you personally?

   _____

   _____

   _____

4. Describe the role and place of emotions?

   _____

   _____

   _____

5. What are three key takeaways from your discipleship time?

   _____

   _____

   _____

   _____

6. Does the disciplee see that they will need to surrender daily (moment by moment) by picking up their cross and choosing to obey as an act of the will, knowing it is possible through the power of the indwelling Holy Spirit?

7. This is a good opportunity to discuss further resources that may encourage the disciplee's ongoing growth.

6. How do you anticipate they will impact your life moving forward?

_____

_____

_____

7. Do you consider your goals for discipleship to have been met? Why or why not?

_____

_____

_____

_____

_____

_____

_____

_____

_____

_____

_____

Life in Christ, Day by Day

It is recommended that **AM I READY FOR STORM?** be read aloud. In this final narrative, we invite the disciplee to consider the foundation and stability of their lives.

The foundation of a house built upon sand is compared to a foolish man who ignores the Word of the Lord, referenced in Matthew 7:24- 27. This admonition is directed to those who are already believers.

An inferior foundation for either a house or a life becomes apparent over time. If we are building or living according to human wisdom rather than the Holy Spirit's guidance, we will not hold up during the sudden storms of life.

An often-repeated theme in *Life in Christ: A Personalized Discipleship Notebook* emphasizes that decisions based on emotions and false beliefs can lead to ruin. Like the lopsided foundation that results in a house out of plumb, an individual who is not directed in daily living choices by God's Word will become increasingly unstable.

AM I READY FOR THE STORM?

Each of us is building a house—our lives. For this analogy, we assume both builders are believers, as the parable speaks to those who *hear* Jesus's words (John 10:27). The parable Jesus told in Matthew 7:24-27 gives us insight into how we are to build that house.

We choose our materials—thoughts, words, and deeds—and fit them together.

A stable foundation is the most essential element when building a house. Are we building through the power of the Holy Spirit or our flesh? The quality of a foundation is not always apparent at first glance, but its strengths and weaknesses reveal themselves over time. Matthew 7:24-27 tells us there are two types of foundations: sand or rock. A solid foundation is essential in weathering the storms of life. Otherwise, our house will crumble.

The Foolish Man

> "And everyone who hears these words of Mine, and does not do them, will be like a foolish man who built his house on the sand. The rain fell, and the floods came and the winds blew and beat against that house, and it fell, and great was the fall of it" (Matthew 7:26-27).

We know sand shifts and is unstable. It moves under our feet, and eventually, particles of sand wash away and leave gaps in the foundation. Building on sand may be faster and less expensive because we do not have to dig as deeply, but it does not provide real strength, support, or security.

Building on sand can be likened to a believer governed by their emotions. We *hear* the words of Jesus, but this is not enough. Our attention is on our circumstances and the concerns of this world. When we face difficult circumstances, we may experience *feelings* based on false beliefs.

What if we *believe* that what we are feeling is true? Because we are usually more comfortable when our thoughts are in sync with our feelings, we now focus in the wrong place. We think and *act* in a way that supports those thoughts and feelings.

At this point, each decision we make throws our house *out of plumb*. The longer we continue to build this way, the further we get from building a secure, sturdy home. The instability we feel from building on the wrong foundation becomes a self-fulfilling prophecy. What we believe becomes

We are encouraged to examine our thoughts and actions to confirm that our daily walk aligns with biblical truth. Believers who know their union with Christ and yield to the Holy Spirit are empowered to reflect these truths consistently.

Nothing I plan or accomplish apart from total dependence on the Holy Spirit will be of any eternal value. Wholehearted surrender is foundational for building a life that realizes and fulfills God's purposes.

This attitude of surrender maintains a *teachable spirit* within the believer. We are mutually submitted in fellowship with our brothers and sisters in Christ, open to constructive feedback contributing to our discernment and spiritual maturity.

"And concerning you, my brethren, I myself also am convinced that you yourselves are full of goodness, filled with all knowledge and able also to admonish one another" (Romans 15:14).

Slowly but surely, a life surrendered to God provides emotional healing. What we know will eventually change our decisions and behavior. Over time, these changes also impact our emotions and testify to our growth in grace.

our perceived *truth,* and we never find the life of peace and safety in Him the Father intended for us (Romans 8:6).

Second Corinthians 13:5 says, "Examine yourselves, to see whether you are in the faith." Because we cannot trust our emotions, we must examine ourselves to see if our thoughts and actions align with the truth. Jesus Christ is in us, and we have a choice to make. We can *hear and know* the truth, but we will not walk in the truth unless we yield to the power of the indwelling Holy Spirit.

The Wise Man

> "Everyone then who hears these words of Mine and does them will be like a wise man who built his house on the rock. And the rain fell, and the floods came, and the winds blew and beat on that house, but it did not fall, because it had been founded on the rock" (Matthew 7:25-26).

What do we know about the rock? Unlike sand, the rock is immovable. The rock is Jesus Christ (1 Corinthians 10:4). He is the Way and the Truth and the Life (John 14:6). The wise man dug deep to find a solid foundation of rock to build on (Luke 6:48). This is much more difficult than erecting a house on sand, and it comes with a cost.

I must surrender my life to Him. I am in Him, and He is in me, and unless He is my foundation, nothing I build will stand. "For no one can lay a foundation other than that which is laid, which is Jesus Christ" (1 Corinthians 3:11). I count this to be true, whether I feel it or not. I examine myself to see whether I am in the faith. Hearing the truth and knowing the truth is not enough. I must *believe* the truth. I believe in who God says I am. I am a conqueror (Romans 8:37). I am a saint (Ephesians 1:1, 15, 18).

When I believe the truth, I will *act* in ways consistent with that truth. I choose with each decision, each wall that is constructed, each nail that is driven. I pray that God will reveal areas of deception to me and that I will willingly receive feedback from godly people. I continue to focus on the truth and yield to the indwelling Holy Spirit. My house becomes more sound with each decision. The walls are straight and plumb (Proverbs 4:23). As I continue to build on the strength and wisdom of the Holy Spirit, the way I *feel* rests on a solid structure and lines up with God's truth. My feelings do not always line up immediately, based on the circumstances that God allows in my life, but I continue to trust in my foundation as I walk forward. Eventually, my feelings line up with the truth.

The second paragraph on page 251 clarifies a vital truth. We may memorize Scripture and know all about Jesus, yet not know Him personally. Without a personal, growing relationship with Jesus Himself, we cannot build our lives in a way that safeguards us during times of crisis.

"You search the Scriptures because you think that in them you have eternal life; it is these that testify about Me; and you are unwilling to come to Me so that you may have life" (John 5:39).

My Daily Walk summarizes the importance of setting the mind. Fleshly thoughts are not to be suppressed but replaced through a mind set on the Spirit. This theme of displacing lies with truth is emphasized in Scripture and repeatedly taught in *Life in Christ: A Personalized Discipleship Notebook*.

When all is said and done, how will we know the difference between the house built on the rock and the house built on the sand? It may not be immediately evident as we look from the outside. First Corinthians 3:13 tells us, "... each one's work will become manifest, for the day will reveal it, because it will be revealed by fire, and the fire will test what sort of work each one has done. If the work that anyone has built on his foundation survives, he will receive a reward." Only what is built on Jesus can survive. The circumstances and trials of our lives are the proving ground where we see the sturdiness of the house we are building. We can choose to walk according to what we know to be true.

What would a building inspector say of my building choices? Am I walking in the truth? Do I hear the truth yet continue living out of my emotions and fleshly desires? Do I yield to the indwelling Holy Spirit and allow Him to live in and through me? Jesus says that the fall of the house not built on the rock (truth) is great. It doesn't matter how well we know the Word of God. If we don't know the Word which became flesh (John 1:14), sin will tear our house down. When your foundation is firm on the rock, you can rest knowing you are on solid ground and can weather any storm.

LIFE IN CHRIST, DAY BY DAY

My Daily Walk

Where I set my mind is a choice of will; I cannot set it on two things at once (Colossians 3:1-2). If I walk by the Spirit, I will not gratify the desires of the flesh, for these are opposed to each other, to keep me from doing what I want to do (Gal 5:16-17). If I focus on my selfish desires, once conceived, they give birth to sin. And sin, when fully matured, brings forth death (James 1:15). If I set my mind on Christ and the things above, my fleshly thinking and desires will be displaced.

At the first hint of fleshly desire, I must make a choice to take my thoughts captive (2 Corinthians 10:5). For the mind set on the flesh is death, but the mind set on the Spirit is life and peace (Romans 8:6). So, do I simply suppress my fleshly desires? No, because they will always bubble back to the surface over time. Instead, I must replace those fleshly thoughts with the truth of God and His Word (Romans 12:2). My feelings will then normally follow where my focus is placed (Philippians 4:8).

God's plans and purposes for my life are accomplished by appropriating life in Christ. Overcoming sin and the destruction it brings is only possible through a life hidden in Christ with God. My union with Him provides victory!

SAMPLE SCENARIOS

Ask the disciplee to read *The Job That Got Away* aloud. This story describes an individual who has worked hard to advance in their career only to be bitterly disappointed. They are angry with their employer but also confused about their own expectations and feelings. Although honest about the broad range of emotions they are experiencing, the situation calls for a decision about where to set their mind.

If I trust God and His Word, I have the power of the indwelling Spirit to choose to live as though what He says is true. Looking to Jesus, I can overcome the sin that threatens to bring death and run the race set before me with endurance (Hebrews 12:1-2). My ability to overcome is not some formula I can apply on my own. Our overcomer is the very person of Jesus Christ. For I have died, and my life is hidden with Christ in God (Colossians 3:3-4).

SAMPLE SCENARIOS

How would I see Christ operating if the following circumstances were to take place in my life?

The Job That Got Away

I have been working for the same employer for ten years and have worked my way up in the ranks. Because I don't have a college degree, I take night courses to advance my career, and a mentor helps me understand the ins and outs of the business.

My company now has an opening for my dream job, and I make it to the final round of interviews. I am stunned when I learn that a younger, less experienced colleague who has only been with the company three years has gotten the job. I was sure God would reward all my hard work. I feel frustrated, cheated, and angry. I want to tell the powers that be what a terrible mistake they have made. I feel ashamed and embarrassed. Did I think they might actually choose me? Why did I apply in the first place?

The time has come for me to choose. Where will I place my focus? Will it be on the emotions raging inside of me or on the truth? What is the truth anyway? The truth is that I am *not my emotions.* My emotional reaction to this disappointing outcome indicates I have something I need to attend to.

The truth is also that, IN CHRIST, I am a new creation. I have all the power and fruit of the indwelling Holy Spirit at my disposal. I start to agree with God that what He says about me, this situation, and Him in me is *true.* I choose to focus on the truth, which is that I have died. I was not entitled to the job. This life is now Christ's, and He does not love me more or less based on any position I hold.

> ❧ It is no longer I who live. I say to the Lord, "In and of myself, I have no capacity to deal with my emotions. I'd really like to give

The surrendered disciple is not entitled to demand a desired outcome. A promotion is not their right to claim, no matter how hard they have worked to be considered for advancement.

We choose to obey the direction given by the Holy Spirit and thank the interviewer for the opportunity to apply for the position.

Our life and future are in God's hands. His plan is always the very best for us. Expressing the life of Christ in every situation, moment by moment, is abundant living.

Emotions are not ignored but displaced by truth.

Read *The Traffic Jams of Life* aloud and discuss the questions with your disciplee.

the interviewers a piece of my mind." However, I *choose* to give up my perceived right to have the job I wanted. The Lord comes back, speaks to my conscience, and tells me to thank them for the opportunity. I reply, "Yes, Lord."

- It is Christ who lives in and through me. "Lord, this is your life and your problem. I trust you to live your life through me. I believe you have a plan and purpose for my life, and that you will accomplish it if I am yielded and obedient to you."

- The life I now live here on earth I live by faith—total dependence and trust in the life of Christ in me (Galatians 2:20). "Lord, faith means agreeing with you and saying thank you. So, by a choice of my will, I thank you for this trial and your sufficiency. I receive this opportunity to learn that I am secure and significant in you. I trust you to work this circumstance for my good (Romans 8:28)."

I have focused on the things above (Colossians 3:1). I understand that trials help me settle the truths of *surrender* in my life. I realize that God is testing me for my benefit and spiritual growth.

Life comes out of death. I go to the Cross and say to the Lord, "I relinquish this to you. I accept that this job was not in your will. I receive this setback as an opportunity from you." I now experience more of His life.

I do not try to suppress my feelings by saying, "I will not be disappointed and frustrated. I won't think about losing out on this job." Instead, I replace the thought by switching my thinking to the real me—the Christ-life. I appropriate what is true about me as I come to understand the implications of my true identity in Christ. I allow the life of Christ, which is now *my* life, to flow through me. I exercise my faith before I focus on my performance.

The Traffic Jams of Life

I am on my way to the concert I bought tickets for some months ago. Prior to the event, I plan to get together with friends for dinner. I meet with a traffic jam on the freeway, bringing my car to a standstill. "Oh no!" I exclaim to no one as my mind begins to race.

- What am I thinking and feeling?

- Where is my mind focused?

- What is the truth about my situation?

Ask the disciplee to read *The Class That Wasn't* narrative aloud.

Go through each question together:

- What are they thinking and feeling? Encourage emotional honesty and transparency.

- Is it true? Do their initial thoughts and feelings correspond to biblical truth?

- Where have they chosen to focus, and is their mind set on what is true?

The final two outcomes of the couple attending the class are entirely different. Do these differences change my perception of the class that was taught?

The Class That Wasn't

I am given an opportunity to teach a class at my church, where I'll share the truths of life in Christ. The class is well-promoted, and I have printed thirty notebooks in anticipation of the Lord changing many lives through me. I have spent untold hours in preparation and eagerly anticipate seeing who attends. I arrive early to greet each attendee and spend a few moments with them. Just as the class is scheduled to begin, a middle-aged couple arrives and sits down in the front row. No one else comes!

- What am I thinking and feeling?

- Is it true?

- Where have I chosen to focus my mind?

- What is the truth about me and my situation?

- Would it change how I feel if the couple who came told me how excited they are because they have learned some truths they have never heard before and can't wait to learn more? Or what if they walk out at the end without saying anything?

DISCIPLER'S NOTES

To conclude the final session, suggest that the disciplee read the closing prayer and thank them for participating in *Life in Christ: A Personalized Discipleship Notebook* sessions.

Possible questions to ask:

- Have they read any books listed in the bibliography on page 278? Recommend one or two titles you think this individual would enjoy and enhance their growth in grace.

- Are there any family members or friends that would benefit from personalized discipleship sessions?

- Would they be interested in training opportunities that would equip them to share these truths with others?

CLOSING PRAYER

Father in Heaven,

I thank you and praise you for knitting me together in my mother's womb, with a plan and a purpose for my life. Thank you that by your doing, I have come to accept the precious gift of forgiveness of my sins through Jesus' death on the Cross, and I now have eternal life in Him.

Thank you, Lord, that, as a believer, I have been crucified with Christ, that I have been made a new creation, and that Christ Himself lives in me through the indwelling Holy Spirit. I praise you, Father, that you knew I could not live the Christian life in my own strength and have provided everything I need to live a godly life. I was once a slave to sin, but now, the authority of sin over me has been broken! Thank you, Lord, that I am now free to choose to obey your will as I yield to Christ's life in me. I am victorious in Him.

Lord, I totally surrender myself to you knowing that you are on the throne and know what is best for me, even when the circumstances may be difficult. Even when my emotions feel like they will overwhelm me, I will choose to focus my thoughts on you and your truth. I thank you that you began the work in me, and you will be faithful to complete it.

Thank you, Lord, that this is your life and as I trust and abide in you, moment by moment, you will show me the way to go. I have complete comfort and rest in you.

In Jesus name I pray,

Amen

SCRIPTURES REFERENCED IN THIS NOTEBOOK

Genesis

Genesis 3:12-13 The man said, "The woman whom You gave to be with me, she gave me some of the fruit of the tree, and I ate." Then the Lord God said to the woman, "What is this that you have done?" And the woman said, "The serpent deceived me, and I ate.

Genesis 32:24-28 Then Jacob was left alone, and a man wrestled with him until daybreak. When he saw that he had not prevailed against him, he touched the socket of his thigh; so the socket of Jacob's thigh was dislocated while he wrestled with him. Then he said, "Let me go, for the dawn is breaking." But he said, "I will not let you go unless you bless me." So he said to him, "What is your name?" And he said, "Jacob." He said, "Your name shall no longer be Jacob, but Israel for you have striven with God and with men and have prevailed.

Genesis 32:29-31 Then Jacob asked him and said, "Please tell me your name." But he said, "Why is it that you ask my name?" And he blessed him there. So Jacob named the place Peniel, for he said, "I have seen God face to face, yet my life has been preserved." Now the sun rose upon him just as he crossed over Penuel, and he was limping on his thigh.

Numbers

Numbers 27:16 May the Lord, the God of the spirits of all flesh, appoint a man over the congregation.

2 Samuel

2 Samuel 12:9-13 Why have you despised the word of the Lord, by doing evil in His sight? You have struck and killed Uriah the Hittite with the sword, you have taken his wife as your wife, and you have slaughtered him with the sword of the sons of Ammon. Now then, the sword shall never leave your house, because you have despised Me and have taken the wife of Uriah the Hittite to be your wife.

2 Samuel 12:11-13 This is what the Lord says: 'Behold, I am going to raise up evil against you from your own household; I will even take your wives before your eyes and give them to your companion, and he will sleep with your wives in broad daylight. Indeed, you did it secretly, but I will do this thing before all Israel, and in open daylight.'" Then David said to Nathan, "I have sinned against the Lord." And Nathan said to David, "The Lord also has allowed your sin to pass; you shall not die.

Psalms

Psalm 9:9 The Lord also will be a stronghold for the oppressed, A stronghold in times of trouble.

Psalm 23 The Lord is my shepherd, I will not be in need. He lets me lie down in green pastures; He leads me beside quiet waters. He restores my soul; He guides me in the paths of righteousness For the sake of His name. Even though I walk through the valley of the shadow of death, I fear no evil, for You are with me; Your rod and Your staff, they comfort me. You prepare a table before me in the presence of my enemies; You have anointed my head with oil; My cup overflows. Certainly goodness and faithfulness will follow me all the days of my life, And my dwelling will be in the house of the Lord forever.

Psalm 42:5-6 Why are you in despair, O my soul? And why have you become disturbed within me? Hope in God, for I shall again praise Him For the help of His presence. O my God, my soul is in despair within me; Therefore I remember You from the land of the Jordan, And the peaks of Hermon, from Mount Mizar.

Psalm 42:11 Why are you in despair, my soul? And why are you restless within me? Wait for God, for I will again praise Him for the help of His presence, my God.

Psalm 59:9 Because of his strength I will watch for You, For God is my stronghold.

Psalm 62:8 Trust in Him at all times, you people; pour out your hearts before Him; God is a refuge for us. Selah.

Psalm 86:11 Teach me Your way, Lord; I will walk in Your truth; unite my heart to fear Your name.

Psalm 90:2 Before the mountains were born or You gave birth to the earth and the world, even from everlasting to everlasting, You are God.

Psalm 94:22 But the Lord has been my stronghold, and my God the rock of my refuge.

Psalm 139:13 For You created my innermost parts; You wove me in my mother's womb.

Psalm 139: 23-24 Search me, God, and know my heart; Put me to the test and know my anxious thoughts; And see if there is any hurtful way in me, And lead me in the everlasting way.

Proverbs

Proverbs 3:7 Do not be wise in your own eyes; Fear the Lord and turn away from evil.

Proverbs 4:23 Watch over your heart with all diligence, For from it flow the springs of life.

Proverbs 5:22 His own wrongdoings will trap the wicked, And he will be held by the ropes of his sin.

Proverbs 6: 1-3 My son, if you have become a guarantor for your neighbor, have given a handshake for a stranger, If you have been ensnared by the words of your mouth, caught by the words of your mouth, do this, my son, and save yourself: Since you have come into the hand of your neighbor, Go, humble yourself, and be urgent with your neighbor to free yourself.

Proverbs 6:16-19 There are six things that the Lord hates, Seven that are an abomination to Him: Haughty eyes, a lying tongue, And hands that shed innocent blood, A heart that devises wicked plans, Feet that run rapidly to evil, A false witness who declares lies, And one who spreads strife among brothers.

Proverbs 14:12 There is a way which seems right to a man, but it's end is the way of death.

Proverbs 16:32 One who is slow to anger is better than the mighty, And one who rules his spirit, than one who captures a city.

Proverbs 22:3 A prudent person sees evil and hides himself, but the naive proceed, and pay the penalty.

Proverbs 25:28 Like a city that is broken into and without walls so is a person who has no self-control over his spirit.

Proverbs 29:11 A fool always loses his temper, but a wise person holds it back.

Ecclesiastes

Ecclesiastes 12:7 ...then the dust will return to the earth as it was, and the spirit will return to God who gave it.

Isaiah

Isaiah 5:20 Woe to those who call evil good, and good evil; Who substitute darkness for light and light for darkness; Who substitute bitter for sweet and sweet for bitter!.

Isaiah 53:6 All of us, like sheep, have gone astray, each of us has turned to his own way; But the Lord has caused the wrongdoing of us all to fall on Him.

Jeremiah

Jeremiah 13:23 Can the Ethiopian change his skin or the leopard his spots? Then also you can do good who are accustomed to do evil.

Jeremiah 32:17 "Oh, Lord God! Behold, You Yourself have made the heavens and the earth by Your great power and by Your outstretched arm! Nothing is too difficult for You....

Lamentations

Lamentations 3:22-24 The steadfast love of the Lord never ceases; his mercies never come to an end; they are new every morning; great is your faithfulness. The Lord is my portion, says my soul, therefore I will hope in him.

Zechariah

Zechariah 12:1 Thus declares the Lord who stretches out the heavens, lays the foundation of the earth, and forms the spirit of man within him.

Matthew

Matthew 5:44 But I say to you, love your enemies and pray for those who persecute you.

Matthew 6:14-15 For if you forgive other people for their offenses, your heavenly Father will also forgive you. But if you do not forgive other people, then your Father will not forgive your offenses.

Matthew 7:2-5 For in the way you judge, you will be judged; and by your standard of measure, it will be measured to you. Why do you look at the speck that is in your brother's eye, but do not notice the log that is in your own eye? Or how can you say to your brother, 'Let me take the speck out of your eye,' and look, the log is in your own eye? You hypocrite, first take the log out of your own eye, and then you will see clearly to take the speck out of your brother's eye!.

Matthew 7:24-25 Therefore, everyone who hears these words of Mine, and acts on them, will be like a wise man who built his house on the rock. And the rain fell and the floods came, and the winds blew and slammed against that house; and yet it did not fall, for it had been founded on the rock.

Mathew 7: 26-27 And everyone who hears these words of Mine, and does not act on them, will be like a foolish man who built his house on the sand. And the rain fell and the floods came, and the winds blew and slammed against that house; and it fell—and its collapse was great.

Matthew 11:28-30 Come to Me, all who are weary and burdened, and I will give you rest. Take My yoke upon you and learn from Me, for I am gentle and humble in heart, and you will find rest for your souls. For My yoke is comfortable, and My burden is light.

Matthew 12:34 You offspring of vipers, how can you, being evil, express any good things? For the mouth speaks from that which fills the heart.

Matthew 14:14 When He came ashore, He saw a large crowd, and felt compassion for them and healed their sick.

Matthew 16:18 And I also say to you that you are Peter, and upon this rock I will build My church; and the gates of Hades will not overpower it .

Matthew 16:24-25 Then Jesus said to His disciples, "If anyone desires to come after Me, let him deny himself, and take up his cross, and follow Me. For whoever desires to save his life, will lose it, but whoever loses his life for My sake, will find it"

Matthew 18:21-22 Then Peter came up and said to Him, "Lord, how many times shall my brother sin against me and I still forgive him? Up to seven times?" Jesus said to him, "I do not say to you, up to seven times, but up to seventy-seven times.

Matthew 18:23-25 "For this reason the kingdom of heaven is like a king who wanted to settle accounts with his slaves. And when he had begun to settle them, one who owed him ten thousand talents was brought to him. But since he did not have the means to repay, his master commanded that he be sold, along with his wife and children and all that he had, and repayment be made.

Matthew 19:26 And looking at them, Jesus said to them, "With man this is impossible, but with God all things are possible.

Matthew 23: 25-26 Woe to you, scribes and Pharisees, hypocrites! For you clean the outside of the cup and of the dish, but inside they are full of robbery and self-indulgence. You blind Pharisee, first clean the inside of the cup and of the dish, so that the outside of it may also become clean.

Matthew 23:27-28 Woe to you, scribes and Pharisees, hypocrites! For you are like whitewashed tombs which on the outside appear beautiful, but inside they are full of dead men's bones and all uncleanness. So you too, outwardly appear righteous to people, but inwardly you are full of hypocrisy and lawlessness.

Matthew 23:29-32 Woe to you, scribes and Pharisees, hypocrites! For you build the tombs for the prophets and decorate the monuments of the righteous, and you say, 'If we had been living in the days of our fathers, we would not have been partners with them in shedding the blood of the prophets.' So you testify against yourselves, that you are sons of those who murdered the prophets. Fill up, then, the measure of the guilt of your fathers.

Matthew 26:39 And He went a little beyond them, and fell on His face and prayed, saying, "My Father, if it is possible, let this cup pass from Me; yet not as I will, but as You will.

Mark

Mark 1:41 Moved with compassion, Jesus reached out with His hand and touched him, and said to him, "I am willing; be cleansed.

Mark 3:4 And He said to them, "Is it lawful to do good on the Sabbath or to do harm, to save a life or to kill?" But they kept silent.

Mark 8:34 And He summoned the crowd together with His disciples, and said to them, "If anyone wants to come after Me, he must deny himself, take up his cross, and follow Me".

Mark 10:14 But when Jesus saw this, He was indignant and said to them, "Allow the children to come to Me; do not forbid them, for the kingdom of God belongs to such as these".

Mark 10:45 For even the Son of Man did not come to be served, but to serve, and to give His life as a ransom for many.

Luke

Luke 6:48 He is like a man building a house, who dug deep and laid a foundation on the rock; and when there was a flood, the river burst against that house and yet it could not shake it, because it had been well built.

Luke 9:23-24 And He was saying to them all, "If anyone wants to come after Me, he must deny himself, take up his cross daily, and follow Me. For whoever wants to save his life will lose it, but whoever loses his life for My sake, this is the one who will save it".

Luke 17:4 And if he sins against you seven times a day, and returns to you seven times, saying, 'I repent,' you shall forgive him.

John

John 1:8 If we say that we have no sin, we are deceiving ourselves and the truth is not in us.

John 1:12 But as many as received Him, to them He gave the right to become children of God, to those who believe in His name.....

John 1:14 And the Word became flesh, and dwelt among us; and we saw His glory, glory as of the only Son from the Father, full of grace and truth.

John 2:13-17 The Passover of the Jews was near, and Jesus went up to Jerusalem. And within the temple grounds He found those who were selling oxen, sheep, and doves, and the money changers seated at their tables. And He made a whip of cords, and drove them all out of the temple area, with the sheep and the oxen; and He poured out the coins of the money changers and overturned their tables; and to those who were selling the doves He said, "Take these things away from here; stop making My Father's house a place of business!" His disciples remembered that it was written: "Zeal for Your house will consume Me".

John 3:3-7 Jesus answered and said to him, "Truly, truly, I say to you, unless one is born again he cannot see the kingdom of God." Nicodemus said to Him, "How can a man be born when he is old? He cannot enter a second time into his mother's womb and be born, can he?" Jesus answered, "Truly, truly, I say to you, unless one is born of water and the Spirit he cannot enter into the kingdom of God. That which is born of the flesh is flesh, and that which is born of the Spirit is spirit. Do not be amazed that I said to you, 'You must be born again'."

John 5:24 "Truly, truly, I say to you, the one who hears My word, and believes Him who sent Me, has eternal life, and does not come into judgment, but has passed out of death into life.

John 6:65 And He was saying, "For this reason I have told you that no one can come to Me unless it has been granted him from the Father.

John 8:44 You are of your father the devil, and you want to do the desires of your father. He was a murderer from the beginning, and does not stand in the truth because there is no truth in him. Whenever he tells a lie, he speaks from his own nature, because he is a liar and the father of lies.

John 10:10 The thief comes only to steal and kill and destroy; I came so that they would have life, and have it abundantly.

John 10:27 My sheep listen to My voice, and I know them, and they follow Me.

John 11:35 Jesus wept.

John 14:6 Jesus said to him, "I am the way, and the truth, and the life; no one comes to the Father but through Me....

John 14:15 If you love Me, you will keep My commandments.

John 14:16-17 I will ask the Father, and He will give you another Helper, so that He may be with you forever; the Helper is the Spirit of truth, whom the world cannot receive, because it does not see Him or know Him; but you know Him because He remains with you and will be in you.

John 14:19-20 After a little while, the world no longer is going to see Me, but you are going to see Me; because I live, you also will live. On that day you will know that I am in My Father, and you are in Me, and I in you.

John 15:4-5 Remain in Me, and I in you. Just as the branch cannot bear fruit of itself but must remain in the vine, so neither can you unless you remain in Me. I am the vine, you are the branches; the one who remains in Me, and I in him bears much fruit, for apart from Me you can do nothing.

John 15:11 These things I have spoken to you so that My joy may be in you, and that your joy may be made full.

John 15:13-15 Greater love has no one than this, that a person will lay down his life for his friends. You are My friends if you do what I command you. No longer do I call you slaves, for the slave does not know what his master is doing; but I have called you friends, because all things that I have heard from My Father I have made known to you.

John 16:7-11 But I tell you the truth: it is to your advantage that I am leaving; for if I do not leave, the Helper will not come to you; but if I go, I will send Him to you. And He, when He comes, will convict the world regarding sin, and righteousness, and judgment: regarding sin, because they do not believe in Me; and regarding righteousness, because I am going to the Father and you no longer are going to see Me; and regarding judgment, because the ruler of this world has been judged.

John 16:12-15 I have many more things to say to you, but you cannot bear them at the present time. But when He, the Spirit of truth, comes, He will guide you into all the truth; for He will not speak on His own, but whatever He hears, He will speak; and He will disclose to you what is to come. He will glorify Me, for He will take from Mine and will disclose it to you. All things that the Father has are Mine; this is why I said that He takes from Mine and will disclose it to you.

John 17:3 This is eternal life, that they may know You, the only true God, and Jesus Christ whom You have sent.

John 17:20-23 I am not asking on behalf of these alone, but also for those who believe in Me through their word, that they may all be one; just as You, Father, are in Me and I in You, that they also may be in Us, so that the world may believe that You sent Me. The glory which You have given Me I also have given to them, so that they may be one, just as We are one; I in them and You in Me, that they may be perfected in unity, so that the world may know that You sent Me, and You loved them, just as You loved Me.

Acts

Acts 2:38 Peter said to them, "Repent, and each of you be baptized in the name of Jesus Christ for the forgiveness of your sins; and you will receive the gift of the Holy Spirit.

Acts 3:19 Therefore repent and return, so that your sins may be wiped away, in order that times of refreshing may come from the presence of the Lord.

Acts 7:51 You men who are stiff-necked and uncircumcised in heart and ears are always resisting the Holy Spirit; you are doing just as your fathers did.

Acts 9:13 But Ananias answered, "Lord, I have heard from many people about this man, how much harm he did to Your saints in Jerusalem.

Acts 9:32 Now as Peter was traveling through all those regions, he also came down to the saints who lived at Lydda.

Acts 9:41 And he gave her his hand and raised her up; and calling the saints and widows, he presented her alive.

Acts 26:10 And this is just what I did in Jerusalem; not only did I lock up many of the saints in prisons, after receiving authority from the chief priests, but I also cast my vote against them when they were being put to death.

Romans

Romans 1:3 ... concerning His Son, who was born of a descendant of David according to the flesh.....

Romans 1:7 To all those in Rome who are loved by God and called to be saints: Grace to you and peace from God our Father and the Lord Jesus Christ.

Romans 1:17 For in it the righteousness of God is revealed from faith to faith; as it is written: But the righteous one will live by faith.

Romans 1:20 For since the creation of the world His invisible attributes, that is, His eternal power and divine nature, have been clearly perceived, being understood by what has been made, so that they are without excuse.

Romans 1:23 ... and they exchanged the glory of the incorruptible God for an image in the form of corruptible mankind, of birds, four-footed animals, and crawling creatures.

Romans 3:23 ... for all have sinned and fall short of the glory of God .....

Romans 5:8-9 But God demonstrates His own love toward us, in that while we were still sinners, Christ died for us. Much more then, having now been justified by His blood, we shall be saved from the wrath of God through Him.

Romans 5:10 For if while we were enemies we were reconciled to God through the death of His Son, much more, having been reconciled, we shall be saved by His life.

Romans 5:12 Therefore, just as through one man sin entered into the world, and death through sin, and so death spread to all mankind, because all sinned .....

Romans 5:16 The gift is not like that which came through the one who sinned; for on the one hand the judgment arose from one offense, resulting in condemnation, but on the other hand the gracious gift arose from many offenses, resulting in justification.

Romans 6:3-5 Or do you not know that all of us who have been baptized into Christ Jesus have been baptized into His death? Therefore we have been buried with Him through baptism into death, so that, just as Christ was raised from the dead through the glory of the Father, so we too may walk in newness of life. For if we have become united with Him in the likeness of His death, certainly we shall also be in the likeness of His resurrection.....

Romans 6:6 ... knowing this, that our old self was crucified with Him, in order that our body of sin might be done away with, so that we would no longer be slaves to sin.....

Romans 6:10-11 For the death that He died, He died to sin once for all; but the life that He lives, He lives to God. Even so consider yourselves to be dead to sin, but alive to God in Christ Jesus.

Romans 6:12 Therefore do not let sin reign in your mortal body that you should obey its lusts.

Romans 6:13-14 ... and do not go on presenting the parts of your body to sin as instruments of unrighteousness; but present yourselves to God as those who are alive from the dead, and your body's parts as instruments of righteousness for God. For sin shall not be master over you, for you are not under the Law but under grace.

Romans 6:16 Do you not know that the one to whom you present yourselves as slaves for obedience, you are slaves of that same one whom you obey, either of sin resulting in death, or of obedience resulting in righteousness?

Romans 6:17 But thanks be to God that though you were slaves of sin, you became obedient from the heart to that form of teaching to which you were committed.

Romans 6:20 For when you were slaves of sin, you were free in relation to righteousness.

Romans 6:23 For the wages of sin is death, but the gracious gift of God is eternal life in Christ Jesus our Lord .

Romans 7:7-8 What shall we say then? Is the Law sin? Far from it! On the contrary, I would not have come to know sin except through the Law; for I would not have known about coveting if the Law had not said, "You shall not covet." But sin, taking an opportunity through the commandment, produced in me coveting of every kind; for apart from the Law sin is dead .

Romans 7:9-10 I was once alive apart from the Law; but when the commandment came, sin came to life, and I died; and this commandment, which was to result in life, proved to result in death for me.

Romans 7:11 ...for sin, taking an opportunity through the commandment, deceived me, and through it, killed me.

Romans 7:15-16 For I do not understand what I am doing; for I am not practicing what I want to do, but I do the very thing I hate. However, if I do the very thing I do not want to do, I agree with the Law, that the Law is good.

Romans 7:17-18 But now, no longer am I the one doing it, but sin that dwells in me. For I know that good does not dwell in me, that is, in my flesh; for the willing is present in me, but the doing of the good is not.

Romans 7:19-20 For the good that I want, I do not do, but I practice the very evil that I do not want. But if I do the very thing I do not want, I am no longer the one doing it, but sin that dwells in me.

Romans 7:21-23 I find then the principle that evil is present in me, the one who wants to do good. For I joyfully agree with the law of God in the inner person, but I see a different law in the parts of my body waging war against the law of my mind, and making me a prisoner of the law of sin, the law which is in my body's parts.

Romans 7:24 Wretched man that I am! Who will set me free from the body of this death?.

Romans 8:1-3 Therefore there is now no condemnation for those who are in Christ Jesus. For the law of the Spirit of life in Christ Jesus has set you free from the law of sin and of death. For what the Law could not do, weak as it was through the flesh, God did: sending His own Son in the likeness of sinful flesh and as an offering for sin, He condemned sin in the flesh.

Romans 8: 4-6 ... so that the requirement of the Law might be fulfilled in us, who do not walk according to the flesh but according to the Spirit. For those who are according to the flesh set their minds on the things of the flesh, but those who are according to the Spirit, the things of the Spirit. For the mind set on the flesh is death, but the mind set on the Spirit is life and peace.

Romans 8:7-10 ... because the mind set on the flesh is hostile toward God; for it does not subject itself to the law of God, for it is not even able to do so, and those who are in the flesh cannot please God. However, you are not in the flesh but in the Spirit, if indeed the Spirit of God dwells in you. But if anyone does not have the Spirit of Christ, he does not belong to Him. If Christ is in you, though the body is dead because of sin, yet the spirit is alive because of righteousness.

Romans 8:11-13 But if the Spirit of Him who raised Jesus from the dead dwells in you, He who raised Christ Jesus from the dead will also give life to your mortal bodies through His Spirit who dwells in you. So then, brethren, we are under obligation, not to the flesh, to live according to the flesh— for if you are living according to the flesh, you must die; but if by the Spirit you are putting to death the deeds of the body, you will live.

Romans 8:14-17 For all who are being led by the Spirit of God, these are sons of God. For you have not received a spirit of slavery leading to fear again, but you have received a spirit of adoption as sons by which we cry out, "Abba! Father!" The Spirit Himself testifies with our spirit that we are children of God, and if children, heirs also, heirs of God and fellow heirs with Christ, if indeed we suffer with Him so that we may also be glorified with Him.

Romans 8:27 And He who searches the hearts knows what the mind of the Spirit is, because He intercedes for the saints according to the will of God.

Romans 8:28-29 And we know that God causes all things to work together for good to those who love God, to those who are called according to His purpose. For those whom He foreknew, He also predestined to become conformed to the image of His Son, so that He would be the firstborn among many brothers and sisters.

Romans 8:37 But in all these things we overwhelmingly conquer through Him who loved us.

Romans 9:1 I am telling the truth in Christ, I am not lying, my conscience testifies with me in the Holy Spirit.

Romans 9:33 ... just as it is written, Behold, I am laying in Zion a stone of stumbling and a rock of offense, And the one who believes in Him will not be put to shame.

Romans 12:1-2 Therefore I urge you, brothers and sisters, by the mercies of God, to present your bodies as a living and holy sacrifice, acceptable to God, which is your spiritual service of worship. And do not be conformed to this world, but be transformed by the renewing of your mind, so that you may prove what the will of God is, that which is good and acceptable and perfect.

Romans 12:12 ... rejoicing in hope, persevering in tribulation, devoted to prayer.....

Romans 12:13 Contribute to the needs of the saints and seek to show hospitality.

Romans 12:17 Never repay evil for evil to anyone. Respect what is right in the sight of all people.

Romans 15:25-26 ... but now, I am going to Jerusalem, serving the saints. For Macedonia and Achaia have been pleased to make a contribution for the poor among the saints in Jerusalem.

Romans 15:31 ... that I may be rescued from those who are disobedient in Judea, and that my service for Jerusalem may prove acceptable to the saints.

Romans 16:2 ... that you receive her in the Lord in a manner worthy of the saints, and that you help her in whatever matter she may have need of you; for she herself has also been a helper of many, and of myself as well.

Romans 16:15 Greet Philologus and Julia, Nereus and his sister, and Olympas, and all the saints who are with them.

1 Corinthians

1 Corinthians 1:2 To the church of God which is at Corinth, to those who have been sanctified in Christ Jesus, saints by calling, with all who in every place call on the name of our Lord Jesus Christ, their Lord and ours.

1 Corinthians 1:30 But by His doing you are in Christ Jesus, who became to us wisdom from God, and righteousness and sanctification, and redemption.

1 Corinthians 2:12 Now we have received, not the spirit of the world, but the Spirit who is from God, so that we may know the things freely given to us by God.

1 Corinthians 2:14 But a natural man does not accept the things of the Spirit of God, for they are foolishness to him; and he cannot understand them, because they are spiritually discerned.

1 Corinthians 2:15 But the one who is spiritual discerns all things, yet he himself is discerned by no one.

1 Corinthians 2:16 For who has known the mind of the Lord, that he will instruct Him? But we have the mind of Christ.

1 Corinthians 3:1-4 And I, brothers and sisters, could not speak to you as spiritual people, but only as fleshly, as to infants in Christ. I gave you milk to drink, not solid food; for you were not yet able to consume it. But even now you are not yet able, for you are still fleshly. For since there is jealousy and strife among you, are you not fleshly, and are you not walking like ordinary people? For when one person says, "I am with Paul," and another, "I am with Apollos," are you not ordinary people?.

1 Corinthians 3:11 For no one can lay a foundation other than the one which is laid, which is Jesus Christ.

1 Corinthians 3:13 ... Each one's work will become evident; for the day will show it because it is to be revealed with fire, and the fire itself will test the quality of each one's work.

1 Corinthians 3:15 If anyone's work is burned up, he will suffer loss; but he himself will be saved, yet only so as through fire.

1 Corinthians 6:17 But the one who joins himself to the Lord is one spirit with Him.

1 Corinthians 6:19-20 Or do you not know that your body is a temple of the Holy Spirit within you, whom you have from God, and that you are not your own? For you have been bought for a price: therefore glorify God in your body.

1 Corinthians 7:23 You were bought for a price; do not become slaves of people.

1 Corinthians 10:4 ... And all drank the same spiritual drink, for they were drinking from a spiritual rock which followed them; and the rock was Christ.

1 Corinthians 10:13 No temptation has overtaken you except something common to mankind; and God is faithful, so He will not allow you to be tempted beyond what you are able, but with the temptation will provide the way of escape also, so that you will be able to endure it.

1 Corinthians 14:33 For God is not a God of confusion but of peace. As in all the churches of the saints.

1 Corinthians 15:3 For I handed down to you as of first importance what I also received, that Christ died for our sins according to the Scriptures....

1 Corinthians 15:45 So also it is written, "The first man, Adam, became a living soul." The last Adam became a life-giving spirit.

1 Corinthians 15:57 But thanks be to God, who gives us the victory through our Lord Jesus Christ.

2 Corinthians

2 Corinthians 5:7 ...for we walk by faith, not by sight—

2 Corinthians 5:17 Therefore if anyone is in Christ, this person is a new creation; the old things passed away; behold, new things have come.

2 Corinthians 10:3-5 For though we walk in the flesh, we do not wage battle according to the flesh, for the weapons of our warfare are not of the flesh, but divinely powerful for the destruction of fortresses. We are destroying arguments and all arrogance raised against the knowledge of God, and we are taking every thought captive to the obedience of Christ.

2 Corinthians 12:10 Therefore I delight in weaknesses, in insults, in distresses, in persecutions, in difficulties, in behalf of Christ; for when I am weak, then I am strong.

2 Corinthians 13:5 Test yourselves to see if you are in the faith; examine yourselves! Or do you not recognize this about yourselves, that Jesus Christ is in you—unless indeed you fail the test?.

Galatians

Galatians 2:20 I have been crucified with Christ; and it is no longer I who live, but Christ lives in me; and the life which I now live in the flesh I live by faith in the Son of God, who loved me and gave Himself up for me.

Galatians 3: 1-3 You foolish Galatians, who has bewitched you, before whose eyes Jesus Christ was publicly portrayed as crucified? This is the only thing I want to find out from you: did you receive the Spirit by works of the Law, or by hearing with faith? Are you so foolish? Having begun by the Spirit, are you now being perfected by the flesh?.

Galatians 4:1,3 Now I say, as long as the heir is a child, he does not differ at all from a slave, although he is owner of everything... So we too, when we were children, were held in bondage under the elementary principles of the world.

Galatians 4:19 My children, with whom I am again in labor until Christ is formed in you.

Galatians 5:16 But I say, walk by the Spirit, and you will not carry out the desire of the flesh.

Galatians 5:17 For the flesh sets its desire against the Spirit, and the Spirit against the flesh; for these are in opposition to one another, so that you may not do the things that you please.

Galatians 5:19 Now the deeds of the flesh are evident, which are: immorality, impurity, sensuality, idolatry, sorcery, enmities, strife, jealousy, outbursts of anger, disputes, dissensions, factions.....

Galatians 5:21 ... envying, drunkenness, carousing, and things like these, of which I forewarn you, just as I have forewarned you, that those who practice such things will not inherit the kingdom of God.

Galatians 5: 22 ... but the fruit of the Spirit is love, joy, peace, patience, kindness, goodness, faithfulness, gentleness, self-control; against such things there is no law.

Galatians 5:25 If we live by the Spirit, let us also walk by the Spirit.

Galatians 6:4 But each one must examine his own work, and then he will have reason for boasting, but to himself alone, and not to another.

Ephesians

Ephesians 1:4 ... just as He chose us in Him before the foundation of the world, that we would be holy and blameless before Him. In love.....

Ephesians 1:6 ...to the praise of the glory of His grace, with which He favored us in the Beloved.

Ephesians 1:17-18 ... that the God of our Lord Jesus Christ, the Father of glory, may give you a spirit of wisdom and of revelation in the knowledge of Him. I pray that the eyes of your heart may be enlightened, so that you will know what is the hope of His calling, what are the riches of the glory of His inheritance in the saints.

Ephesians 1:20-21 ... which He brought about in Christ, when He raised Him from the dead and seated Him at His right hand in the heavenly places, far above all rule and authority and power and dominion, and every name that is named, not only in this age but also in the one to come.

Ephesians 2: 1-3 And you were dead in your offenses and sins, in which you previously walked according to the course of this world, according to the prince of the power of the air, of the spirit that is now working in the sons of disobedience. Among them we too all previously lived in the lusts of our flesh, indulging the desires of the flesh and of the mind, and were by nature children of wrath, just as the rest.

Ephesians 2:4-7 But God, being rich in mercy, because of His great love with which He loved us, even when we were dead in our wrongdoings, made us alive together with Christ (by grace you have been saved), and raised us up with Him, and seated us with Him in the heavenly places in Christ Jesus, so that in the ages to come He might show the boundless riches of His grace in kindness toward us in Christ Jesus.

Ephesians 2:8-9 For by grace you have been saved through faith; and this is not of yourselves, it is the gift of God; not a result of works, so that no one may boast.

Ephesians 2:10 For we are His workmanship, created in Christ Jesus for good works, which God prepared beforehand so that we would walk in them.

Ephesians 4:5 ... one Lord, one faith, one baptism.

Ephesians 4:26-27 Be angry, and yet do not sin; do not let the sun go down on your anger, and do not give the devil an opportunity.

Ephesians 4:32 Be kind to one another, compassionate, forgiving each other, just as God in Christ also has forgiven you.

Ephesians 5:15 So then, be careful how you walk, not as unwise people but as wise.....

Ephesians 5:18-21 And do not get drunk with wine, in which there is debauchery, but be filled with the Spirit, speaking to one another in psalms and hymns and spiritual songs, singing and making melody with your hearts to the Lord; always giving thanks for all things in the name of our Lord Jesus Christ to our God and Father; and subject yourselves to one another in the fear of Christ.

Ephesians 17: 20-21 These are in accordance with the working of the strength of His might which He brought about in Christ, when He raised Him from the dead and seated Him at His right hand in the heavenly places, far above all rule and authority and power and dominion, and every name that is named, not only in this age but also in the one to come.

Philippians

Philippians 1:6 For I am confident of this very thing, that He who began a good work among you will complete it by the day of Christ Jesus.

Philippians 2:3 Do nothing from selfishness or empty conceit, but with humility consider one another as more important than yourselves .....

Philippians 2:5-8 Have this attitude in yourselves which was also in Christ Jesus, who, as He already existed in the form of God, did not consider equality with God something to be grasped, but emptied Himself by taking the form of a bond-servant and being born in the likeness of men. And being found in appearance as a man, He humbled Himself by becoming obedient to the point of death: death on a cross.

Philippians 2:13 ... for it is God who is at work in you, both to desire and to work for His good pleasure.

Philippians 3:4-7 ... although I myself might have confidence even in the flesh. If anyone else has a mind to put confidence in the flesh, I far more: circumcised the eighth day, of the nation of Israel, of the tribe of Benjamin, a Hebrew of Hebrews; as to the Law, a Pharisee; as to zeal, a persecutor of the church; as to the righteousness which is in the Law, found blameless. But whatever things were gain to me, those things I have counted as loss for the sake of Christ.

Philippians 3:10-11 ... that I may know Him and the power of His resurrection and the fellowship of His sufferings, being conformed to His death; if somehow I may attain to the resurrection from the dead.

Philippians 3:12 Not that I have already grasped it all or have already become perfect, but I press on if I may also take hold of that for which I was even taken hold of by Christ Jesus.

Philippians 3:21 ... who will transform the body of our humble state into conformity with the body of His glory, by the exertion of the power that He has even to subject all things to Himself.

Philippians 4:6-7 Be anxious for nothing, but in everything by prayer and supplication with thanksgiving let your requests be made known to God. And the peace of God, which surpasses all comprehension, will guard your hearts and your minds in Christ Jesus.

Philippians 4:8 ... whatever is true, whatever is honorable, whatever is right , whatever is pure, whatever is lovely, whatever is commendable, if there is any excellence and if anything worthy of praise, think about these things.

Philippians 4:11 Not that I speak from need, for I have learned to be content in whatever circumstances I am".

Philippians 4:13 I can do all things through Him who strengthens me.

Philippians 4:19 And my God will supply all your needs according to His riches in glory in Christ Jesus.

Colossians

Colossians 1:12 ... giving thanks to the Father, who has qualified us to share in the inheritance of the saints in Light.

Colossians 1:13-14 For He rescued us from the domain of darkness, and transferred us to the kingdom of His beloved Son. In whom we have redemption, the forgiveness of sins.

Colossians 1:15-17 He is the image of the invisible God, the firstborn of all creation. For by Him all things were created, both in the heavens and on earth, visible and invisible, whether thrones or dominions or rulers or authorities—all things have been created through Him and for Him. He is before all things, and in Him all things hold together.

Colossians 1:25-27 I was made a minister of this church according to the commission from God granted to me for your benefit, so that I might fully carry out the preaching of the word of God, that is, the mystery which had been hidden from the past ages and generations, but now has been revealed to His saints, to whom God willed to make known what the wealth of the glory of this mystery among the Gentiles is, the mystery that is Christ in you, the hope of glory.

Colossians 2:10 ... and in Him you have been made complete, and He is the head over every ruler and authority.....

Colossians 2:13-14 And when you were dead in your wrongdoings and the uncircumcision of your flesh, He made you alive together with Him, having forgiven us all our wrongdoings, having canceled the certificate of debt consisting of decrees against us, which was hostile to us; and He has taken it out of the way, having nailed it to the Cross.

Colossians 2:18-19 Take care that no one keeps defrauding you of your prize by delighting in humility and the worship of the angels, taking his stand on visions he has seen, inflated without cause by his fleshly mind, and not holding firmly to the head, from whom the entire body, being supplied and held together by the joints and ligaments, grows with a growth which is from God.

Colossians 2:20-23 If you have died with Christ, to the elementary principles of the world, why, as if you were living in the world, do you submit yourself to decrees, such as, "Do not handle, do not taste, do not touch!" (which all refer to things destined to perish with use)—in accordance with the commandments and teachings of man? These are matters which do have the appearance of wisdom in self-made religion and humility and severe treatment of the body, but are of no value against fleshly indulgence.

Colossians 3:1-2 Therefore if you have been raised up with Christ, keep seeking the things above, where Christ is, seated at the right hand of God. Set your mind on the things above, not on the things that are on earth.

Colossians 3:3-4 For you have died and your life is hidden with Christ in God. When Christ, who is our life, is revealed, then you also will be revealed with Him in glory.

Colossians 3:15 Let the peace of Christ, to which you were indeed called in one body, rule in your hearts; and be thankful.

Colossians 4:2 Devote yourselves to prayer, keeping alert in it with an attitude of thanksgiving.

1 Thessalonians

1 Thessalonians 3:13 … so that He may establish your hearts without blame in holiness before our God and Father at the coming of our Lord Jesus with all His saints.

1 Thessalonians 5:23 Now may the God of peace Himself sanctify you entirely; and may your spirit and soul and body be preserved complete, without blame at the coming of our Lord Jesus Christ.

2 Timothy

2 Timothy 2:15 Be diligent to present yourself approved to God as a worker who does not need to be ashamed, accurately handling the word of truth.

Titus

Titus 3:5-6 He saved us, not on the basis of deeds which we did in righteousness, but in accordance with His mercy, by the washing of regeneration and renewing by the Holy Spirit, whom He richly poured out upon us through Jesus Christ our Savior.....

Hebrews

Hebrews 1:1-2 God, after He spoke long ago to the fathers in the prophets in many portions and in many ways, in these last days has spoken to us in His Son, whom He appointed heir of all things, through whom also He made the world.

Hebrews 1:3 And He is the radiance of His glory and the exact representation of His nature, and upholds all things by the word of His power. When He had made purification of sins, He sat down at the right hand of the Majesty on high.

Hebrews 4:12 For the word of God is living and active and sharper than any two-edged sword, and piercing as far as the division of soul and spirit, of both joints and marrow, and able to judge the thoughts and intentions of the heart.

Hebrews 10:15 And the Holy Spirit also testifies to us.

Hebrews 10:30-31 For we know Him who said, "Vengeance is Mine, I will repay." And again, "The Lord will judge His people." It is a terrifying thing to fall into the hands of the living God.

Hebrews 12:2 … looking only at Jesus, the originator and perfecter of the faith, who for the joy set before Him endured the cross, despising the shame, and has sat down at the right hand of the throne of God.

Hebrews 12:14-15 Pursue peace with all people, and the holiness without which no one will see the Lord. See to it that no one comes short of the grace of God; that no root of bitterness springing up causes trouble, and by it many become defiled.

Hebrews 13:8 Jesus Christ is the same yesterday and today, and forever.

James

James 1:2-3 Consider it all joy, my brothers and sisters, when you encounter various trials, knowing that the testing of your faith produces endurance.

James 2:17 Even so faith, if it has no works, is dead, being by itself.

James 4:1-2 What is the source of quarrels and conflicts among you? Is the source not your pleasures that wage war in your body's parts? You lust and do not have, so you commit murder. And you are envious and cannot obtain, so you fight and quarrel. You do not have because you do not ask.

James 4:10 Humble yourselves in the presence of the Lord, and He will exalt you.

1 Peter

1 Peter 1:3-5 Blessed be the God and Father of our Lord Jesus Christ, who according to His great mercy has caused us to be born again to a living hope through the resurrection of Jesus Christ from the dead, to obtain an inheritance which is imperishable, undefiled, and will not fade away, reserved in heaven for you who are protected by the power of God through faith for a salvation ready to be revealed in the last time.

1 Peter 1:6-7 In this you greatly rejoice, even though now for a little while, if necessary, you have been distressed by various trials, so that the proof of your faith, being more precious than gold which perishes though tested by fire, may be found to result in praise, glory, and honor at the revelation of Jesus Christ.

1 Peter 2:24 ...and He Himself brought our sins in His body up on the cross, so that we might die to sin and live for righteousness; by His wounds you were healed.

1 Peter 5:6-7 Therefore humble yourselves under the mighty hand of God, so that He may exalt you at the proper time, having cast all your anxiety on Him, because He cares about you.

1 Peter 5:8-9 Be of sober spirit, be on the alert. Your adversary, the devil, prowls around like a roaring lion, seeking someone to devour. So resist him, firm in your faith, knowing that the same experiences of suffering are being accomplished by your brothers and sisters who are in the world.

2 Peter

2 Peter 1:3 Seeing that His divine power has granted to us everything pertaining to life and godliness, through the true knowledge of Him who called us by His own glory and excellence.

2 Peter 1:4 For by these He has granted to us His precious and magnificent promises, so that by them you may become partakers of the divine nature, having escaped the corruption that is in the world by lust.

2 Peter 3:9 The Lord is not slow about His promise, as some count slowness, but is patient toward you, not willing for any to perish, but for all to come to repentance.

2 Peter 3:18 ... but grow in the grace and knowledge of our Lord and Savior Jesus Christ. To Him be the glory, both now and to the day of eternity. Amen.

1 John

1 John 1:1-2 What was from the beginning, what we have heard, what we have seen with our eyes, what we have looked at and touched with our hands, concerning the Word of Life—and the life was manifested, and we have seen and testify and proclaim to you the eternal life, which was with the Father and was manifested to us.

1 John 1:8 If we say that we have no sin, we are deceiving ourselves and the truth is not in us.

1 John 2:15 Do not love the world nor the things in the world. If anyone loves the world, the love of the Father is not in him.

1 John 2:17 The world is passing away and also its lusts; but the one who does the will of God continues to live forever.

1 John 3:1-3 See how great a love the Father has given us, that we would be called children of God; and in fact we are. For this reason the world does not know us: because it did not know Him. Beloved, now we are children of God, and it has not appeared as yet what we will be. We know that when He appears, we will be like Him, because we will see Him just as He is. And everyone who has this hope set on Him purifies himself, just as He is pure.

1 John 5:4 For whoever has been born of God overcomes the world; and this is the victory that has overcome the world: our faith.

1 John 5:11-12 And the testimony is this, that God has given us eternal life, and this life is in His Son. The one who has the Son has the life; the one who does not have the Son of God does not have the life.

1 John 5:20 And we know that the Son of God has come, and has given us understanding so that we may know Him who is true; and we are in Him who is true, in His Son Jesus Christ. This is the true God and eternal life.

Jude

Jude 24 Now to Him who is able to keep you from stumbling, and to make you stand in the presence of His glory blameless with great joy.

Revelation

Revelation 2:5 Therefore, remember from where you have fallen, and repent, and do the deeds you did at first; or else I am coming to you and I will remove your lamp stand from its place—unless you repent.

BIBLIOGRAPHY

There are many excellent books that have been written about life in Christ, but here are some of the very best!

So Great Salvation. . . . . Barabas, Steven

Exchanged Lives . . . . Best, John

They Found the Secret . . . . Erdman, V. Raymond

Ultimate Intention. . . . . Fromke, Devern

Bone of His Bone. . . . . Huegel, F. J.

The Law of Liberty in the Spiritual Life . . . . Hopkins, Evan

Victory Through Surrender. . . . . Jones, E. Stanley

Born Crucified . . . . Maxwell., L.E.

Absolute Surrender. . . . . Murray, Andrew

The Ins and Out of Rejection . . . . Solomon, Charles

From Pastors to Pastors . . . . Testimonies

Victory in Christ . . . . Trumbull, Charles

Man as Spirit, Soul, and Body . . . . Woodward, John

The Worthy Walk . . . . Woodward, John
Miller, Bryan

For further study on the impact of trauma on the brain, mind and body, we recommend:

The Body Keeps the Score. . . . . van der Kolk, Dr. Bessel

DISCIPLER'S SESSION NOTES

Disciplee: _____

Session Number: _____ Date: _____

Homework: Complete? Y___ N___ Questions/Areas of misunderstanding:

New material: What new information was introduced this session?

Session Notes:

Next session:

    To be covered:

    Homework assigned:

Key Concepts to Be Grasped: What information emerged in these areas?

- Further **Who Do You Think You Are?** insights?

- What **Fleshly Identity** (coping behaviors) have been realized?

- Areas of clarification of the **Wheel and Line** diagrams?

- How does the disciplee exhibit a heart attitude of **Surrender**? What might be held back?

- What **Belief Systems** might be limiting appropriation of the Holy Spirit?

- What **Forgiveness** issues might interfere with their spiritual walk?

www.ingramcontent.com/pod-product-compliance
Lightning Source LLC
Chambersburg PA
CBHW080643270326
41928CB00017B/3178

Is the Grace of God Effective?

We know grace is the most powerful force in the universe, but why are there so many anxious and depressed Christians?

Christ is the answer, and the Bible is sufficient, but how do we lay hold of these truths?

Life in Christ: A Personalized Discipleship Notebook was designed for this very purpose. The twelve sessions have proven transformational in church and parachurch settings. The notebook contains everything needed: weekly teachings, interactive materials, "Consider This" homework assignments, Scripture verses, and even designated space for written responses. The new discipler may particularly appreciate the structure and ease of sharing in this way.

Here's What Others Have Discovered

"This 12-week course can and does change lives. It has changed mine. It is not new truth, it is existing truth brought to light. This material uniquely guides the student to come to their own conclusions through the Holy Spirit's illumination." —J. S.

"Have you ever experienced burdens beyond your strength, to the point you despaired of living? If you have, where did you seek help? I began this 12-week discipleship course at my local church six years ago. Gradually, my depression lifted, and I experienced joy as a child of God. I understood His transformational grace in a way I had never known before." —S. A.

"Far beyond knowing that I've been forgiven for my sins, the truths presented here are what every Christian needs to know if they sincerely want to abide and find rest for their souls." —L. E.

GRACE FELLOWSHIP INTERNATIONAL

ISBN 978-1-963542-03-5

9 781963 542035